COGNITIVE
EDUCATION
AND
TESTING

Recent Titles in
Contributions to the Study of Education

Getting Down to Business: Baruch College in the City of New York, 1847–1987
Selma C. Berrol

The Democratic Tradition and the Evolution of Schooling in Norway
Val D. Rust

Diffusion of Innovations in English Language Teaching: The ELEC Effort in
Japan, 1956–1968
Lynn Earl Henrichsen

Improving Educational Quality: A Global Perspective
David W. Chapman and Carol A. Carrier, editors

Rethinking the Curriculum: Toward an Integrated, Interdisciplinary College
Education
Mary E. Clark and Sandra A. Wawrytko, editors

Study Abroad: The Experience of American Undergraduates
Jerry S. Carlson, Barbara B. Burn, John Useem, and David Yachimowicz

Between Understanding and Misunderstanding: Problems and Prospects for
International Cultural Exchange
Yasushi Sugiyama, editor

Southern Cities, Southern Schools: Public Education in the Urban South
David N. Plank and Rick Ginsberg, editors

Making Schools Work for Underachieving Minority Students: Next Steps for
Research, Policy, and Practice
Josie G. Bain and Joan L. Herman, editors

Foreign Teachers in China: Old Problems for a New Generation, 1979–1989
Edgar A. Porter

Effective Interventions: Applying Learning Theory to School Social Work
Evelyn Harris Ginsburg

COGNITIVE
EDUCATION
AND
TESTING

A Methodological Approach

———

EUGENE J. MEEHAN

Contributions to the Study of Education, Number 47

GREENWOOD PRESS
New York · Westport, Connecticut · London

Library of Congress Cataloging-in-Publication Data

Meehan, Eugene J.
   Cognitive education and testing : a methodological approach /
Eugene J. Meehan.
      p.   cm. — (Contributions to the study of education, ISSN
0196-707X ; no. 47)
   Includes bibliographical references and index.
   ISBN 0–313–27889–X (alk. paper)
   1. Thought and thinking—Study and teaching.   2. Cognition—Study
and teaching.   3. Thought and thinking—Testing.   4. Cognition–
–Testing.   5. Knowledge, Theory of.   I. Title.   II. Series.
BF411.M44   1991
155.9—dc20   91–3

British Library Cataloguing in Publication Data is available.

Library of Congress Catalog Card Number: 91–3
ISBN: 0–313–27889–X
ISSN: 0196–707X

First published in 1991

Greenwood Press, 88 Post Road West, Westport, CT   06881
An imprint of Greenwood Publishing Group, Inc.

Printed in the United States of America

The paper used in this book complies with the
Permanent Paper Standard issued by the National
Information Standards Organization (Z39.48–1984).

10   9   8   7   6   5   4   3   2   1

Contents

Preface		vii
Acknowledgments		xiii
1	Introduction	1
2	The Theory of Knowledge	17
3	Cognitive Skill Testing	81
	Appendix 3-A: Cognitive Skill Test: Generalized Version	107
	Appendix 3-B: Skills Explored by Each Test Question	109
	Appendix 3-C: Coding and Weighting Instructions: Cognitive Skill Test	111
4	Cognitive Improvement	121
	Appendix 4-A: Sample Unit—University	169
	Appendix 4-B: Sample Units—Elementary	177
5	Summary and Conclusions	181
	Bibliography	189
	Index	201

Preface

My immediate purpose here is to communicate to the reader as clearly and precisely as possible the essentials of a very promising approach to measuring and improving cognitive performance, and to summarize the excellent, and even exceptional, results obtained thus far from experimental applications, both in the United States and abroad. The approach depends primarily upon two basic constructs: (1) a concept labeled "cognitive skill" or "cognitive competence," which is identified with the individual's capacity to acquire, assess, and apply knowledge; and (2) a "theory of knowledge," which is limited in scope and focused on the development and use of knowledge in the conduct of human affairs. The theory serves to sharpen and constrain the meaning of cognitive competence, by specifying the structures and processes required in successful efforts to acquire, assess, and apply knowledge, and since it has been established on external grounds, provides a justification for accepting the overall approach as a legitimate point of departure. The concept of cognitive competence provides the needed focus for efforts to develop a measurement for, and ways to improve, overall cognitive performance.

My extended purpose, the reason for being concerned with measuring and improving cognitive competence, is to call attention to the glaring inadequacy of the intellectual performance of those educated in contemporary educational institutions, in the United States and elsewhere, compared to current needs. Regarded as a measure of that overall performance, the significance of cognitive competence in human affairs can hardly be exaggerated. That being the case, the need to produce a valid measure of cognitive capacity, which is an essential prerequisite to developing the ability to both improve competence levels and show that an improvement has been made, could hardly be more urgent.

The fundamental assumption on which the approach to measurement and improvement of intellectual performance depends is that skill at acquiring, assessing, and applying knowledge (here labeled "cognitive skill" or "cognitive competence") is the major factor that determines the level of achievement of the individual in real-world affairs. Knowledge, in other words, truly is "power" in the sense that it accounts for most of what humans have achieved on earth. However, knowledge, like any other form of power, must be acquired, assessed, and applied before it has any impact on human affairs, and the skill with which knowledge is handled can be as significant as the knowledge itself, other things equal. Of course, other things are not usually equal, but if information levels, motivation, and resources, among other factors, can be stabilized, that assumption allows the use of real-world achievement as a prime indicator of the individual's cognitive skill or competence. Achievement can therefore serve as the primary indicator for developing measures of cognitive skill as well as a basis for testing any proposed programs for improving performance. Identifying high-level achievers in areas of human activity that clearly depend on a significant level of acquired intellectual skill (which cannot be performed using just the inherited physical or intellectual capacity) provides the essential testing ground for proposed measures of cognitive skill; education programs meant to improve cognitive performance are validated by the performance or achievements of those who have been trained.

The importance of the theory of knowledge that provides the base for the approach is also beyond exaggeration, despite the limited conception of knowledge that it deals with. Knowledge-in-general is much too broad to serve as a base for rigorous criticism. By limiting the meaning of "knowledge" to those products of "thinking" that can be used to fulfill real-world human purposes—or, more precisely, to direct human actions to the attainment of such human purposes—nothing of any consequence is lost or omitted and skill in acquiring, assessing, and applying such knowledge (cognitive skill) is opened to pragmatically based testing and improvement at least in principle. Because the human purposes sought through action themselves become part of the knowledge structure, the ability to deal with them critically and effectively is included in the concept of cognitive skill or competence.

In that context, the two necessary preconditions to success in measuring and improving intellectual performance are: the availability of an appropriate and adequate "theory of knowledge" or analytic framework, and the capacity to identify "high-level achievers" in real-world affairs. The meaning of the concept "theory of knowledge," which will be articulated fully in Chapter 2, needs some preliminary elaboration. A "theory," as the term is used here, is simply a set of generalized assumptions that assert the necessary or sufficient preconditions for achieving a given purpose in the environment. More narrowly, those assumptions serve to relate some set of two or more events by rule under specified limiting conditions—so that action that produces a change in one event can be used to alter the other. That is, a theory will incorporate either the necessary (no *B* unless *A*) or the sufficient (if *A* then *B*) conditions for a given event *(B)* to occur. Given such a theory, if the purpose of the action is to achieve a particular purpose (produce event *B*), then at a minimum, all of the elements stipulated in the theory, including all of the limiting conditions specified, must be available before the purpose can be fulfilled.

The theory of knowledge set out in Chapter 2 satisfies those requirements fully. It consists of a set of assumptions that are, taken collectively, necessary and/or sufficient for directing human actions to the achievement of the overall purpose for which knowledge is sought (within the limits of human capacity as presently understood). By convention, philosophers call such structures a "theory of knowledge." Whether they are properly labeled "theories" is not particularly important (though it is perfectly reasonable given the way those terms are used here) so long as the meaning intended is clear.

On the approach adopted here, a theory of knowledge comprises the set of assumptions necessary for achieving the overall purpose for which knowledge is sought—a purpose that remains to be specified. Such a theory can provide the needed base for the kind of justification that is required for accepting a claim to knowledge. Justification, in other words, depends on reaching agreement through a systematic articulation of successive layers of assumptions (relating to the nature of knowledge, the intellectual capacity of species members, and the purposes that should be achieved by the exercise of human capacity, among other factors). Taken collectively, those assumptions make up the theory of knowledge. Because the overall structure is inductively based, it is contingent ultimately on the fit between inferences drawn from the set of assumptions and the content of particular human experiences—and the experience is always decisive. The full set of assumptions comprised in the theory of knowledge is beyond reach, but as the overall structure is inductively based, the selection actually applied in a justification is a function of the particular knowledge claim being justified, and can usually be specified.

Unfortunately, most discussions of knowledge creation and validation arising in specific fields of inquiry, and even in philosophy, tend to ignore or overlook the element of conditionality that marks every knowledge claim—the fact that there is no way to test any assumption except by reference to other assumptions. Yet a theory of knowledge (of a particular kind, of course) is an essential element in any defensible knowledge system. One of the major functions of this volume is to explore some of the more significant implications of a specific theory of knowledge for cognitive education and testing—and particularly the role that the theory must play in the criticism and improvement of knowledge quality or its uses or applications. Such methodological criticism, so long as it is based on a theory that includes at least some of the necessary conditions for achieving a given purpose, can be used to assess the apparatus suggested for achieving it. For if the necessary conditions for the event to occur have been identified correctly, the absence of any one of them will, necessarily, preclude success and that provides the critic or knowledge-user with a very powerful evaluative tool. If the sufficient conditions for the event to occur are included in the theory, which is a question of evidence rather than intent, then if all of those conditions have been met, the expectation that the event will occur is justified. Because it serves to inform the inquirer precisely what he or she is looking for, a theory of this kind assists the inquiry positively by restricting areas of search, and by providing both guidance for developing a search strategy and criteria for knowing when the inquiry has been successful.

To make the point in a different way, an inductively based theory of knowledge of the kind described can serve the same function with respect to purposeful thinking that a theory of play created by those who coach such well-developed sports as football or golf serves for those who play, or coach, the game. Each provides a basis for assessing performance as well as defensible grounds for suggesting ways of improving it. Both in sports and in thinking, theories function by linking human actions, under specified limiting conditions, to the achievement of particular purposes. The need to achieve those purposes is derived from the overall purpose of the game being played. The principal difference between the two is found in the source of the overall purpose sought through action: in sports, that purpose is given as part of the rules of the game; with respect to thinking, an overall purpose must be assumed—it becomes the central element in the normative apparatus on which the theory of knowledge depends. Once an overall purpose has been accepted, it serves to order subordinate purposes where they come into conflict. A theory of knowledge that can fulfill those requirements for "thinking in general," that is not field- or subject-matter specific, is set forth in Chapter 2, and is available in greater detail elsewhere in my previous books.[1]

The approach to cognitive education or testing recommended here is actually quite simple: the theory of knowledge is taken as a base; the characteristics of the thinking products necessary for successfully directing human actions to the achievement of human purposes are extrapolated or inferred from the theory of knowledge. They are tested against the actual performance of high-level achievers. The results of such testing become evidence useful for: (1) amending and improving the test of cognitive skill, (2) correcting or modifying the basic theory of knowledge, and (3) developing education programs meant to improve cognitive performance using the improved theory of knowledge as a source. This procedure has been used to create a generalized test of cognitive skill, to improve the theory of knowledge set forth in Chapter 2, and to generate a variety of educational programs, targeted at a range of different populations.

The approach does not imply or require any particular technique or method; and it should not be confused with any form of logical reasoning, whether deductive or informal. Of course, logical operations play an important part in the overall process of acquiring, assessing, and applying knowledge. Indeed, knowledge is quite usefully construed as a special kind of applied logic or mathematics. But the process of acquiring, assessing, and applying knowledge is not merely logical. To illustrate, a test produced inductively should be able to fulfill at least two major purposes: first, to serve as a predictor of success in the environment; and second, to function as a diagnostic tool, able to show aspects of cognitive performance that need improvement. Neither function is logical in the formal sense of the term.

Some of the more significant findings to emerge from the preliminary experiments with cognitive testing and training can be summarized quickly. At a minimum, they suggest: (1) the importance of having an adequate measure for the concept of cognitive skill; (2) the need to create education or training courses able to increase such skill levels substantially; and (3) the value of the theory of knowledge in the enterprise as a whole. More specifically, the link to high-level performance in real-world affairs is extremely powerful. High-level achievers, in a variety of cultures and subcultures, invariably display high levels of cognitive skill as measured by the cognitive skill test; those who do not are rarely if ever found among society's high-level achievers. That relation has thus far held across a wide range of cultural, linguistic, environmental, and other differentials. Perhaps even more important, cognitive skill as defined can be improved substantially (judged by reference to the scores attained by those whose achievements in real-world affairs were regarded as outstanding) despite differences in IQ scores, or grades received in the public schools or the universities. At the extremes of the IQ range, there are persons whose performance is not improved by any amount of cognitive training, as well as other persons who will do very well without any outside assistance. In fact, intelligence seems to function best as an indicator of individual ability to learn how to learn without assistance from others. The relative efficiency of such learning may be suspect, but that remains a matter for future inquiry.

In sum, it is clear from the testing already conducted that the concept of cognitive skill relates very strongly to real-world achievement, that a useful measure of the concept can be created and stabilized, and that the skills measured can be improved selectively and systematically by using

education or training based on or extrapolated from the theory of knowledge. Moreover, that training carries over into everyday activities much
better, for example, than training in formal or "informal" logic or in
mathematics. The principal areas of uncertainty remaining, which are due
mainly to the limited resources available for experimentation, have to do
with such things as the long-range effects of cognitive training, and the
factors that influence retention, particularly in societies that maintain a
generally antiintellectual environment or where methodological or analytic
criticism is not a regular part of everyday practice, even among the well-
educated.

NOTE

1. See Eugene J. Meehan, *Reasoned Argument in Social Science: Linking Research to Policy* (Greenwood Press, 1981), and *Ethics for Policymaking: A Methodological Analysis* (Greenwood Press, 1990).

Acknowledgments

More than two decades have passed since this study began, and it has involved the active cooperation and assistance of a number of agencies and organizations in several different countries. It would be quite impossible to enumerate all of the individuals who have contributed, either directly or indirectly, to the enterprise—even a full list of groups and institutions would be cumbersome and impractical. The best that can be managed is an expression of heartfelt thanks to everyone who has taken part, and in particular to the relevant members of the following organizations: the Agency for International Development in Washington, D.C. and the Guatemala office; the Instituto Nacional de Administración Para el Desarrollo (INAD) in Guatemala City; the University of Costa Rica in San Jose, and the Ministry of Education of that country; the Department of International Education at Indiana University in Bloomington; the Normandy School System, and especially the Bel Nor Elementary School, in St. Louis; and the Center for Metropolitan Studies at the University of Missouri–St. Louis. Those cooperating in one way or another ranged from government administrators to personal friends and colleagues, from preschool children to graduate students. I welcome the opportunity to thank them all, and I hope they may find some slight recompense for their time and effort in the very hopeful prospects for the future of cognitive education and testing outlined in the pages that follow.

COGNITIVE
EDUCATION
AND
TESTING

1

Introduction

Whether other living things on earth besides humans can "think" may be open to dispute, depending on how "thinking" is defined; that no other known creature can think fractionally as well as humans is beyond cavil. The overwhelming superiority of the human intellect over that of any other living creature is well established. Indeed, it is generally accepted that the products of that superior human intellectual capacity (knowledge), suitably harnessed to human actions, have been largely if not entirely responsible for the dominant position of the human species, taken collectively, on the planet. The collection of intellectual capacities required in successful efforts to harness knowledge to action (to acquire, assess, and apply knowledge adequate for directing actions on defensible grounds), which is one of the two central elements directing the inquiry, has been labeled "cognitive skill."

Given the importance of the cognitive dimension of human performance (of the role that knowledge acquisition, assessment, and application plays in human affairs), it is somewhat surprising to note how little effort has been made to improve the quality of cognitive performance systematically and extensively—to raise levels of cognitive skill. Enormous sums have been expended on education, of course, but the narrowly cognitive dimension of human capacity has generally been neglected, both in the schools and in the society at large. The contrast to the systematic efforts that have been made to improve performance in physical activities by appropriate coaching and practice is particularly striking. In the intellectual domain, there is at present no equivalent to the kind of capacity to measure and improve performance widely available in physical education, in athletics, or in physical therapy. There are few if any intellectual "coaches" worthy of the name, despite the thousands and thousands of educators found in most societies, and no sign of the kind of "theory of play" on which competent athletic coaching depends. If the work carried out in recent years under such rubrics as "critical thinking," "informal logic," "problem solving," or simply "management" has produced a plethora of experts, the precise nature of their expertise remains uncertain and the reasons offered for regarding them as experts are usually unconvincing. It is very unlikely, for example, that a coach in a well-developed sport such as football could obtain employment on the basis of the kinds of credentials and track record currently accepted in the area of cognitive or intellectual analysis or training.

The problem has, of course, been recognized. The following assessment of the situation, made by the National Institute of Education (NIE) in 1980, is typical:

In a rapidly changing technological environment, it is difficult to predict what knowledge students will need and what problems they will have to solve twenty years from now. What they really need to know is how to learn the new information and skills that will be required throughout their lives. . . . Skill in learning and reasoning itself is almost entirely neglected by the schools. . . . It is assumed, or hoped, that repeated attempts to learn or to solve problems will automatically result in improvement in general ability to reason and solve problems.[1]

Furthermore, it is now generally accepted by those working in the field that development of an adequate theoretical/conceptual framework, a theory of knowledge in which the meaning of knowledge is linked firmly to real-world actions, is the essential prerequisite to improving cognitive assessment and training. Indeed, the NIE circular quoted above solicits proposals for creating such an apparatus. In that context, the basic purpose of this volume is simply to provide an adequate theory of knowledge, a "theory of play" for the "knowledge game," and to show how it can be used to measure and improve cognitive performance.

A theory able to fulfill those requirements will consist of the set of assumptions that makes possible, though it cannot guarantee, the fulfillment of an agreed set of intellectual functions or purposes within the limits of human capacity as presently understood. The basic elements of an apparatus adequate for systematically assessing the quality of cognitive performance and for producing improvements in such performance through particular kinds of education and training is set forth in Chapter 2. It remains tentative and uncertain, like all such structures, and the evidence and argument available to support its use as a basis for measuring and improving cognitive skill are less decisive than one might wish. But the results obtained thus far have been uniformly positive and the theoretical apparatus is clearly corrigible in use, open to criticism and improvement on the basis of experience and argument, and that is all that can reasonably be demanded given the present state of development of the field.

PRELIMINARY CONSIDERATIONS

The lexical meaning of "cognition" (the process or the product of knowing) is too broad to serve as a basis for systematic criticism and improvement of human intellectual performance. But it does provide support for locating cognitive skill or cognitive competence (in the discussion that follows, the two terms are used interchangeably) in the relation between the human individual and the knowledge supply. Cognitive skill, as the term is used here, is an evaluative concept; it refers in context to the skill or effectiveness with which an individual acquires, assesses, and applies or uses knowledge. The overall construct includes a large number of particular skills; its meaning cannot be completely stipulated. But because that meaning can be established within a theory of knowledge, an adequate measure can be created for it and tested in application. The best analogue available for clarifying the procedure is the concept of skill as it appears in sports: overall skill in a particular sport can be assessed and improved without identifying all of the particular skills that contribute to the total performance, providing that an adequate theory of play or "coaching theory" is available in which at least some of the particular skills involved can be identified.

In sum, if the task at hand is to find defensible ways of measuring and improving cognitive skill in the sense employed here, the key to success is the development of a theory of knowledge in which the meaning of knowledge is firmly and clearly linked to the intellectual requirements for directing human actions on defensible and/or corrigible grounds within the limits of human capacity as it is presently accepted or understood. The implications of that requirement are formidable. The need for defensibility/corrigibility enjoins a statement of the purposes for which knowledge is sought and used; human actions, whether mental or physical, cannot be criticized qualitatively except by reference to the purpose to which they are directed. That requirement in turn forces identification of an overriding purpose for intellectual performance, an ultimate purpose for which knowledge is sought and employed, that can serve as a baseline for evaluating analyses, justifications, and criticisms. Curiously enough, articulating the ultimate purpose for which knowledge is to be used, and in terms of which knowledge claims can be assessed, turns out to be much simpler than might be expected. Given the overwhelming importance of human life to members of the species (if only of their own), maintenance and/or improvement of the conditions of life of *some* human population can safely be assumed as the ultimate purpose of all forms of human activity, whether physical or intellectual. The connecting link between knowledge (and cognitive skill) and that overall purpose is supplied by human actions, which serve to reify purposes in the world of experience. It follows that the intellectual requirements for evaluating/improving cognitive performance are identical to the intellectual requirements for directing human actions on defensible and corrigible grounds. A conception of knowledge that will fulfill one of these purposes will therefore fulfill the other. That provides the needed leverage point for assessing or measuring and improving cognitive performance.

Once an overall purpose to be fulfilled by the use or application of knowledge has been agreed, a fuller and more precise meaning for knowledge, and for the related conception of cognitive skill—or more precisely, for the functions to be performed by the use of such skill—can be created by systematic analysis of the agreed overall purpose into the set of contributory or subordinate purposes whose fulfillment is prerequisite (necessary and/or sufficient) to achieving the overall goal. Those ancillary purposes can be subjected to still further analysis until the limits of analytic capacity (or of the available time and resources) have been reached—again noting that no absolute statement of either intellectual purposes or cognitive skills is possible. The analysis to be carried out exactly parallels the procedure followed by coaches of sports such as football, where the overall purpose of winning a game is broken down through successive levels to show that success depends on fulfilling such purposes as scoring points according to the rules and preventing the opponent from doing so, and that fulfilling those second-order purposes is facilitated by using the results of further analysis (into such actions as passing, blocking, and so on). Still more analysis may then show that satisfaction of those purposes in turn is facilitated by fostering certain physical abilities and mental attitudes through appropriate practice and training. In football, the complete analytic apparatus amounts to a theory of play that can be used to guide both coaches and players in the performance of their respective functions. That theory of play provides the criteria needed for assessing, and improving, the performance of individual players as well as teams (and coaches). For assessing and improving cognitive skill, a theory of knowledge is needed that is equivalent to such a theory of play. That theory will focus on the fulfillment of an overall purpose or goal—in the present case, maintenance and/ or improvement of the conditions of life of some human population. That is the sense in which it can be said quite properly that all of human knowledge rests upon a normative foundation.

Maintaining and improving the human condition by using knowledge to direct actions requires the individual to fulfill three major second-order purposes (the equivalent of running, passing, and kicking in football). First, knowledge must be *acquired* (and therefore must be recognized); second, it must be *assessed* or evaluated; and third, it must be *applied,* or used to direct actions. Although these three subordinate purposes seem to be both necessary and sufficient for maintaining and improving the human condition, that strong claim need not be made in order to satisfy the goals set for the inquiry. So long as it can be agreed that they are *necessary* for the task, an analytic apparatus that is able to show that those requirements are indeed necessary and to suggest ways of fulfilling them is an invaluable intellectual tool. Cognitive skill, as the term is used here, is simply a measure of the relative effectiveness with which these functions are performed.

The full analysis of the requirements for directing human actions, which may comprise several levels or layers of purposes, provides the needed grounds for justifying or arguing the adequacy of the theory of knowledge. That in turn provides a way of measuring and comparing cognitive performance, and a basis for designing education or training programs to improve that performance. The results obtained by applying the analytic apparatus can be tested further against pragmatic criteria developed externally to the theory—within the particular field of action involved. The three primary skills required, which can be referred to as the "Three As" of cognitive education, are largely if not completely independent, both analytically and empirically, of native intelligence. The concept of cognitive skill does, however, include the individual's ability to make and defend judgments, and particularly judgments of the kind needed to assess the significance and acceptability of knowledge claims.

As in sports, the necessary precondition to determining the quality of cognitive performance is the use of knowledge to direct actions. Knowledge that cannot be acted upon, directly or indirectly, is opaque to qualitative assessment. Using "action" as the primary focus for assessing cognitive performance might appear to introduce an additional source of ambiguity and uncertainty into the analysis, and more particularly into the measurement and assessment procedures developed from it, for action can be conceptualized in an enormous number of different ways and it is well known that actions almost always involve a number of complex factors such as motivation, the availability of resources, awareness, and so on. Further, cognitive performance cannot be judged simply by reference to success in achieving its overall purpose of maintaining and improving the conditions of life of some part of the human population, for the same reasons that the quality of athletic coaching is not necessarily measured accurately by the number of games won or lost by the team that has been coached.

Fortunately, such problems are readily avoided by defining action in terms of an actor's capacity to produce change in the environment. The analytic apparatus can then be tailored to fit any way of classifying actions, whether as mental actions, verbal responses, paper and pencil functions, the exercise of abstract social or economic authority, and so on, without difficulty.

The complexities arising out of the multicausal character of human actions are avoided by basing assessments of cognitive competence on the reasons that are offered for acting in a particular way, rather than on the objective characteristics of the actions. That avoids reliance upon such risky practices as attributing psychic characteristics to the person and then using them to account for behavior—which comes very close to postulating a "spirit" within a tree that is responsible for its movements. Instead, criticism can focus on the *action* taken or recommended and not on the actor. Criticism of actions therefore remains possible even in those cases where the actor fails, or refuses, to give reasons for acting in a particular way, for the reasons that *could be* offered to support one or another of the options available to an actor in a particular situation can be generated by the critic. In effect, criticism is concerned to produce the best argument possible (as judged by the critic) in favor of acting in a particular way— or choosing one of the available outcomes—and to use that argument as a basis for criticizing the action that is actually taken. Of course, the critic then has a responsibility to open the criticism to further criticism, but that responsibility is adequately fulfilled by articulating the reasons for particular actions or preferences as completely and accurately as possible.

An action focus is particularly important in any analysis intended to produce the instruments needed for assessing and improving cognitive performance because the primary cognitive skills need not be exercised self-consciously or in the full realization that something labeled "knowledge" is being acquired and/or used. The individual can and does possess, evaluate, and apply knowledge whether or not the structures and processes are conceived in "knowledge" terms. The transmission of knowledge from one person to another can take place without awareness of "what" is being transferred. Indeed, it seems very likely that most human knowledge is transmitted, and acquired, embedded in particular substantive propositions, even within formal education, and that cognitive competence or skill is developed from the same base. The results obtained in a number of university-level testing programs conducted in the United States and Costa Rica, which indicate that the field of study is the single most important factor in determining the level of cognitive skill developed by members of a college-level population, not excluding even native intelligence, support the same conclusion.[2]

However, without self-conscious awareness that knowledge is being sought, acquired, and applied, there is no way for the individual to develop an analytic framework that can be used for criticizing knowledge produced or employed on methodological grounds. But adequate criticism of any knowledge claim necessarily involves reference to both substantive and methodological or analytic requirements, and the latter are contingent upon the availability of an appropriate theoretical base. Absent such a critical base, cognitive skill levels tend to be a function primarily of native intelligence and accident. In fact, the relation between intelligence and performance is then so strong that it commends the underlying wisdom of what is best labeled the "Harvard syndrome" in American higher education—recruiting students with very high levels of native intelligence and taking credit for their intellectual achievements. For if intelligence is taken as an indicator of the individual's capacity to learn how to learn unaided (how to acquire and use knowledge without external assistance), as seems reasonable, then a university system that is unable to assist the student to learn how to learn systematically and self-consciously cannot improve on that policy.

The most serious consequence for the individual of not having an analytic framework for dealing with knowledge and its applications, of not having a self-conscious awareness of "what is being done" intellectually, is that the person is then unable to defend or criticize knowledge claims on adequate grounds. Yet the need to subject every knowledge claim to criticism on both experiential or substantive and methodological grounds before it can be accepted renders it essential that this be done. Agreement with experience is not enough. A simple illustration is found in the case of the child who learns that one cannot add apples and pears but does not understand why the operation cannot be performed. In the circumstances, the child cannot say which other "things" can or cannot be added. More importantly, it cannot deal critically with such additions when they are performed by others. For in the absence of an adequate analytic or theoretical framework, specific propositions cannot be tested against the available body of generalized knowledge. For example, to know that a particular light bulb glows if attached with two specific wires to a particular battery is to have knowledge, but that knowledge can be tested only against the particular apparatus so long as the linkages or relationships involved are conceptualized in that way. The necessary connection to the body of cumulated knowledge is provided by the abstract and generalized character of an analytic/critical framework or theory. The concepts employed in such structures refer to classes of events and not to particulars; when correctly applied, such concepts serve to create a formal and calculable relation between the particular case and the body of generalized past experience currently accepted within a field of inquiry (or a society) and thus make testing of the particular case against the cumulated body of knowledge, suitably generalized, possible at least in principle.

LIMITS AND QUALIFICATIONS

Given the need to focus on acquiring, assessing, and applying knowledge, the conception of knowledge employed as a base for inquiry (the theory of knowledge that is assumed), becomes the central factor determining the validity or acceptability of proposed procedures or programs for testing or improving cognitive performance. The conception of knowledge on which the analytic framework depends must therefore be assessed before evaluations of cognitive competence—the capacity to acquire, assess, and apply knowledge—can themselves be evaluated. That in turn forces reference to actual experience, to systematic efforts to achieve specified real-world purposes by accepting and applying particular generalized assumptions through an appropriate set of formal connections. Which brings us eventually to the importance of having an identifiable set of high-level achievers available for testing the validity of at least some of the theoretical assumptions included in the apparatus.

The primary requirement for successful isolation of the performance attribute here labeled cognitive skill is therefore the development of a conception of knowledge, a generalized theoretical framework, to which the meaning of the term "cognitive skill" can be linked. Acceptable criteria for assessing cognitive skill, and for augmenting that skill by suitable training, can then be created and tested pragmatically. That requirement rules out the use of a number of approaches to cognition that may be perfectly valid in another context. Thus a neurological construction of cognitive processes, using concepts that refer to their physical or physico-chemical dimensions, would be of little assistance given the purpose to be fulfilled here. If the aim is to assess and improve cognitive performance rather than simply observe or measure it, using that conceptual framework would be equivalent to making a systematic analysis of the electromagnetic wave patterns produced by human voices in an effort to assess the validity of an argument conducted by telephone. Such analysis can be valuable for some purposes, as in modern communications, where it is necessary to know the functioning of the system that carries information in order to maintain and improve it, but is useless for assessing the quality of the substantive messages that are carried.

Other limits and qualifications to be observed in the development of the theoretical apparatus are a function of the peculiar character of the intellectual enterprise in its self-examination mode. Thus most of the really difficult conceptual/theoretical problems to emerge during efforts to measure and improve cognitive performance are a function of the holistic character of the nervous system as a functioning entity. Like intelligence, cognitive skill cannot be directly perceived; the intellectual system is opaque to human observers, including the person in whom the system resides. Nor can cognitive performance be analyzed completely into its constituent elements and processes, in the same way as a watch or other piece of machinery. So far as the quality of cognitive performance is concerned, the human intellectual apparatus must be treated as a unit or, to use the language of engineering, regarded as a "black box." It follows that there is no alternative to focusing on the products of intellectual processes in efforts to evaluate and improve intellectual performance. At best, inputs and outputs (stimuli and responses) can be linked in useful ways by creating a suitable analytic framework—which can then be tested experimentally and pragmatically. And in those situations where even very limited forms of experimentation are difficult or impossible, the only assessment procedure available is to link system outputs to external events. When that occurs, it may be useful to postulate particular processes within the overall apparatus, and by suitable experimentation provide support for accepting the postulated apparatus, but it cannot be shown that the system really operates in any particular manner. The evidence that is available and can be cumulated is only sufficient to *rule out* particular forms of system organization or functioning.

The difference between treating cognitive processes as postulates and regarding them as established internal processes becomes particularly important when the critic must deal with nonanalyzable performance characteristics, particularly of the kind usually labeled "judgments." Such functions are translogical, meaning that they cannot be reduced to formal inferences from specific premises and must instead be treated as a function or product of the complete (unspecified) nervous system. A good metaphor is found in the relation between "telling time" and the physical functioning of a watch that cannot be opened or analyzed. The nervous system is so enormous, and contains so many propositions or assumptions, that every human performance requires a selection of assumptions or beliefs as operating premises on which to base the required judgments. In principle, the full set of assumptions actually employed in any given case cannot be identified; even the individual involved cannot be certain on the point. Further, since the content of the system has not been and cannot be rationalized completely, serious inconsistencies may be present within the overall system—even if the person is sensitized to the need to avoid contradiction. A practical resolution to the problem can be achieved by first seeking to articulate as fully as possible the set of premises used in particular cases, and then *assuming* that they constitute a complete set—on the clear understanding that the assumption may be mistaken. Due regard must also be given to the logical coherence of the enumerated set, of course, but logical coherence is not in itself an adequate justification for accepting some set of assumptions as the complete set needed to deal with a particular case.

Put somewhat differently, the *process* of judgment lies beyond human capacity to replicate fully and perfectly—or to incorporate into a formal logical structure and be certain that it will function perfectly. Human judgments are in a sense "creative" actions; they are usefully construed as the use of the total intellectual apparatus to make a measurement. The only available test of a human judgment is another human judgment—in effect, a comparison must be made of the reasoning and evidence that *can be* marshaled to support different judgments, carried out by competent human judges. Such tests proceed by pushing back the argument, uncovering successive layers of assumptions until one or both of the protagonists (the process may involve only one person) reach a point where no further evidence, or relevant knowledge, can be produced. If no agreement has been reached at that point, nothing more can be said unless additional evidence comes available—or unless the fundamental assumptions accepted as a basis for argument change. In both the physical sciences and the study of human affairs (including normative inquiry), the court of last resort with respect to judgments is a consensus of the community of informed and competent persons, a consensus arrived at by that relatively simple process. The members of the well-informed community may be very difficult to identify, and in some cases at least they may not agree. When that occurs (absent a consensus) the point in question must be regarded as moot.

The formal limit imposed by the need to rely on judgments is immutable; some way of evading it must therefore be produced and accepted, otherwise efforts to create knowledge or, more precisely, to assess its validity, cannot succeed—or cannot be known to have succeeded. The "solution," which is a commonplace, is to ignore the processes by which judgments are reached and concentrate on replicating the conclusions. Since that is the only procedure available for dealing with black boxes, at least to the extent that they are truly opaque, it must be accepted as one of the fundamentals in every knowledge system. The task of producing knowledge appears from that perspective as an effort to create a logical apparatus that reproduces the external characteristics of black box performance. There is no justification for assuming that the axioms incorporated into the logical system replicate the internal logic of the black box, nor is there any need to do so. So long as such knowledge is created with a specific purpose in mind, and linked firmly to the conduct of human affairs, successive applications (and the elimination of discrepancies as they appear) can produce intellectual tools of immense power and accuracy.

The Lack of Agreement on Fundamentals

A major goal of this study is to develop and justify an analytic or theoretical framework that is adequate for dealing with cognitive performance. Unfortunately, that cannot be done by building upon established elements or sets of elements in the existing literature on cognition or cognitive performance. Although the amount of published material relating to cognition is enormous, it is also extremely diverse, particularly with respect to fundamentals. Put differently, there is at present no single "paradigm" that guides cognitive inquiry, no common conceptual or theoretical framework that could be elaborated or refined and applied. Nor would it be feasible to try to summarize the results of past inquiries and thus provide a base for future research, or a justification for particular conclusions or recommendations. An analytic framework adequate for cognitive assessment and performance improvement will in fact be a theory of knowledge of a particular character. The failure to produce an agreed epistemological base has been, and remains, the greatest impediment to the development of adequate instruments for testing cognitive competence or skill, and the creation of education and/or training programs for improving it. Filling that gap is therefore a primary concern.

Absent agreement on a set of fundamental assumptions, the best way to proceed is first to produce a theory of knowledge that is *adequate* for the task, supply a justification or rationale for accepting it, and then summarize the evidence obtained by using it. The key to an adequate theory is a construction of knowledge that makes it possible to assess its quality. The solution employed here construes knowledge instrumentally, as a humanly created tool for achieving human purposes that are themselves instrumental to maintaining and improving the conditions of life of some human population. The link between the two is provided by human *actions,* which are defined as the exercise of human capacity to produce change (or prevent change) in the environment. In these terms, an analytic apparatus that is adequate for assessing and improving cognitive performance must be able to show how the kind of knowledge required for directing human actions on defensible grounds can be created, and assessed, within the limits of human capacity.

A theoretical structure able to fulfill those requirements is set out below. There may, of course, be others, but that does not affect the validity and usefulness of the proposed theory, or of the results obtained by applying it. There can be any number of different but equally valid theories for a given phenomenon. What is most important in the present context is that the criteria of adequacy entailed by one valid theoretical apparatus must satisfy the requirements of *all* other valid theories. To illustrate, a number of different conceptual frameworks can be used to theorize about "freezing" (changing from a liquid to a solid state). But fulfilling the minimum requirements for freezing as established by one valid theory that employs such concepts as molecular activity will automatically, and necessarily, satisfy the requirements for freezing developed within another valid theory that made use of the concept "temperature" instead. Indeed, having two theories that account for the same phenomenon actually serves to make them mutually reinforcing.

The theory of knowledge used to identify and criticize efforts to direct human actions is detailed in Chapter 2. A test derived from the theory that can serve as a measure of cognitive skill is set forth in Chapter 3. The use of the theory for education or training intended to increase cognitive skill, and thus improve overall cognitive performance, is examined in Chapter 4. The results obtained to date by applying the test, and by experimental training, carried out in a variety of different cultural settings at various age levels, are included in the discussion and detailed in the chapter appendixes.

Unacceptable Constructions

To avoid needless disagreements about the kinds of evidence and argument that are needed to support the theory of knowledge, it may be useful to identify a small set of assumptions and practices that appear quite frequently in cognitive inquiries (either explicitly stated or implicit in the supporting evidence and argument offered for a conclusion) but are explicitly rejected here. Five are particularly important: (1) focusing inquiry upon procedures or processes rather than outcomes or products, often coupled with reliance on "stage theories" of intellectual (or moral) development that are taken as nature-imposed and immutable; (2) identification of "thinking" with logical functioning, or with "rational" procedures; (3) assuming that physical science, and more specifically modern physics (sometimes confused with Newtonian mechanics), provides the best available model for emulation in efforts to improve cognitive performance; (4) assuming that traditional constructions of ethics are adequate, hence that the fundamental normative problem is to learn how to use an already-available intellectual apparatus; and (5) interpreting the logical gap between empirical and normative propositions to mean that cognition has little or no role in normative affairs.

The reasons for rejecting these particular assumptions/practices are relatively straightforward:

1. No process, whether identified as some kind of scientific method practiced by physicists or merely generalized from the practice of ordinary mortals carrying on their daily affairs, can guarantee the quality of human performance. The *only* arena in which process guarantees product is formal logic or mathematics. Further, the kind of evidence needed to separate what is necessary behavior in a creature that is capable of learning from what is merely an observed regularity, which is essential for identifying immutable developmental stages, cannot be determined completely.

2. Although formal calculation or logic has an important role to play in thinking, it is a serious, though common, mistake to equate the two. For thinking, as it appears both in everyday affairs and in the cognitive psychologist's laboratory, is always thinking *about* something; it involves more than a process. To illustrate, the same difference appears between addition, which is an arithmetical (purely formal or logical) process, and addition *of*, say, "apples" or "pears," which is analogous to thinking. The latter involves the *application* of arithmetic, and thus depends upon considerations that are additional to, and not part of, that specialized branch

of logic—the process differs significantly from thinking carried on *within* the boundaries of any logic such as arithmetic.

3. The use of natural science, and physics in particular, as a prototype for intellectual inquiry, is particularly unfortunate because of its superficial plausibility—and the immense prestige those fields of study enjoy in contemporary society. At a minimum, using the (assumed) characteristics of the natural sciences as a model for emulation by other disciplines greatly increases the danger, if it does not ensure, that the normative dimension of the thinking processes and knowledge structures involved will be overlooked or ignored—with potentially disastrous consequences. For it is much easier to avoid the normative when dealing with a world made up of atoms and molecules, or elements and chemical reactions, than when dealing with medicine or even with agriculture. Since the normative aspect of thinking purposefully is ignored at peril, such fields as medicine or agriculture, or even athletic coaching, which combine a concern for the empirical with explicit attention to the normative dimensions of the activity involved, offer a far better model for the overall cognitive enterprise than fields such as physics, where the need to rely on a normative base, though no less real, is much less obvious—a point to be elaborated at some length in Chapter 2.

4. The concept of "ethics" or "morality" presently taught and practiced, in the universities as well as in society at large, is almost never adequate for assessing and improving cognitive performance. For reasons that will be considered in detail below, what is required of a useful and defensible ethic is a way of justifying a preference for one of the outcomes available for choice by a given actor at a particular time and place. Such justifications depend absolutely on systematic comparisons. In contrast, the objective of traditional ethical inquiry has usually been to evaluate or measure some "normative" quality (goodness, rightness, justice, and so on) of particular actions, intentions, or, occasionally, outcomes. If a comparative basis for justification is essential, as is readily demonstrated, then such an evaluative tool, even if it could be produced and justified (and thus far, philosophers and moralists have failed to accomplish this), would still be inadequate. That is, being able to argue that one outcome in an available set of options is "good" or "right" or "just" is not enough, for if one of the alternatives is "better" than the others, the normative apparatus must be able to make that distinction.

Further, most of the imperatives that have been developed in moral philosophy simply *cannot* be applied to human affairs given the meaning normally attached to that term. To "apply" an assumption means to accept and act upon it, and therefore to accept (and act upon) all of its implications. Such constructs as "do the right thing," "perform just actions," and so on, have no content, hence cannot in principle be accepted and acted upon. They are tantamount to such instructions as "take no fish from this lake if doing so will harm the ecological balance." So long as the "ecological balance" cannot be determined, what appear to be "instructions" are actually meaningless. The same criticism should be leveled against such "normative" devices as Kant's "categorical imperative," which advises us to "act only on that maxim which you can at the same time will to be a universal law." The effect is to shift the focus of argument to the reasons that should be offered for proposing a universal law—which is equally unattainable.

One of the best illustrations of what is involved in such normative legerdemain appears in Antoine de Saint-Exupery's *The Little Prince,* a wonderful fairy tale for adults about a little prince who leaves his tiny planet and comes to visit earth.[3] An aviator, who befriends the little prince, is asked by the visitor to draw a sheep (the prince wants a particular sheep to take home to his distant planet). After numerous efforts fail to satisfy the prince, the aviator hits on a winning strategem: he draws a box and explains to the little prince that the sheep can be found inside. The prince then populates the box from his memory/imagination, leaving the aviator free to claim success and the little prince with an exaggerated and unwarranted assessment of the aviator's artistic competence. Not surprisingly, the technique finds great favor among those who live by dispensing empty formulas for guiding human behavior. Traditional ethics has in general foundered on the difficulties that appear when abstract formulas must be linked to concrete human situations and provided with an experience-based justification. Twentieth-century English-language philosophy largely abandoned the effort and turned, perhaps out of despair, to a form of metaethics that is almost insistently lacking in content. And in those cases where the content of the ethic is stated, particularly in terms that imply concrete actions or choices, it turns out almost invariably to be either Delphic and ambiguous or beyond any possibility of justification.

5. Finally, the total separation of cognitive process and normative judgment is far and away the most important of the assumptions to be rejected here—the more so, perhaps, because of the inherent vagueness of meaning of the phrase "normative judgment." That propositions expressing preferences ("value" statements) cannot be deduced formally from factual propositions is beyond dispute. But that prohibition refers only to logical processes; it does not mean that such propositions are unrelated in the world of experience. Analysis suggests that normative questions are not only part of the cognitive domain, but that they are actually *the most important* kind of problem to be resolved by cognitive functioning, and a type of problem that can be resolved acceptably *only* by cognitive functioning.

NOTES

1. National Institute of Education, *Request for Proposal: NIE-R-80-0014.* April 21, 1980, Section I, p. 1.

2. See Eugene J. Meehan, "The Impact of AID-Sponsored Training on Development-Related Attitudes and Behavior," in Roy C. Macridis and Eugene J. Meehan, *Value Systems of Youth in Developing Countries: A Report Submitted to the Agency for International Development,* AID Contract ced-824, November 15, 1969.

3. Antoine de Saint-Exupery, *The Little Prince,* tr. Katherine Woods (Harcourt, Brace, and World, 1943).

2

The Theory of Knowledge

The importance of being able to assess and increase the amount of cognitive skill available within society, to determine whether or not an intellectual performance was the best possible by current standards, and to estimate, however crudely, the credence that should be attached to a knowledge claim could hardly be greater, particularly in self-governing society. At a minimum, the individual must be able to identify, and to avoid, gross errors in reasoning and argument, and that requires knowledge of the necessary and/or sufficient conditions for success in the enterprise at hand. A theory of knowledge that parallels the theory of play created by coaches in well-developed sports can provide the necessary critical apparatus. Such theories perform their critical function by linking purposes sought to the structural, procedural, and evidentiary requirements for fulfilling them. The purposes sought must themselves be both worth attaining (a matter for independent judgment and argument), and attainable within the limits of human capacity. If real-world purposes can be identified within such a theoretical structure, the analytic requirements can be transferred to the world of experience. They can then assist the individual to: (1) develop knowledge (because they identify the preconditions to be satisfied before the purpose in hand can be fulfilled); and (2) criticize knowledge claims (because they include at least a statement of the necessary conditions for success). Applying the theory to the world of experience, because it produces consequences that are open in some degree to observation, provides an opportunity to test the theory against pragmatic criteria that can also be developed and justified out of past experience.

To illustrate the process in a simple way, if some of the analytic preconditions for successful prediction can be established, then efforts to produce a real-world prediction can use them as guidelines for developing the needed instrument—to know the kind of instrument required, and thus be able to assess its quality to some degree at least before actually using it. The predictions generated using the instrument then provide a further test of the analytic apparatus as well as a test of the specific forecasting device. Because successful predictions have to satisfy the specified preconditions, failure to do so would be sufficient grounds for rejecting the prediction in advance of actually making it or acting upon it. The individual who wishes to make use of such a critical apparatus must first know its content (the necessary/sufficient conditions for successful prediction) and then be able to identify the real-world purpose as the kind of predicting to which the apparatus applies.

An analytic framework of the kind required, a theory of play for the knowledge game, is developed in precisely the same manner, and according to the same criteria, as a theory of play in athletics. Like the football coach, those seeking to create a theory of knowledge that can serve as a theory of play for the effort to produce and apply knowledge must begin by identifying the overall purpose of the "game" being played. The possibilities and limitations that can influence the performance of the players, including both the attributes of the players themselves and the relevant conditions that characterize the environment in which the game is played, can then be established or stipulated. That much accomplished, systematic analysis and reasoning can, in principle at least, produce a statement of the necessary, or even the sufficient, conditions that must be fulfilled in order to achieve the overall purpose of the game—and perhaps suggest optimal strategies for doing so. Knowing the necessary preconditions for fulfilling the purpose one is trying to achieve is, of course, an enormous improvement over proceeding in ignorance, whether the goal is creation or criticism of knowledge. Further, the overall structure, since it is not field-specific, can be tested by almost anyone against his or her own past experience.

The exposition of the analytic framework or theory of knowledge is organized in this chapter under five major headings. It begins with the overriding purpose to be achieved through the use of knowledge, maintenance, and improvement of the conditions of life of some human population. The three major second-order purposes that must be fulfilled in order to achieve that overriding purpose (prediction, control, and choice) are then examined serially. The discussion turns next to the human capacities available for achieving those purposes, and the limitations that must be observed while doing so. After setting out the intellectual requirements for directing action, discussion focuses on the so-called induction problem and a recommended way of evading it. A more detailed examination of the way in which two types of empirical knowledge (descriptions and predictions) are created is followed by a careful exposition of the kind of instrument needed for controlling future events (theories). That leads to a summary of the normative requirements for directing actions and the way in which they can be fulfilled and the result argued or justified. Particular emphasis is placed on the problems of measurement involved in comparisons of outcomes and the implications of the equality assumption—both prime considerations in development and justification of normative knowledge. The chapter ends with a brief discussion of the implications of being forced to function in a social context, within the boundaries of a nation-state located in the existing international state system.

PURPOSES

Unlike the athletic coach, those seeking a theory of knowledge must, as it were, invent their own game and justify the effort to learn it. As noted earlier, every form of human activity, including the development and use of knowledge, can legitimately be regarded (analytically at least) as directed toward a common overall purpose. In general terms, that purpose is relatively easy to establish or justify: for the species as a whole, the satisfaction of the fundamental normative assumptions or premises that are accepted by those who take part in the game, the assumptions that make up the normative system accepted and applied in that situation by those involved, is basic. To illustrate, it is an overriding purpose of that nature, the set of fundamental normative premises accepted by those involved (whether knowingly or self-consciously is irrelevant) that constrains the high school football coach from risking the health and future welfare of the players in the interests of fulfilling the purpose of the game of football being played (winning). The overriding purpose accepted as a basis for the quest for knowledge must be regarded as autonomous (not subject to qualification, though only temporarily), otherwise it could not perform its essential function in analysis and criticism. So long as that overriding status is maintained, all other human purposes are contingent and their significance can therefore be judged in terms of their contribution to fulfilling it. The ultimate purpose accepted as a goal for human actions serves as the primary ordering instrument for organizing the hierarchy of purposes needed for adequate criticism—and serves to adjudicate among them in the event of conflict.

However, the overall purpose accepted at any given point in time cannot be regarded as immutable; it may be superseded if persuasive reasons ("persuasive" to the established body of informed opinion) can be offered for accepting a different overall purpose for human actions. Furthermore, different individuals, or societies, may accept quite different overall purposes or premises as a basis for their respective normative structures, despite the fact that many subordinate purposes are widely shared. Finally, agreement on an overall purpose need not produce agreement on the relative importance of particular ancillary or contributory purposes, although differences on such questions can in principle be resolved once an overriding purpose has been accepted.

In more general terms, a knowledge system meant for directing human actions will be predicated on a bedrock of normative premises and no *defensible* knowledge system can be created without prior agreement on the content of that base. Each set of normative premises must contain one overriding assumption. Once agreement is reached at that level, perhaps openly and self-consciously but more often tacitly, it becomes possible to argue persuasively for or against accepting particular subordinate purposes as necessary and/or sufficient for achieving the overall purpose, and to produce reasons for assigning priority to one or another of them in particular situations where they must be reconciled. Ambiguities aside, much of the difficulty that arises in real-world arguments, particularly over collective affairs, can be traced directly to the absence of agreement on an overriding normative premise of this kind.

The Overriding Purpose of Human Actions

In practical terms, an overriding purpose for the human enterprise, the purpose that controls every subordinate "game" in which humans engage, is remarkably easy to establish. Perhaps the simplest way to clarify the line of reasoning on which the selection depends, and to support the particular assumptions that are employed in the process, is to construct a "model" of the human enterprise that can serve as a reference point. An excellent model can be produced by focusing on the predicament of a single individual riding a hypothetical boat down a river of time. The boat is located at the juncture between past and future, and its occupant is condemned by the built-in limitations on human capacity to face backward toward the past. The flow of the river of time cannot be stayed; the person cannot turn and observe future events directly. Information available to the individual is assumed to be limited by the capacity of the human sensory apparatus, and is therefore singular, static, and related strictly to the past. Finally, the individual is exposed to a range of events in the external environment (not least the actions of other human individuals)—some beneficial, others harmful, and some lethal. The need to identify at least some of these external events, classify them accurately, and manage them in an appropriate manner is built into the human situation.

The presence of other individuals, similarly situated, and sometimes occupying "the same boat," in the world occupied by the individual, will for the moment be ignored, although the question when and how people come to recognize themselves as occupants of the same vehicle is a matter of considerable importance. The overriding purpose that controls and guides the individual isolated in that situation is the absolute need to maintain and/or improve the conditions of life of the person involved—beginning, of course, with sustaining the life, since everything else is contingent. Other persons can be incorporated into the model by a simple extension of the principle to maintaining and/or improving the conditions of life of *some* group of individuals. The group may comprise only the self or it may extend to include everyone living on the planet earth. In those terms, some of the more difficult questions to be decided in ethics are related to the principles that will be employed in deciding the population to be taken into account when decisions are made, and the relative "weight" to be attached to different human lives in a variety of circumstances. The problem is complicated by the presence of, and absolute need for, social organization.

Summarily, then, given the overwhelming significance of human life in human affairs, it can be argued quite cogently that the ultimate purpose of every form of human activity is to maintain and/or improve the conditions of life of *some* human population. The first reason for accepting the primacy of human life as a basis for assessing significance is that if the assumption is rejected, human affairs then lose their significance for humans, and that is patently absurd. The *reductio ad absurdum* argument is buttressed by the realization that rejecting the assumption would force members of the species to judge relative significance using criteria derived from some extrahuman sources, but so far as can at present be determined, humans have no access to such data. In positive terms, given an absolute need to assume *some* basis for assessing significance if normative knowledge and human affairs generally are to be placed on a defensible foundation, there is, for the moment at least, no feasible alternative to using human life as the basic unit of assessment. The possibility that an alternative may appear in due course, and be defended successfully, need not be denied, but for the present no serious competitor is at hand. Further, it is difficult to believe that human life would at some future time lose all of its significance for members of the species; therefore, efforts to augment, or further articulate, that basic assumption seem a more likely future outcome than total replacement.

The assumption that if anything has significance for members of the human species, it is human life (*homo mensura,* in classic terms) performs two major functions within the analytic framework. First, by limiting significance to human life, it provides the essential leverage point for developing the criteria of significance that any knowledge system must contain. Once assumed, anything unrelated to, or having no effect upon, human life is by definition trivial or insignificant. More important by far, however, is the implication that if nothing more is known of two lives than that each is human, there can be no basis for preferring one to the other.

That assumption turns out to be a critical tool of enormous power, amounting in practice to a primary statement, in defensible form, of the principle of human "equality." It becomes the second fundamental premise in the normative apparatus. In that limited form, the claim is fairly narrow: it asserts only that if nothing more is known of two lives than that each is human, there can be no grounds for preferring one to the other. Obviously, additional information may provide such grounds, but that is another matter (and one of the more intractable problems facing those concerned with the quality of ethical reasoning or argument). Put differently, the assumption that human life is prime turns out to have as one major corollary the assumption that human lives are of equal worth, *ceteris paribus.* Of course, other things are not always equal, and the equality assumption does *not,* when stated in this form, require absolutely equal weighting or treatment of every individual. The most important implication, as will appear in due course, is that departures from equal treatment must be justified. That implication turns out to have enormous importance for the kind of justification that can be offered, and should be accepted, for a preference, particularly in the management of collective affairs.

Second, assuming that "man is the measure" provides a justification for transforming the quest for knowledge in general into a search for the intellectual apparatus needed to direct human actions on defensible/corrigible grounds—a much less difficult task than seeking a justification for something identified only as "knowledge." Actions can provide the needed connection between a knowledge system that is created by human efforts and the goal of maintaining and improving the conditions of human life for which the knowledge was developed. In that limited sense, the normative apparatus becomes testable, though that term must be used with extreme caution because the "testability" available with respect to normative assertions is quite different from the kind of testability that is possible with respect to empirical propositions.

The Major Second-Order Purposes

If the overall purpose to be served by creating knowledge is to maintain and/or improve the conditions of life of some human population, then only four major second-order purposes need be satisfied in order to fulfill the task. Again, the validity of the selection of subordinate purposes can best be argued by reference to the basic model of the human predicament: the individual afloat on the river of time facing toward the past. Before any kind of intellectual processing can occur, an individual in that situation must have the data (and the knowledge, of course) needed to assess and modify the conditions of life enjoyed or endured by those involved—the data needed to direct future actions. Such data need not be created by the actual user (though there are good reasons for regarding the separation of data-creator and data-user as unfortunate, particularly in certain kinds of inquiries), but each user is in principle responsible for assessing the quality of the data accepted and employed. In any case, as the model of the individual isolated on the surface of a river illustrates all too well, it would be madness to ignore the quality of the information on which actions are premised. Since most people are today born into a world that is awash with information, the primary requirement is in most cases likely to be for some ability to assess or evaluate the quality of the data being used rather than the ability to create it. However the question of production and use is decided, the commonplace that the quality of the products of calculation is a function of both calculating performance and the quality of the data manipulated, which is nicely captured in the old homily "Garbage in means garbage out," cannot be overlooked or forgotten because it is a commonplace. Further, efficient fulfillment of the other second-order purposes involved in the overall enterprise is contingent on success in obtaining data of requisite quality; without such information, the task cannot be accomplished.

Assuming an adequate supply of data of the right kind, and a user capable of evaluating or assessing its quality, three other second-order purposes that must be fulfilled in order to achieve the overall goal for which knowledge is required can be identified (and tested roughly and crudely against the model of the overall human enterprise suggested above). All three are essential if the overall purpose set for the human enterprise is to be achieved. They are enumerated below in order of ascending complexity.

First, and perhaps most obvious, the individual who is open to the influence of events in the environment must be able to *predict* at least some of them, if only to ensure survival. The model of a person riding down a river of time facing backward allows a clear illustration of the point. In those circumstances, the individual must be able to anticipate forthcoming disasters, or potential disasters, such as treacherous rapids or waterfalls of great height, otherwise the risk of perishing suddenly and unexpectedly would increase dramatically. Ordinarily, predictions will refer to the future, which cannot, given established limits on human capacity, be observed; but they can also be used to deal with the as-yet-unobserved past (by predicting that a road has been rendered impassible by recent bad weather, for example). Events already observed, such as the outcome of a horse race, cannot be predicted—they can only be described. For obvious reasons, putting forward a descriptive account as a prediction is indefensible, not least because the practice is sometimes very difficult to detect.

Prediction alone is insufficient, however, for achieving the overall purpose sought through the creation of knowledge, for maintaining and improving the human condition. Indeed, "maximum human frustration" may be quite usefully and accurately defined as the condition in which a forthcoming disaster can be foreseen with confidence but nothing can be done either to prevent it or escape from its effects—that is one reason why the death penalty is regarded with such abhorrence by the sensitive. To maintain the condition of life of a person or group of persons, a basis for action is essential, and that must include the knowledge required for *controlling* future events (the past can be predicted but cannot be controlled) in foreseeable ways, for either causing events to occur or preventing their occurrence by deliberate action. In effect, a link must be found or created between one or more of the actions available to the individual (where "action" is defined as the capacity to produce change in the environment that can be exercised voluntarily by the person) and the consequences of the action that are expected to follow in the environment. No more may be possible than a connection between climbing a tree and thus escaping a lion's jaws, but some relation must be established and available to the individual in advance of need, otherwise the capacity to predict is of very limited worth.

Finally, given some capacity for voluntary action, if only the ability to climb a tree when faced with an approaching (and presumably hostile) lion, the individual is forced to *choose,* hence must also possess the knowledge required for fulfilling that purpose. The choice between climbing a tree and not climbing a tree when a furious lion is approaching at a high rate of speed may not appear as much of a choice, but so long as capacity can be exercised voluntarily, a decision is required whether or not to use it. Further, the illustration provides a good lesson in the importance of choosing not to act, since the consequences are reasonably foreseeable and the outcome clearly undesirable if the lion's perspective is ignored. Analytically, having the capacity to act is precisely equivalent to making a choice and the decision *not* to use that capacity counts as an action equally with its positive exercise. Every action is precisely equivalent to a choice; the content of the choice includes all of the outcomes available to an individual actor through voluntary action at a given time and place.

This set of second-order purposes (description, prediction, controlling events, and choosing among alternative futures) does not exhaust the list of purposes that are pursued, self-consciously or not, by individuals in a real-world environment. Further, there are any number of purposes whose fulfillment can contribute indirectly to the overall enterprise—development and clarification of language, extension of mathematical capacity, and so on. The four primary second-order purposes are no more exhaustive of the human intellectual game than running, passing, kicking, and blocking exhaust the set of activities involved in playing football. Happily, the need is not an *exhaustive* list of purposes but a set that provides an adequate basis for criticism and improvement of efforts to achieve the overall purpose of the game being played. That set then becomes a launching pad for present actions as well as a base on which future improvements can be constructed.

CAPACITIES AND LIMITATIONS

Most of the difficulties encountered in efforts to fulfill the basic purposes of systematic inquiry are a function of the natural limits on human capacity. Human dependence on the sensory apparatus for information about the world, including the self, is particularly important because it produces what is commonly referred to as the "induction problem"—the logical gap between the data that are available through the senses and the kind of knowledge needed for dealing with the environment. If "reality" could be observed directly, or be known to have been observed accurately, the "problem of knowledge" would be much easier to solve and might disappear altogether. Developing a way of bridging or avoiding that logical gap is perhaps the most important and difficult step in the justification of knowledge claims and their applications. Formally, the problem cannot be resolved; there can be no "logic of induction" in the ordinary meaning of the term. But an evasion can be arranged, and a discussion of how that can be done with respect to both empirical and normative matters will occupy the next two parts of this chapter. In addition, since the assumptions that must be made in order to achieve the evasion greatly restrict the activities of those who seek to create and apply knowledge, those assumptions too will be identified as fully and accurately as possible.

The Intellectual Requirements for Directing Actions

To simplify the argument, the discussion will focus fairly narrowly on the intellectual requirements for directing human actions in ways that can be defended out of human experience within the limits of human capacity. Those requirements cover the prerequisites to fulfilling all of the primary purposes that contribute to maintaining and improving the human condition. The main reason for concentrating upon actions is fairly obvious: if the conditions of life of species members are to be regarded as primarily a function of the available knowledge and resources, then some medium or instrument is needed through which knowledge can function to maintain or alter those conditions. Action provides that connecting link. Action, as here defined, occurs any time that an actor has the capacity to produce change in the environment that can be exercised voluntarily—in that sense, each of us "acts" almost continuously during life. Analytically, capacity is a sufficient condition for action to occur, whether the actor is an individual or a collectivity. The indicator of action is a world that is in some respect different than it would have been had capacity been employed differently. In effect, actions can either produce change in the environment, or prevent changes from occurring that would otherwise take place—both meanings will henceforth be assumed under the general term "change."

And capacity is "exercised," an action occurs, whether or not positive actions are taken by the person who possesses or controls the capacity.

The minimum conditions to be fulfilled before actions can be justified, criticized, or improved are easily stated though hard to satisfy. The capacity to produce change in the environment, which provides the analytic definition of action, must be available for voluntary use. A theoretical framework linking action to purpose in generalized terms must already have been established and tested; and the action taken must be a logically forced consequence of accepting a known set of empirical and normative assumptions. The latter point is particularly important because it is the set of assumptions that is tested in application and not the action per se. Improved performance requires a *change* of actions rather than an improvement in actions. Indeed, actions cannot be "improved" in any meaningful sense of the term; they are what they are. Since what is tested by action is the full set of assumptions used to direct the action, it may be difficult to locate erroneous assumptions if an application of the knowledge fails to achieve the intended purpose.

Beyond such fundamentals, it must also be assumed that the set of priorities applied to the action or choice has been ordered transitively; otherwise, the priority system is ambiguous and cannot be calculated or applied. Certain other assumptions that relate to human intellectual capacity, to the limiting conditions imposed by natural processes, to the availability of resources (including both time and knowledge) must be agreed upon. Finally, a set of conventions is needed that stipulate the grounds on which decisions are made relating to what constitutes evidence (what is relevant and what is not) in particular situations.

The justification offered for an action will be based upon a systematic comparison of the outcomes available for choice, carried out in terms of past human experience, both direct and vicarious. It will include, but cannot be limited to, the affective reaction to past experience with the various outcomes. No effort to assess or evaluate a single outcome in normative terms (to determine whether or not a given outcome is "good" or "right," for example) can succeed given the limited human capacity available for the task. The performance of the emperor serving as judge in a singing contest, who after hearing the first of two finalists promptly awarded the prize to the second, lies beyond the capacity of ordinary humans. Moreover, as noted earlier, even if a way to assess a single outcome could be found, it would not provide an adequate basis for action. Another one of the available outcomes might be "better" or "more right," and a systematic comparison would in any case be necessary to determine whether or not that was the case. Moreover, the sensory dependence of the species rules out efforts to assess the quality of knowledge or models by comparing them directly to the content of reality. The only available basis for assessing the quality of a given item of knowledge, while avoiding the induction problem, is to compare the results produced by accepting and using it to achieve a specified purpose with the results anticipated or produced by accepting any of the competing alternatives—an essentially normative or evaluative function that is employed in the normative realm as well. The applications can, of course, be made indirectly, by accepting patterns of relations already established, or by arguing analogically from one case to another.

Even if all of these specific assumptions are accepted without quarrel, and most are relatively uncontentious or easily justified, the intellectual requirements for fulfilling the overall purpose sought through the use of knowledge (for directing actions in ways that can be defended out of human experience within the limits of human capacity) remain complex and difficult to satisfy. The nature of the complexity emerges from even a fairly cursory summary of the minimum prerequisites for success:

1. The actor's capacity, the range of actions available to the actor at a given time and place must be specified. This can be very difficult to do, particularly when the "actor" is a collectivity such as a legislature. Even with respect to an individual, the need to estimate capacity can raise some complex and difficult questions: how to treat psychological incapacity, for example. It follows that the person directing or evaluating actions needs to be acutely aware of the quality of the estimates of capacity that control the selection of outcomes taken into account in the comparisons used to establish or to justify preferences.

2. The consequences expected to follow from each of the available actions are then projected on the future as far as current knowledge permits, and the accuracy/reliability of the projections estimated. How adequately that can be done is a function of various factors, of which the time, resources, and knowledge available for the task, and the relative significance of the outcomes as assessed using the accepted normative apparatus, are the most important.

3. The set of concepts used to structure the available outcomes should capture all of their normatively significant dimensions. If the concepts incorporated into the apparatus used to make the projections are not adequate for normative purposes, which is very likely to be the case, then other instruments are needed that can translate the concepts actually used in the projections into suitable normative terms. This can be a troublesome problem, as most persons who have struggled to assess the human significance of economic changes projected in terms of income data or the size of the gross national product can testify.

4. The preferred outcome within the set of available outcomes must be identified, and the preference justified. If an established priority is already available, it can be applied to the set of outcomes. Otherwise, an instrument must be created, and that can be a very formidable problem, particularly given the need to maintain the transitive ordering of the whole set

of priorities included in the normative system. Development proceeds inductively, by generalizing solutions to specific choice problems. To complicate the task, the priority system as a whole, which is generalized in form, must be marked by cutoff points that identify outcomes regarded as either trivial and unimportant or of overwhelming significance. Since it is conceivable that *all* of the available outcomes may be either trivial or of great importance given the accepted normative system, the normative apparatus applied must be capable of identifying and dealing with such situations.

5. Once the preferred outcome is identified (whether by applying an established priority, or by creating a new one), an action program or *policy* must be created that will produce the preferred outcome in that situation, or, more precisely, that can be expected to produce that outcome with some estimated measure of reliability. Because testability is essential if the overall apparatus is to be justified and improved out of experience, the preferred outcome must be a *logical* as well as an empirical consequence of accepting the proposed action program—a requirement that is too often overlooked by those engaged in policymaking, both public and private.

6. Finally, it is very unlikely that any policy, whether it is produced and applied by an individual or by a collectivity, will function exactly as designed, or produce the anticipated results perfectly, therefore a monitoring system is needed that can keep track of the effects of applying it. To complicate the requirements, the monitoring system must be capable of capturing any significant consequences that can be anticipated; it cannot be limited to those that have been included in the projection of outcomes made by the actor involved. Further, the monitoring apparatus should be linked closely to the decision-making unit that controls the administration or application of the action program. Needed adjustments may be made in the action program, leaving the priority system intact, but it may be considered preferable to alter the preference system, leaving the action program unchanged, and that possibility should be allowed for by the designer. To illustrate, all those living on a small private lake may favor a policy that allows the use of power boats on the lake at a time when they are few in number because they prefer maximum opportunities for recreation to expected levels of noise (even though the accepted normative system also enjoins generating excessive amounts of noise). If the number of such power boats increases over time to a point where the noise causes so much serious dissatisfaction, a choice must be made between changing the policy (restricting the use of power boats) or maintaining the policy and altering the normative apparatus (enduring greater amounts of noise). It does not follow necessarily that the established priority system will be maintained—that a preference will be expressed for limiting the use of power boats. A new decision must be made to deal with the situation as

it appears at that point in time. In effect, the need to monitor the effects of action is complicated by a need to hedge against two possibilities: first, that unanticipated effects may be far more important in human terms than those taken into account; second, normative systems may change with time, thus altering the content required of an adequate monitoring system.

In addition to these six major requirements, systematic direction of actions depends upon a number of additional elements or factors. They include, among others: a supply of information or data; a conceptual apparatus that includes both normative and empirical concepts adequate for dealing with the situations being treated (omitting nothing of empirical or normative significance); measurement standards or conventions for each of the continua used to organize the data employed; the calculating capacity needed to perform all of the logical operations required; and an appropriate language. Each is a potential source of error or inadequacy in the development and use of the overall apparatus.

Human Capacities, Human Limits

The human capacity available for satisfying those requirements is adequate, but only barely so—at best, the results are neither totally accurate nor completely reliable. Two major factors need to be examined given the purpose sought here: first, the scope and limits of human capacity as understood at present; second, the relevant characteristics of the natural world as agreed within informed opinion. Both are, of course, subject to change as knowledge expands or improves.

The Induction Problem. The so-called induction problem provides what is perhaps the best working focus for discussing the human capacities and limitations relating to the development and use of knowledge. There are various ways to state the problem, some more useful than others. The source of the induction problem is absolute human dependence upon the sensory apparatus for information; its prime implication is the need to develop an alternative to the correspondence theory of truth as a basis for justifying knowledge claims. The data that the sensory apparatus produces are singular and static; they relate strictly to the past. Logically, nothing can be inferred from data stated in that form. If the data are generalized, inferences from the resulting propositions are possible, but such generalizations will then contain more information than the sum of all of the observations made previously. They must be justified prior to use or application, yet they cannot be justified by reference to, or by inference from, past experience alone. Finally, even if an acceptable justification could be produced for generalizations based on past observations, logic would not allow inferences from empirical generalizations to the kinds of normative statements that are required for directing actions. At the level of logic, such problems lie beyond human capacity to resolve.

For present purposes it is much more useful (and less misleading) to regard induction as a statement about the direction of contingency between particular and general propositions rather than as a process. In a deductive system, particular statements are derived from, and therefore contingent upon, general propositions; in the event of a conflict, the particular proposition is abandoned. In an inductive system, particular propositions are analytically prior to general statements, the direction of contingency is reversed, and in the event the two are incompatible, the general, not the specific, must be abandoned. That creates no special problems for inquiry, but it does require the user of knowledge to be aware of the need to tailor all generalizations to experience and hence to regard inconsistencies as evidence of inadequacies in the generalized pattern. That alters very substantially the nature of the resulting induction problem and opens the way to an acceptable evasion.

One potential escape route can be abandoned immediately. The induction problem cannot be avoided or resolved by comparing knowledge claims to the content of reality. The data that reach the central nervous system are an unanalyzable fusion of the characteristics of the content of reality, the effects of the transmitting medium on those characteristics, and the further effects of the operation of the sensory apparatus on the prior combination. In practical terms, the three elements are again most properly regarded collectively as a black box, in the engineering sense of the term. There is no way to identify the relation between the internal structure of the system and system outputs. Even if the internal apparatus can be analyzed into some of its elements, that limit still holds, particularly in cases where the internal apparatus includes feedback mechanisms.

In that context, the induction problem forces inquirers to devise a nonlogical way of dealing with the future using data that refer only to the past. Somewhat more technically, a way must be found to deal with the disjunction between the time focus of the available data and of the needs or purposes for which knowledge is sought. The requirement is both real and serious. Life is future-oriented to a rather surprising degree: the hopes, fears, and aspirations of the individual refer entirely to the future; the effects of present actions are felt there; efforts to control the flow of events must refer to the future; choices are directed to alternative, attainable future states, and so on. Of course, it can be argued that acting on the basis of a given body of knowledge will in due course provide a test of the validity of projected futures, but that is not sufficient. The quality of the knowledge must be assessed *before* it is applied at least part of the time, otherwise validation becomes merely a program for post hoc rationalization.

Evading the Logical Impasse

A working evasion, adequate for human purposes, can be created, but *only* by and for those concerned with achieving some overall purpose in the world through systematic inquiry. Indeed, the major price to be paid for the evasion is loss of absolute control over the kinds of purposes that can be sought through inquiry, and over the kinds of claims that can be put forward based on the results produced—the meaning of "knowledge" must be restricted. That may annoy the free spirits within the intellectual community, but the effect is hardly catastrophic. The other major intellectual cost of the evasion is an unavoidable loss of certainty, or reliability, with respect to any knowledge that is produced and justified inside the prescribed limits. Within the framework of a coaching language developed for directing human actions, the quality of knowledge claims can be judged in terms of their usefulness for achieving specified purposes under stipulated conditions within given limits. For maintaining and improving the human condition, such pragmatic criteria will suffice.

Pragmatic criteria will not, of course, satisfy everyone, or serve as an adequate base for fulfilling every and any purpose that human ingenuity can conceive. Two groups in particular are unlikely to accept a pragmatic approach to knowledge justification: first, those who seek absolute knowledge, who refuse for various reasons to accept a relativistic and uncertain construction of the concept; second, those who will not be bound by a commitment to applying knowledge to human purposes in order to test its significance and quality. There are others, of course, who deny altogether the possibility of anyone producing anything worthy of the label "knowledge," but they are usually unwilling to specify what knowledge means to them. The first two groups can be left free to provide their own justification for the position they have adopted and seek acceptance for it; the intellectual Luddites can simply be ignored.

The effects of forced reliance upon sensory data can be overcome given a relatively small set of assumptions relating to human capacity, to the intellectual requirements for directing actions, and to the conditions that obtain in the human environment now understood. None of these assumptions is particularly contentious with respect to the species as a whole, though they may be untenable in particular cases. The required human attributes include, among others, the ability to react affectively, some capacity for creativity, some capacity to organize and/or generalize experience into patterns, some calculating capacity, and the ability to make and defend what are best labeled "judgments," or nonlogical or nonformalizable decisions. With respect to the conditions of application of knowledge, two requirements are preeminent: first, the individual must function in an ongoing system in which at least some of the knowledge in use is valid for directing actions; second, the capacity to deal with recurring events, directly or by transposition (analogy or metaphor), must suffice for attaining the purposes sought through knowledge production and use. Each of these requirements or limitations is fulfilled regularly and as a matter of course in human affairs.

Caring. Although it may seem too obvious to require an explicit statement, it is nonetheless a matter of prime importance that individual members of the species react differentially to differences in the environment, that they prefer some situations to others. Some such reactions are more or less built-into the neural system, of course, but that does not lessen their importance. The initial basis for caring may be affective; ultimately even direct affective reactions are at least partly an intellectual product. However they may be created and justified, the capacity to produce them is one absolutely essential element in the human armory. Without it, the quest for knowledge would be bound to fail, and its achievement would in any case be pointless.

In effect, knowledge functions primarily as an instrument for expressing, refining, and pursuing preferences—which is only another way of saying that all knowledge rests upon a normative foundation. The minimum requirement for the continued existence of living things in a potentially lethal environment is a set of differentiated reactions functioning in a Darwinian-controlled relationship with that environment. The ability to alter behavior through intellectual activity or learning, to override affective reactions by cognitive processes, vastly expands the potential for continued survival, and accounts very largely for human predominance among the earth's life forms. Put differently, cognitive control over affective reactions serves to identify the normative apparatus as a human creation rather than a gift of nature, as a sign of human capacity, however limited in ultimate terms, to control the human destiny. The function of science, in that context, is to extend and enhance the human capacity to improve and apply its own normative apparatus. The function of the normative apparatus is to assess the effects produced by applied science (the only kind of science open to assessment) and use that assessment to justify directing future efforts in particular ways for the benefit of some or all of humanity.

Organization. The key to knowledge development is the human capacity to organize experience, to impose calculable patterns upon it. In a sense, the best analogue to the human neural system is an enormous electronic discriminator coupled to an even more enormous retention and recall system. Even the basic flow of incoming perceptions, which has been organized to some extent by the transmitting medium and the functioning of the sensors, must be organized further before it makes sense or can be used by the individual. Two types of organization are essential: first, the things or entities that are observed in the environment must be grouped into recognizable patterns or classified—the boundaries of a tiger are established within the human neural apparatus, though the tiger can, to some extent at least, influence such decisions; second, concepts that define the relations among those entities or classes that are found to be significant for human purposes must be created and labeled, producing what are variously called "logical" or "relational" terms. These first-order organizing patterns or concepts provide the "spectacles" through which the world around, and inside, the person is perceived.

The prime implication of the overall organizing process, from the perspective of the kind of inquiry undertaken here, is that every account of human experience, every description that is produced, is selective. The principles on which the selectivity is based are in large measure inherited and are usually, though not invariably, applied without awareness. It follows from the logic of the process that there can be no *complete* description of any event. In principle at least, an event could be viewed through any one of an infinite set of spectacles, each providing slightly different, though not contradictory, information.

To create the kinds of knowledge required for directing actions, humans must generalize, must create generalizations. Formally, a generalization states a relation between two or more classes of events, or between two or more things or aspects of things. The events that are linked may be abstract or concrete, real or imaginary, observable or hypothetical, and so on. But the generalized character of such propositions means that they are not limited in application to any specific time and place, and that feature makes them invaluable in the quest for a route around the induction barrier. Perhaps equally important, the process of generalization serves to condense or summarize enormous amounts of information into a form that is readily transmitted and applied. Consider the difference between learning that dogs bite, and learning that dog A has bitten another dog, that dog A has bitten a human, or even that dog A bites, which is already generalized information.

Five types of generalizations, five basic organizing patterns, are needed for directing human actions on defensible grounds, presuming, of course, that the patterns themselves can be defended by reference to experience. The five patterns are sketched only summarily here, for they actually identify the basic forms that knowledge required for directing human actions must take and will therefore be examined in much more detail later. Each pattern consists of a set of entities or "variables" and a set of rules that link the values of those variables in particular, and in some cases calculable, ways. It will normally have attached to it a set of limiting conditions governing application, a statement of the conditions under which it can be expected to hold. The nomenclature employed to identify the different kinds of patterns has not been completely standardized, therefore the labels attached to them may be somewhat peculiar or even misleading, depending on the reader's area of specialization, hence the terminology employed here should be examined carefully.

1. Patterns that generalize the attributes of a particular entity will be called *classifications*; technically, they are a special case of classes that contain only one member, such as "my brother" or "that house." The rules in such cases will link the class member to a particular generalized attribute or set of attributes—my brother is a smart person, or my brother has behaved badly in recent weeks, for example. Such classifications are widely used in personal affairs but have only limited utility for dealing with the environment in general.

2. Patterns that specify the distributed properties of classes of things, such as dogs, or typewriters, will also be labeled *classifications*—the nomenclature is fairly standard in this case. The rules included in the pattern will state the selection of variables that identify the distributed properties of the class and the range of values that each variable can take. All members of the class "dogs" have four feet, one head, two ears, and so on, for example. If the enumeration of the class is only partial, if it refers to "some dogs . . . ," the result is a subdivision of a full classification that is much less useful for dealing with the environment, not least because very little can be inferred from it about particular class members—because some dogs are small does not allow the inference that the unseen dog who is growling in a threatening manner is small.

3. Two types of patterns can be distinguished that assert the empirical or observed relations that hold among two or more classes of events or things. The first (to be labeled a *forecast*) includes all such patterns that generalize past observations or experience with members of the class, that either link one event to another, or link changes in the value of one variable of observable to changes that occur in the value of another variable, whether concurrently or serially. Forecasts do not include or assume a causal relation among events, do not assume that one event is a necessary or a sufficient condition for another to occur. The rules included in forecasts link the values of some selection of variables in a calculable way, thus transforming a descriptive account of past experience into a generalized proposition that is expected to hold in future. For our purposes, the most important characteristic of such patterns is that no causal connection is assumed between the events connected by rule, meaning in practical terms that the user *cannot* assume that the pattern will continue to hold if it is acted upon or applied.

4. The fourth type of pattern (here labeled a *theory*) is identical in structure to a forecast, but includes a causal assumption linking the events or variables, meaning that the rule(s) of interaction is expected to hold regardless of the way that change is introduced into the pattern—that one change will lead to another regardless of the way in which the first change is induced. That assumption allows, and is in fact necessary for, the pattern to serve as a basis for action, since it follows that the rule(s) can be expected to hold even if the initial change in the value of one of the vari-

ables included in the pattern is induced deliberately by human action. Put differently, theories incorporate the necessary or the sufficient conditions for a specified event to occur (and therefore for achieving a particular purpose) under given limiting conditions. Forecasts do not.

Theories and forecasts are structurally identical; each consists of a set of variables, one or more rules of interaction, and a set of limiting conditions that governs the application of the pattern (that states the conditions under which the pattern can be expected to hold). An example may help to differentiate their uses and show the significance of the very limited causal assumption incorporated into theories. If the date of blooming of two species of flowers is observed and recorded over time, the relation between dates can be summarized statistically as a descriptive statement about the past—recognizable by the past-tense verb included in the statement. If that past relation is then generalized, freed of time constraints, the resulting pattern can be used to predict the date of blooming of the second flower in the sequence, often quite accurately. But efforts to speed the blooming of the second flower by force-feeding the one that historically has bloomed earliest are not likely to succeed; no causal linkage can be justified by reference to past experience with the two events in the world of experience alone. If, however, the date of blooming can be linked causally to the sustained temperature of the environment (as seems to be the case on the basis of observed and recorded past experience with flowers), that relation can be tested both historically and experimentally, and the pattern can in principle be used to control the blooming date of either flower by controlling the temperature in the environment. To repeat, such a causally linked set of events, captured in a suitable and calculable pattern, will be referred to as a theory; a pattern that contains no causal assumption will be labeled a forecast. The reader is again warned that the usage has not been standardized, but there are strong reasons for recommending it, particularly in social science.

5. Finally, patterns asserting that one outcome in a specified set of alternatives is preferable to any of the others are essential for making choices, and therefore for directing actions, since they are analytically identical functions. Such patterns, which will be labeled *priorities,* are created, as noted earlier, by generalizing solutions to particular choice problems. Such solutions are themselves contingent upon other priorities already accepted or established. The process will be discussed more fully later in the chapter (see "Preferences and Priorities").

Calculation. The dynamic force that drives every human knowledge system is the capacity to calculate, to manipulate patterns of rigorously defined symbols and carefully specified relations. For present purposes, the most useful construction of the meaning of calculation is "a process for determining the full content of generalized propositions, or combinations of generalized and particular propositions." Unless at least one generalized proposition is available, calculation is ruled out. Nothing can be inferred from a static description; it states its own content fully. For the most part, the formal calculations involved in applying knowledge are here taken as given; in real world affairs, the adequacy of the calculations may require very careful scrutiny. The criteria to be applied to the formal aspect of calculation are, however, a function of logic and mathematics, and not amenable to the kind of methodological criticism that engages us here.

Judgment. The process to be labeled "judgment" is very difficult to capture precisely in language, though its use is commonplace in human affairs. Somewhat simplistically, judgments are made whenever a decision is reached that cannot be produced by the application of formal rules or patterns to a stated set of assumptions or propositions. Any diagnosis, any action that involves identification of a class member (Is that a cat? Does that child have measles?) requires an act of judgment. Similarly, every effort to evaluate the adequacy of the body of supporting evidence provided for a generalized proposition depends on judgment. And most important of all, every normative decision, every statement of preference, reflects a judgment of the same order. Although the process is the same in all three cases, the content of the experience taken into account when judgment is rendered will, of course, be very different as will the criteria of adequacy applied to the result.

Judgment can also be defined residually by treating it as one of three fundamental processes that humans employ to reach conclusions. Two of the available processes for reaching conclusions can be tested, up to a point, in the scientific sense of the term: first, conclusions reached by direct observation or measurement; second, conclusions produced by logical inferences from known assumptions ("If you accept these propositions, then you must accept that proposition"). In all other cases, a judgment is required to reach a conclusion. Indeed, even the first two procedures depend ultimately on judgments, though the judgment may be several levels removed from the conclusion reached. The process of judgment cannot be formalized, but a variety of conventions can be established for making judgments, as in much of modern medical diagnosis, or in statistics generally. However, the decision whether to accept or apply the convention, either in general or in a particular case, always involves an act of judgment—which may not be consciously made.

Judgments are essential in every knowledge system, and therefore commonplace. Briefly, it appears that over time, a body of experience can be combined within a single person to produce a decision tool able to transcend the limits of formal logic, and thus to create solutions to a range of formally insoluble problems. No one can say how this is done, for the present at least, but there is no question that the process occurs every day for nearly everyone, or that such judgments play a key role in the development and use of knowledge. That raises a very difficult evaluation problem, for the only available check on a human judgment is another human judgment, made by a fully competent person. The court of last resort in the event of sustained disagreement is the body of persons fully informed and competent on the matter in question, and that group may be very difficult to identify. Worse, if those who comprise informed opinion cannot agree, arguments about judgments cannot be settled. That is quite a different matter from the old and mistaken adage which says: "That's my opinion, and it cannot be criticized because it's only my opinion," implying that the individual is fully entitled to hold *any* opinion about any subject. Freedom of opinion in intellectual matters holds only for points that cannot be decided on adequate grounds, and that depends on what the opinion refers to. It is not acceptable to maintain an opinion, however labeled, that runs contrary to, say, the Law of Gravity, and expect to be taken seriously. Even if that sort of gross error is avoided, the need to deal with judgments remains a major problem for those concerned with the evaluation of knowledge claims or applications.

Environmental Conditions. The two limiting conditions required of the environment by the theory of knowledge are not very controversial and can be summarized quickly. First, the effort to fulfill the requirements for directing action must take place in an environment that contains some knowledge that is adequate for the task, in an ongoing knowledge system that is at least partly successful. If inquiry had to begin with a blank slate, the slate would in most cases remain blank. Second, no more can be required for success than the capacity to deal with recurring events. There is no way to create an intellectual apparatus able to cope with an event that is wholly divorced from prior human experience. Such events are, of course, very unlikely to occur, but if they did, that would exclude both analogical and metaphorical reasoning as a basis for dealing with them. At this stage in human history, the limitation has been in effect for a very long time, and is unlikely to cause serious practical difficulties, but the principle involved needs to be made clear. The knowledge system is limited to dealing with recurring events. To make the point somewhat differently, every event will have some characteristics that are unique (alone or in combination) and some that are shared with other events. The crucial question is usually whether two or more events are sufficiently alike to allow the transfer of knowledge from one to the other. Whether they are wholly unlike any other event or perfectly identical to another event is not a matter of great concern; both extremes are impossible in principle to establish with certainty.

Given an individual endowed with these capacities, functioning in an intellectual environment that contains at least some knowledge adequate for directing actions, a four-step procedure is sufficient to direct actions by the self, or to deal critically with the actions of others.

First, the purpose sought must be identified within an analytic framework that contains a statement of the necessary or the sufficient conditions for its fulfillment.

Second, either experience must be organized into patterns of the form specified within the analytic framework for achieving the purpose at hand, and the result provided with a justification out of experience, or previously organized and justified patterns that fit the situation in which the purpose is being sought must be located in the existing knowledge store.

Third, the pattern is applied to the situation, meaning that it is combined with one or more specific observations, and the implications of the combination are calculated and transferred to the world of experience. If the purpose is valid, the diagnosis correct, and the calculations properly made, acting in accordance with the calculations should fulfill the purpose at hand within the limits of reliability estimated for the pattern.

Fourth, comparing the results produced by the application with the expectations generated by the calculations (which necessarily involves suitable monitoring of the effects of action) produces the evidence needed to reinforce, modify, or reject use of the pattern for that purpose when and if the same situation recurs.

Knowledge so conceived evolves in unending cycles of observation, generalization, calculation, application (action) and observation/reaction/testing. Agriculture provides a particularly good illustration of the process, for cycles of planting, tilling, harvesting, and consuming/evaluating/adjusting have over time led to improvements in what is produced, in production methods, and in the criteria of evaluation applied to the outcome as well as the processes involved in creating it. The key to success is the creative procedure known as generalization, for it produces the patterns of relations, not restricted in application to a particular time and place, that are essential for evading the induction problem. How they are created cannot be determined. Once created, however, they can in some cases, mainly those that are empirical, be tested more or less conclusively, and in all cases they can be argued before the bar of informed opinion.

FULFILLING EMPIRICAL REQUIREMENTS

The various knowledge patterns used for directing human actions on defensible grounds must be able to fulfill a number of purposes, perform a number of difficult functions, to achieve the overall goal set for the enterprise. At a minimum, experience must be organized to produce: (1) the descriptive information (data) required for developing, applying, and testing the different instruments required for the task; (2) instruments able to predict at least some of the future conditions that can be expected if the flow of events is allowed to continue uninterrupted—if the capacity to intervene is not exercised; (3) instruments able to project what amounts to a "film clip" of the future to be expected from each of the actions lying within the actor's capacity, either using concepts that capture the normatively significant dimensions of the future outcomes or translating the concepts used to make the projections into an adequate set of normative concepts; (4) an instrument able to identify the preferred outcome from among the available set; (5) an action program or policy that can be expected to lead to the preferred outcome with some known level of reliability; and (6) a monitoring system that will supply the information needed for adequate evaluation and/or modification of the action program or policy. Various additional supporting requirements—a set of logics or calculi, an adequate language, and a body of organized prior experience that is sufficient to allow evaluation and/or justification of the instruments produced, among others—are here taken for granted. Any pattern that is essential for achieving real-world purposes can be located at some point in the overall framework, and therefore exposed to criticism in methodological terms.

Only a very summary account of the manner in which those requirements can be fulfilled, of the structures and processes involved in the performance of each of the needed functions, can be provided here. The prime concern is to expose the major obstacles to be overcome in creating or applying the needed instruments, stated in methodological terms, and to locate the principal sources of error, since they are the crucial points to be taken into account by anyone seeking to create, apply, or criticize the necessary tools. The empirical apparatus used for description, prediction, and projection of the consequences of action, is dealt with immediately below; the normative requirements, both conceptual and instrumental, are reserved for discussion later in the chapter (see "Fulfilling Normative Requirements").

The analysis begins with a brief examination of the initial organization of perceptions into the descriptive accounts. Since descriptions are the raw materials from which all of human knowledge is created, assessment or evaluation of descriptive quality is a common concern for everyone seeking to use knowledge to achieve purposes in the environment, whether those purposes are identified in empirical, normative, or methodological terms. As might be expected, there is a considerable amount of overlapping in the structures and processes involved in producing the various instruments used to fulfill the basic purposes of inquiry. The instruments themselves tend, understandably, to be complex combinations of a number of different elements. Indeed, their complexity is one of the major reasons for undertaking methodological analysis. If the overall apparatus can be broken into elements, and criteria of adequacy developed for each element, it becomes possible to evaluate even very complex instruments, and improve their overall performance. With respect to intellectual tools, as with mechanical tools, the whole is no stronger than its weakest link. Locating and strengthening the weakest link in a complex apparatus should, other things equal, produce improved performance from the whole or, at the very least, increase the level of reliability that can be attached to the implications generated by applying the instrument.

Description

The basic building blocks in every knowledge system are descriptive propositions, statements in the form "X is the case at time t," which transform automatically, and almost instantaneously, into the form "X *was* the case at time t." They can be labeled "information" to distinguish them from the generalized patterns that are more commonly called "knowledge." They constitute what is somewhat misleadingly referred to as "the facts." Almost everyone has access to an enormous body of such observed and recorded descriptive accounts, propositions that are, or can be, supported by observations. Descriptions are the strongest, and the most easily tested, of all of the propositions created by the human intellect. Nevertheless, it is a profound error to speak of "the facts" as though they were either self-evident, indubitably true, or complete or exhaustive. Descriptions, like all other intellectual products except logic and mathematics, are always to some degree imprecise or inaccurate, and in some cases they are flagrantly inadequate or mistaken. Some descriptive errors are the result of human fallibility; the more important descriptive inadequacies, however, are a function of the nature of the descriptive process, and of the limitations enforced by the human perceptive apparatus. Knowledge intended for use in the direction of human affairs must, for obvious reasons, take such limitations into account.

In general, as noted earlier, descriptions are created by organizing the flow of perceptions entering the neural apparatus, by observing events through a set of spectacles (consisting of concepts and relational terms) and recording the result. Structurally, a descriptive proposition consists of a set of variables that represent the concepts and relational terms used to make the observations, plus the "fillers" needed to complete grammatical and syntactical requirements. The values taken by each of the variables used to make the description are determined using a process that can be labeled either "observation" or "measurement." A description, then, is a set of variables (concepts and relational terms) whose values are set by observation or measurement.

It is useful, within limits, to regard a description as a "snapshot" of what was observed at a specific time and place. Like snapshots, descriptions refer only to past events. And like snapshots, they are static, the equivalent of a single frame in a movie film; change is an inference from two or more descriptions of "the same" event or object. Descriptions are also particular or specific in focus; selectivity is unavoidable given the nature of the perceptive apparatus. Metaphorically, the world can be construed as a stage on which an infinite (in principle) set of plays is taking place. The play that is seen depends on two factors: first, what is actually occurring upon the stage; second, on the spectacles (the set of concepts and relational terms), worn by the observer. Everyone wears a set of such spectacles at all times; each person has a number of sets and they can be exchanged quickly and easily, or even worn simultaneously. All of them can be misleading, in some cases because of bias or ideological commitment, but in others because they focus improperly, on the wrong aspect of things—"wrong," that is, given the purpose in hand.

In the circumstances, two types of errors can be expected to occur in the descriptive process. First, what is asserted may in fact be mistaken, the description may not be *accurate.* Second, and much more important for the purposes of this volume, the description may be *inadequate,* may contain the wrong information. Two major sources of error are worth noting: first, the spectacles or concepts used to make the observations may have been ground to the wrong formula, leading to inaccuracy; second, the observer may have focused on the wrong point. To extend the picture-taking metaphor, accuracy is a function of the quality of the lens, but adequacy is a function of either the way the lenses are ground or the way in which the camera is pointed. All descriptions are inaccurate at some standard of accuracy; no description can be perfect.

The adequacy of any description depends on the purpose for which it will be used. Purposeless descriptions cannot be evaluated except by reference to their accuracy. The purpose for which the description will be used is therefore an integral part of the assessment machinery. To illustrate the role of purpose in descriptive evaluation, consider the case of an automobile repair shop asked to set a price for repairs but given a description of the damage caused by an accident that was guaranteed to be accurate, but nothing more. Descriptions may also contain otiose information, data that are irrelevant to the purpose for which the description is used, but that is only an annoyance and does not affect the quality of the description unless there is too much of it to be handled efficiently.

The Basic Problem Areas. In a limited space, only a few of the major problems encountered in the process of creating, evaluating, and employing descriptions can be examined. The primary sources of error are usually conceptual; they relate mostly to the meaning of concepts and relational terms, and/or measurements made of their values. Other major problem sources include: (1) the processes used to create descriptions (and particularly the characteristics of the human perceptive apparatus); (2) the need to rely upon a language to record and transmit descriptive information; (3) the role that subjectivity plays in observation; and (4) the need to rely upon translogical judgments, among others. Anyone either producing or using descriptive data should be aware of the kinds of errors that can occur, and their sources; they should also know the measures that can be taken to guard against them. All that is possible here is a very summary account of a selection of major points.

Conceptual Problems. The need to use spectacles, to rely on concepts for observation, is a potentially dangerous nuisance, a constant source of worry, in systematic inquiry as in everyday life. Basically, concepts are classification devices, ways of bounding and identifying entities and stating the relations that are observed among them. If concepts are inadequate, the propositions in which they appear are not to be trusted, and in some cases, should be rejected immediately. The two most common conceptual faults or inadequacies are *vagueness,* uncertainty about the meaning of propositions that include the concept (e.g. "John is schizophrenic"), and *ambiguity,* which appears if more than one meaning can be attached to a proposition ("the apple is green"). Many other kinds of conceptual problems can be found in everyday practice, but none has as much importance for systematic inquiry as vagueness and ambiguity.

Conceptual problems relating to meaning are in most cases due to poor or inadequate definition, for that is where meaning is to be found. There are various ways of defining terms, not all of them appropriate or adequate for every situation. Thus the *lexical* definitions that appear in dictionaries simply summarize current usage uncritically and cannot be treated as definitive, or even useful, in all cases. Current usage can be tightened by what are called *precising* definitions, which limit meanings in specific ways but open the way to another error—both user and reader may forget to use *only* the limited meaning of the term. Thus if "political participants" are limited for purposes of a specific inquiry to those who both take part in the work of political parties and who vote in elections, the author must remember to use the term only in that way, and the reader must bear in mind the special meaning attached to it. If the terms chosen have well-established meanings in everyday use, as is the case with "political participants," that can create a serious gap in the flow of information and reasoning between author and reader.

Perhaps the most important kind of error in meaning commonly found in descriptive accounts results from a failure to differentiate adequately between *real* and *nominal* definitions. Technically, a real definition summarizes human experience with a particular class of events, while a nominal definition is a statement of the author's intention to substitute one phrase for another.[1] The definitions found in a medical dictionary, for example, are "real"; those that appear in mathematics or logic are "nominal." Real definitions can be challenged on the basis of experience, and they can be used to deal with experience. Nominal definitions need have no relation to experience, and cannot be questioned on experiential grounds. Nominally defined terms, in other words, cannot be used to deal with real-world affairs. If I choose to define a frog (nominally) as an animal with four legs and a blue beak, I can defy anyone who questions the definition *because* it is nominal, but I am also unable to identify the label "frog" with any real-world creature. Before nominally defined terms can be applied to real-world affairs, their meanings must be transformed into real definitions.

The problems associated with the use of nominally defined terms cannot be avoided by simply abandoning their use. So long as they are properly employed, nominally defined terms can perform a number of very useful functions. They are essential for introducing new concepts into a field of inquiry, for simplifying complex proposals (let X stand for . . .), and for avoiding bias in discussion (employing such labels as "country X" and "country Y" when discussing national behavior rather than identifying the countries involved, for example), among other things. Most of the problems arising from the use of nominal definitions appear when terms that have well-established real-world meanings are given nominal definitions (not precising definitions). It is then very easy, but unacceptable, to slip from one meaning to another. The term "market," for example, is nominally defined as it appears in economic theory, yet is quite commonly (and mistakenly) equated with the "markets" that appear in everyday affairs—by economists as well as by nonspecialists.

Conceptual standardization is often suggested as a practical cure for the problems of meaning that appear in the social sciences, and those who urge that course of action usually point to the physical sciences and their accomplishments to support their position. But premature conceptual standardization could have a more deleterious effect on such disciplines as political science and economics than the vagueness and uncertainty of meaning they are intended to cure. Standardization tends to fix meanings more or less permanently, and in a relatively undeveloped field of inquiry, that can be a recipe for disaster.

Efforts to *apply* concepts to experience, however adequately they may be defined, create problems of a different order. First, because all concepts are generalized terms, their application requires an act of judgment. In some cases, that creates no serious problems for either inquirer or critic. It is fairly easy to demonstrate that the assertion "There is a cow in that field" should be accepted. But what of "John is anxiety ridden" or "Peter is a very unstable person"? Such judgments sometimes provoke unending arguments among experts or specialists in the field. To make matters worse, judgment is not easily separated from extrapolation, contextualization, or interpretation, and all three should be minimized if not eliminated altogether if the goal is accurate description. To illustrate, consider the meaning or implications of the following notation in a ship's log: "The Captain was sober this morning." Taken alone, it qualifies as a flat descriptive statement, but it is very difficult to read without making some effort to work out the "meaning," of the entry, the "reason" for including it.

The process of observation, or making measurements, produces a different type of problem for those who must deal systematically with descriptive accounts. For one thing, concepts do not always refer directly to the world of observation. Most concepts require "indicators," sets of observables that serve as an indirect means of measuring the value taken by a particular variable or concept. Thus the indicator of "viscosity," which refers to the amount of friction among the molecules that make up a liquid, is the rate of flow of liquids through a tube of a given manufacture and size, compared to the rate of flow of water. For such measurements to be valid, a strong theory must be available that links the concept to the indicator(s). When the concept is a classification, such as a particular species of birds, the indicator will commonly be one or more of the distributed attributes of the species, and the linkage is found in the actual classification. But in other cases, it may be very difficult indeed to produce an adequate and reliable indicator for concept, particularly if its meaning is vague or fuzzy. Arguments among experts still rage, and seem likely to continue, about the validity of the tests used to measure intelligence, for example.

A second fundamental type of intellectual problem has to do with the products of measurement, with the content of a description; it is most easily clarified by using the standard notion of scaling. Although there are other ways of dealing with the information content of measurements, the division into nominal, ordinal, interval, and ratio scales is widely used and it will suffice for clarifying the nature of the problem. In general, the type of scale used to make a measurement is determined by the characteristics of the continuum being measured and the purpose for which the data will be used. A decision to make use of a particular type of scaling usually determines the kind of mathematical manipulations that can be carried out on the results. The reason is simply that mathematical analysis cannot extract more from a given body of information than it contains. Unless and until a logic of creation is developed, which seems highly unlikely, the amount and kind of information that a description contains depends on the kind of scaling used to produce it, and every mathematical technique requires data of a particular quality before it can properly be applied. Applying any mode of formal calculation to data that cannot satisfy the scaling requirements of the calculus is a serious mistake. Measurement is not simply the assignment of numbers to a set of entities.

Various other methodological issues can be expected to arise in systematic discussions of descriptions. The subjectivity of *all* observations, for example, raises fundamental questions about the validity of the selection of characteristics that is attributed to things observed. The margin of error can be reduced, but not eliminated (if the object of observation is external to the person) by using instruments to stabilize the set of stimuli that produce the perception, and by using multiple observers, suitably trained. But such techniques have little value when applied to personal observations of the subjective dimensions of the person. Yet those data are essential for meaningful social inquiry. Affective reactions or opinions, for example, which are reported as descriptions of subjective states by those who experience them, can hardly be ignored in certain kinds of studies.

The use of collective terms, and in particular the need to differentiate carefully between organized and unorganized collectives, is yet another source of conceptual problems, particularly in the social sciences. To treat society as analogous to a watch, or to any other mechanical system, for example, is a gross though common mistake. Similar problems associated with the use of organic analogies in efforts to deal with social problems are equally well known but such analogies are frequently used and abused nonetheless. Finally, the use of collective terms facilitates the commission of the all-too-common fallacies of division and composition.

At a slightly different level, the need to develop conceptual frameworks, sets of theoretically linked concepts that can be used to deal with complex events, creates yet another major source of descriptive inadequacy. That a dentist or physician must have a reasonably well-integrated set of concepts to perform effectively is readily established. Citizens of every political society, and members of every family, need and develop a similar apparatus. Such structures are extremely useful, and even essential. But they are also potential intellectual prisons, for they are usually transmitted institutionally and only partly self-consciously. A common result, most readily observed in a social context, is a marked tendency to preserve outmoded and even dangerous assumptions long after their validity has been effectively destroyed. Understandably, conceptual frameworks are perhaps the most powerful vehicle available for transmitting untenable forms of bias from one generation to the next.

The last major source of conceptual error common in description is a function of the full set of concepts available and in use, of what can be called a description's "potential for omissions." The first problem created for users of descriptive data determining *what*, if anything, has been omitted that is significant for the user's purpose. Difficulties of that order will be well known to anyone who has set out to answer a significant question using data taken from the field of history. The most difficult question is of course whether anything of importance has been omitted, but that does not end the matter. If an omission is found, was it deliberate? Does the fact that X does not appear in the historical record mean that X did not occur? Or was X simply not noticed by the observer? Or was it noted but considered insufficiently important to include in the historical account? Was the omission due to bias on the historian's part? The answers to these and other similar questions can have a profound effect on the significance, and the meaning, that is assigned to a particular body of information. The critic must therefore be seriously concerned with the general question: How and why was the omission noted in the first place?

Prediction

To predict, stated precisely, means to project the content of an observation or description that has not yet been made. The event that is predicted may have already occurred but not been observed, but more commonly it will lie in the future. In everyday language, predictions appear in a wide variety of forms, ranging from statements that begin "I believe that . . . ," to dogmatic assertions about the future that commence "It will . . . ." To be testable, predictions must follow logically from applying a particular pattern to a given situation—in practical terms, from combining a pattern with an observation and calculating the result. The form is quite simple:

$$\text{Observation (Description)} + \text{Pattern} + \text{Calculation} = \text{Prediction}$$

If either the pattern or the content of the observation is not known and specifiable, the result is prophecy. In such cases, all that can be used as a basis for deciding whether or not to accept the prediction is the track record of the prophet, or a Kierkegaardian act of faith.

The type of pattern accepted and applied, and its relation to past experience, is the key to both successful prediction and sound criticism or evaluation of the pattern used to make it. The pattern must precede the prediction; human experience must antedate the pattern. The primary task for those who wish to predict future events is to locate a set of two or more events that have related or interacted systematically in past experience; that relation is generalized to produce a pattern. In effect, a formal pattern or calculus is imposed upon the selection of events. The pattern must connect the event to be predicted to some antecedent event(s) regularly and systematically in a way that corresponds to past experience with those events. The pattern simply organizes or generalizes prior experience with a particular set of events. There is no magic involved; the pattern can be used to predict *because* it generalizes past experience. The only major assumption required is that past experience will hold in the future. Since that assumption is usually suppressed, it is a common and persistent source of error.

Two basic types of patterns can be used to generate defensible or testable predictions: the first is a classification; the second includes both forecasts and theories. Because theories and forecasts are identical in structure, and function in precisely the same way when used to make predictions, the discussion will deal only with forecasts, reserving theories for the discussion of instruments used to control future events.

Predicting with Classifications

A classification states the set of attributes or properties that are in logic distributed to or, in everyday language, shared by all members of the class. The pattern consists of a set of variables and the rules that specify the range of values that can be taken by each variable. Each classification has the same basic form:

$$\text{If } A, \text{ then } b,c,d,e \ldots \ldots n$$
$$\text{or All } A \text{ is } b,c,d,e \ldots \ldots n$$

Within the form, A represents class membership and the lowercase letters are the various attributes shared by each member of the class. The structure may be quite large and complex, including a variety of subdivisions, sub-subdivisions, and so on. The class of creatures identified as "birds" will be used to illustrate the processes by which classifications are created and used to make predictions, since it is widely known and its applications are not particularly complicated.

The overall process of predicting actually begins with the *creation* of a classification; that in turn depends on prior observations of things, as yet unclassified and unlabeled, in the environment (for purposes of illustration, things that are now called "birds"). Assume that at first only one such thing, differentiable from the remainder of the environment, is seen. If it remains visible for some time, its attributes can be generalized, and that produces a classification with only one member, not a trivial tool, actually, but limited in usefulness. Everyone needs, and produces/applies, such classifications when dealing with particular events, or the specific persons encountered in their daily lives.

Suppose, however, that a second and third and Nth thing appear in the observed world. The first problem is how to decide they are members of "the same" class or group. What makes the observer say "That is another one of *them?*" for that phrase once said, a classification has been claimed. It cannot occur, obviously, until someone notices the similarities that link or relate the different entities that have been observed. Some at least of the specific properties of the first thing (properties that may already have been generalized) must also characterize the others. It is unlikely, however, that every characteristic observed in the first bird will be shared by all of the others, hence some of the defining terms of the initial classification of a single bird will have to be dropped, for the meaning of the class labeled "birds" is limited to attributes shared by all of its observed members. Over time, as the number of observations increases, one can expect the range of differences to narrow, the precision and usefulness of the classification to increase, and so on. Understandably, the influence of technological improvements, as they affect human capacity for increasingly precise observation, is very important in that phase of classification development.

Application of the classification, its use for making predictions, depends on an initial assumption to the effect that a member of the class has been observed. That assumption will be based on observation of some attributes of class membership in an as-yet-unclassified "thing." In some cases, seeing one or two attributes of a thing can be enough; in Missouri, for example, a black bird more than twelve inches tall with a flaming red topknot is almost certainly a pileated woodpecker. In other cases, such as the identification of fall or spring warblers, diagnosis may be difficult and the results very uncertain, no matter how many attributes of the thing being classified are observed. Once the initial assumption of class membership is made and justified, all of the class attributes can be transferred to the particular individual, using a very primitive logical procedure:

1. All members of class A have properties $a,b,c,d,e,f,g,h,i \ldots n$
2. X is a member of class A (based on seeing a,b,c,d,e)
3. Therefore X can be expected to have properties $f,g,h,i \ldots n$

The principal suppressed assumption is that attributes or characteristics observed in the past will remain constant in the future, and evidence can be produced to support, or attack, that assumption as well.

The use of classifications to make predictions can itself be generalized into a four-step procedure:

1. Identify the real-world purpose to be fulfilled as a prediction. For example the question, "Will that bird stay in the backyard all winter?" requires a prediction. If the question were, "Can we get that bird to remain in the yard over the winter?" a theory would be needed to produce a defensible answer.

2. Locate or create a pattern of the type needed to fulfill the purpose that fits the situation being observed. In the case of a bird, it can be either: (a) a classification that includes the bird in question and contains a generalized statement information relating to its migratory habits—the feature to be predicted, or (b) a forecast linking migration to other observable factors such as weather conditions. In some cases, the same data may be found in both kinds of patterns.

3. Calculate the effect of assuming that the content of the pattern applies to the present case. If all birds of a particular species migrate, any bird that is assumed to belong to that species can also be expected to migrate, *unless,* and it is a very important caveat, the limiting conditions

governing the application of the pattern apply. It may be, for example, that the pattern does not hold invariably for states in the border region of the United States. Otherwise, a syllogism is constructed as follows:

- All birds of a species S have characteristic A (migrate annually).
- This bird is a member of species S (assumption or judgment).
- Therefore, this bird will migrate.

The justification for accepting the prediction is found, in the first instance, in the content of the classification and the content of the observation.

Although competent criticism of predictions extends beyond accepting the observations and classification used to make them, the critic will usually deal with those factors first. The problems inherent in observation have already been touched upon; it remains to look briefly at the other points that can affect the quality/acceptability of predictions made with the use of a classification.

The first danger point is the initial diagnosis: Does the pattern fit the case? Is this really a bird of species S? That requires a competent critic to have: first, a sound knowledge of the distributed attributes of the species (if *all* of the attributes of the species appear in observation, then the thing observed must by definition belong to the class); second, knowledge (or information) about the content of observations on which the diagnosis was based; and third, enough familiarity with the alternative possibilities to be confident that nothing significant was overlooked, that a better fit with observations was not ignored.

The second aspect of a pattern where error occurs often is the content or, more precisely, the validity of the content or substance. Is the generalized content assumed in the prediction fully justified by past experience? In the illustration, have birds of species S really migrated without exception? That judgment depends primarily on knowledge of the content of historical experience with such birds.

Finally, the logical or mathematical quality of the calculations involved bears examination. Does the conclusion reached actually follow from the premises stated? In a simple case of the kind used for illustration, that is not a serious concern; in more complex predictions, expert advice may be needed before a decision is made.

One last point: there are aberrations and exceptions to every pattern or classification that can be produced, some minor and others not. The uncertainty that is attached to every form of inductively based knowledge applies, and it is always possible that the diagnosis is correct, the classification is sound, yet the prediction fails. How are aberrations and discrepancies separated from inadequacies in the pattern itself? Further, the diagnosis may be wholly mistaken, yet the predicted event may occur. How, in such cases, is the user to learn that an error has been made? There is no simple answer to such questions; what makes an answer acceptable is a function of the state of the discipline in which the prediction is made. The point to remember is that predictions based upon classifications serve as a test of a number of elements in the predictive process, and it may be exceptionally difficult to determine where error occurred when predictions fail and it cannot be assumed as a matter of course that a prediction was correctly made merely because it succeeded. In effect, there is no way to be certain that an adequate assessment has been made of all of the elements involved in a complex prediction. All that can be done is to make the inquirer aware of the points where errors can occur, and thus make it possible in principle for such errors to be avoided, or their effects minimized.

Predicting with Forecasts or Theories

The second type of pattern that can be used to make defensible predictions is the forecast. Forecasts are created and applied in much the same way as classifications, but the two forms of knowledge differ greatly in both structure and content. Each instrument is produced by generalizing relations among events observed regularly in the past; each consists of a set of variables and rules, together with a set of limiting conditions governing application. But the rules in a forecast link the values of the set of variables, whereas the rules in a classification state the selection of variables that indicate the distributed properties of the class and the range of values that each variable can take. In both cases, however, predictions are generated by combining the pattern with one or more specific observations, calculating the implications, and transferring the result to the world of experience.

Understandably, forecasts and classifications are created by quite different procedures. Development of a classification begins with a specific thing, and generalizes the results of observing its behavior, or its relations with the environment; a forecast is created by locating two or more events in the environment that covary, or recur systematically, separated by a time lag that is adequate for the purpose of the predictor. If event A regularly precedes event B by a fixed time, that is already a sufficient base for predicting event B once event A is observed. Further, that relation can be generalized to produce a pattern in the form: $A + t = B$, where A is the date/time when event A occurs, t is the time that elapsed between the two events in the past, suitably generalized, and B is the observed time of event B. Once established, that structure can be used to predict B's time of occurrence once the time of A has been observed (or postulated). An extended chain of such relations can be constructed, if time and resources permit, to bring predictive capacity within almost any reasonable time frame.

In effect, forecasts are produced by generalizing descriptive accounts of correlations or covariance observed in the past.

A forecast connects changes in the values of two or more variables over time; in a simple variant, a single variable is used and the rule links its values over time, as a store owner may predict future sales by direct extrapolation from sales in the past. Predictions will usually link a target variable to a different indicator variable, preferably to an event assumed to be linked empirically to the variable whose value is being predicted. However, no causal connection between the events included in the pattern need be postulated. The justification required for a pattern used to make predictions is the same regardless of whether or not it includes a causal relation; the requirements are a function of the purpose for which the instrument is used. Thus, if a sophisticated computer is used to do problems in addition, its validity as an adding machine is all that counts when performance capacity is being assessed with respect to that specific purpose.

Predictions generated with the use of forecasts are subject to many of the same limitations that apply to predictions generated using classifications. The strength of a forecast depends entirely on historical evidence; the absence of a causal assumption effectively precludes experimental testing. Such factors as the length of time for which the relation has held in the past, the variety of circumstances in which the pattern has continued unchanged, the absence of past failures, or of any reason to expect a different outcome in particular circumstances, and so on, can all serve to increase confidence in the results. Perhaps the most useful technique for strengthening confidence in forecasts is to increase the number of predictions made of an event, employing different factors in each case. A manufacturer who needs an accurate prediction of sales for a given future time period may ask for a number of forecasts, each based on a different set of correlations. If they tend to agree, that is usually the best reason possible for accepting the estimate.

Controlling Events in the Environment

To this point, a fairly conventional approach to the methodology of social inquiry has been adequate to the purposes set for the theory of knowledge. The first major departure from convention is forced by the need to control events in ways that are adequate for directing human actions. The reason is fairly straightforward: the conventional or traditional conception of "theory" found in philosophy of science,[2] even if it could be satisfied within the social sciences (which is unlikely for the immediate future), would not in any case provide instruments that could be used to control the flow of events accurately and reliably. Not all of the theories in physical science, not to say social science, are adequate for that purpose.

If the methodology of inquiry is to be controlled by the overall normative purpose sought through the creation of knowledge (by the effort to maintain and/or improve the conditions of life of some human population), then some major changes in emphasis, and in the criteria of adequacy applied to the instruments produced, are required. The result of those changes is an approach to creating the tools needed for directing actions that differs from conventional or philosophic methodology in a number of fundamental ways. Perhaps the most important difference is found in the commitment to the use of pragmatic criteria for assessing the knowledge created within a discipline. For example, the fact that a valid theory must include a causal assumption does not imply that theories should be used primarily to determine the cause of events, nor that inquiry should focus primarily on the causes. Indeed, given a commitment to producing knowledge that can be used for directing actions, theories are more fruitfully regarded as devices for producing *cures* through human actions than as instruments for locating causes. The only circumstances in which an inquirer need be concerned with causes is when a cause must be known in order to effect a cure, and that seems to be an uncommon situation, even in physical science.

A second major departure from conventional usage required by the commitment to directing human actions follows from the consequent need to assess the full set of options available for choice. To justify a preference, the consequences anticipated to follow from each of the actions available to a specific actor at a given time and place must be projected as fully as time, resources, and knowledge allow. Actions usually trigger sequences of consequences, lead to a branching effect; ideally each of the branches or offshoots produced by the initiating action should be explored for normatively significant consequences. Theories usually appear as two- or three-element structures whose interactions are rule controlled; to satisfy the causality assumption, the rule need only be expected to hold regardless of the way in which the initial change is produced. Projecting the full effects of a major human action will usually involve the use of a number of such theories. If an action focus controls the quest for theories, that minimizes the risk of serious omissions. That is, theories should be sought that will produce the widest and most accurate picture of the repercussions expected to follow from specific actions. Given the overall purpose accepted for inquiry, the quest for theory is more accurately stated as the quest for theories that are sufficient to project the future effects of complex actions on human populations.

Put another way, the significance of any given theory will depend on the kinds of human actions whose outcomes it can assist in projecting or achieving (the theories used to project outcomes are also used to develop policies for achieving them). In terms of the overall purpose for inquiry accepted here, the quest for theory can be expected to begin at one of three basis points: (1) with a condition in the environment that requires change on normative grounds; (2) with an actor who has some capacity to produce change, and seeks reasons for selecting one course of action rather than another; or (3) with a gap in the present theoretical apparatus that needs to be filled. If the need to produce an apparatus adequate for directing human actions on defensible grounds is accepted as fundamental, the third of these reasons for seeking theory, which is dominant in some thinking about the nature of physical science, can usually be disregarded or avoided.

Developing Theories. In some ways, the development of an instrument useful for controlling future events in the environment proceeds in much the same manner as the creation of a forecast. Each is based on observed regularities in past experience, suitably generalized; each consists of a set of two or more variables and a rule that links their values, together with a set of limiting conditions that control applications. But the pattern required for controlling events must include, in principle at least, a human action as the starting point in the chain reaction, and that forces some major differences in procedure and emphasis. For example, forecasts usually focus on the event to be predicted, the variable whose future value is to be estimated. Optimal strategy of inquiry then suggests a close examination of the antecedent conditions of the event to be explained, seeking other events that have covaried in time and could be used to predict the phenomenon in question. The so-called methods suggested by John Stuart Mill in his *System of Logic*[3] provide a classic example of common practice. But for developing the kinds of theories needed for directing actions in defensible ways, the focus should in principle change. If the central concern is the effects of action, inquiry can usually, though not invariably, be expected to begin with actions and seek to determine their consequences rather than the converse.

The major reasons for focusing on actions and their consequences are essentially normative: first, that focus is prerequisite to producing the information needed to make defensible choices; second, and far more important, it tends to eliminate or at least reduce the likelihood that the patient will be killed in order to cure the cancer. Such considerations give strength to the basic assumption that inquiry should begin with an action and seek to follow the chain reactions it triggers as far as knowledge, time, and resources permit (to the limits of human capacity to project) rather than beginning with the event to be predicted and examine preceding events for covariance, as in the effort to produce a forecast or determine a "cause."

The elements in the sequence of changes triggered by human actions must be linked causally if they are to be controllable in principle, meaning that the pattern of interactions should be expected to hold (within the limits of established reliability) regardless of the way in which the initial change is introduced. In effect, control over events is achieved only if a pattern can be created that contains either the necessary and/or the sufficient conditions for a specific event to occur—for achieving a specified purpose. Any instrument that can perform that function will be labeled a theory. That meaning corresponds fairly well with usage in the experimental sciences, but the reader is warned that few of the intellectual tools labeled "theories" in social science, and even in some of the physical sciences, can be used to control the flow of events. Put somewhat differently, theories of the kind sought here are able in principle to supply answers to the three questions that must be dealt with if human actions are to be directed on defensible grounds: What caused event E to occur? How can condition C be altered by human actions? and What changes will follow from action A?

Structurally, a theory is identical to a forecast, consisting of a set of two or more variables whose values are linked by rule(s) and a set of limiting conditions that control application or use. If the theory states conditions necessary for an event to occur, it will take the form "No X unless Y under condition C"; if it incorporates the sufficient conditions for the event to occur, the form is "If X then Y under condition C." The apparatus is created by first solving a particular case, or a set of cases, and then generalizing the result; the generalized pattern is tested against *other* particular cases. A sound model is found in medicine, where physicians can only develop and test proposed treatments with individual patients.

Because of the causal assumption they include, theories always provide a basis for action, but only in principle for the technology and resources needed to implement them may not be available. The causal assumption makes experimentation possible; applying and/or acting on a theory is one major way to test it. The causal assumption also influences the kind of justification required for a theory in some very important ways. Although theories require stronger evidence to justify acceptance and use because of the implied causal connection, that assumption also makes it easier to provide. It is worth noting in passing that the validity of theories must be separated from their usefulness or applicability. So far as the direction of human actions is concerned (policymaking), validity is not enough. If the technology and resources needed to act upon or apply a theory are not available, the theory simply cannot be used by policymakers.

In principle, a theory isolates a set of variables so completely that once the initial change introduced into a pattern or situation is known, all changes that occur in their values can be accounted for perfectly by applying the rules incorporated into the pattern. In practice, that is rarely if ever possible. Indeed, if it did occur, measurement error would usually suffice to destroy the perfection of the apparatus. It follows that the rules included in theories cannot be nomic in form *(All X is Y)* yet fit observations precisely. The alternative limited form *(Some X is Y)* is more accurate, technically speaking, but also virtually noncalculable. That is, unless the theory is applied to very large numbers of events for which a Poisson distribution can be assumed, virtually nothing of value can be inferred from propositions stated in that form.

A fairly simple resolution to the problem is achieved by retaining the nomic form within the theory but inserting a *ceteris paribus* (c.p. clause or Fudge Factor) between the theory and its applications. In effect, all of the external influences on the variables included in the theory are lumped in the c.p. clause. The total influence of those factors can then be estimated out of experience gained by applying the theory, and that becomes a measure of the theory's reliability (in use). The c.p. clause performs several valuable functions for the theorist: first and foremost, it eliminates a formal anomaly in the theoretical apparatus (no "law" in science fits data perfectly); second, it allows the use of weaker theories, which in many fields is all that can be produced; finally, it focuses on the user's purposes in judgments of acceptability, illustrated classically by the physician whose patient will predictably die in a fairly short period of time if nothing is done to help. In the latter case, a treatment that is effective only 5 percent of the time is nonetheless a defensible alternative to simply allowing the patient to die. In that sense, the significance of the purpose that can be achieved with its use is as important as its absolute reliability in the assessment of any theory.

Criticism and Justification. Criticism and justification of theories intended to project the effects of action is a difficult task, made somewhat more complex by the kind of conditionality that attaches to all such intellectual instruments. A range of elements and features must be taken into account in assessment or evaluation. First, the theory itself is subjected to direct visual inspection; it must contain two or more variables that have *real* (and not nominal) definitions and a set of rules of interaction that are applicable or calculable. Second, the limiting conditions should be unambiguous, and the influence of the factors incorporated into the c.p. clause or Fudge Factor estimated with reasonable accuracy. Third, the evidence must justify assuming that the whole of the theory is isomorphic to the whole of past experience, with due regard for aberrations. It is not enough for *some* of the events that are entailed by a theory to coincide with practice, nor for the theory to fit only some past experience (which is only illustration). Both the elements in the theory, the things that are related and the processes incorporated into the rules, must fit experience with some known level of accuracy and reliability, else the apparatus is useless. Although the level of assurance that can be achieved may be in principle controlled by the nature of the knowledge-creating process, of generalizing, in practice theoretical reliability is determined mainly on pragmatic grounds. Finally, if the theory includes what are somewhat misleadingly called "feedback" relations, calculability becomes a serious problem as the number of variables increases. In general, theories that include feedback cannot include more than three variables without losing their calculability. However, instead of increasing the number of variables in the theory, the limiting conditions controlling application can be tightened, producing the same effect at much less (intellectual) cost.

From a different perspective, theories can be used only for purposes that lie within their capacity. As defined here, theories can show *why* a change occurred, *how* to produce a particular change, and *what effect* can be expected to follow from making a given change. The purpose of the user must fall within those limits. The quality of the theories needed will depend very much on the way in which the purpose is stated. Rough and general statements of purpose, such as simply "altering the conditions of life of a small population," are relatively easy to satisfy, for the action taken can vary widely yet fulfill the stated purpose to the letter. For example, the conditions of life of a given population could be altered by providing better food and shelter, by execution, by supplying intoxicating liquor, and so on. In ordinary discourse, such peculiarities are eliminated by the suppressed assumptions built into the context in which the discussion occurs. More formally, purposes need to be defined fairly narrowly to be effective either for directing the quest for theories or for assessing actions taken. But the more narrowly and precisely that purposes are drawn, the more complex the theoretical requirements become and the more difficult they are to fulfill. Finally, the question whether any of the changes that *can* be introduced into a given situation are actually more desirable than allowing the drift course of events to continue must be decided before actions can be justified; that very basic problem in applied ethics will be considered in some detail in the section that follows.

In some respects at least, theories can be treated as though they were intellectual maps of a particular territory, in the sense that both maps and theories are used to represent a body of observations and both make use of conventional symbols to record them. Many of the criticisms that can be directed at maps are also useful for assessing theories. Both are selective, for example, and selectivity is in each case controlled by the user's purposes. What is included or excluded depends on purpose, and its significance; the cost of additions and extensions must be justified by reference to the importance of what they make possible. Further, theories, like maps, can serve a number of purposes, but no theory, and no map, can serve all purposes equally well for all persons. Neither maps nor theories need to be abandoned if they fail occasionally; like a map, a theory can be altered, or its conditions of application can be changed, to eliminate problems caused by occasional lapses. Finally, theories, like maps, are assessed in terms of their fit with experience (with history), particularly as that experience has been incorporated into the fundamentals of the discipline in which the theory is employed. A proposed theory in physics that violated the Law of Gravity, for example, would be regarded with great skepticism by the body of informed opinion, pending a detailed discussion of the reasoning and evidence available to support it. As the available supply of theory increases, it tends to become the primary reference point for testing proposed additions to the body of knowledge in the field. The tendency to rely on the established body of knowledge in that way serves to increase disciplinary stability, but at a price, for major revisions proposed in the fundamental structure may find it increasingly difficult to gain acceptance, or even an unbiased hearing.

As might be expected from the foregoing discussion, the role that experimental evidence plays in testing and justification of theories, although very great, depends to some extent on the amount of well-established knowledge available in a field. In a relatively weak field, experimental evidence is likely to play a much stronger role in justification than in a stable and well-established discipline such as chemistry or physics. The best test of any empirical theory is, of course, to act on it, but the conditions of application may be difficult to control, and if the situation cannot be isolated sufficiently, the results of acting on the theory may be indeterminate, or even seriously misleading. In some cases, theories that cannot be acted upon directly can be tested in action indirectly, through other related theories; when that occurs, the quality of all the theories employed must be examined when validity is being estimated.

In that context, the uses and limitations of laboratory and natural-state experiments, which depend on the use to be made of the results in the conduct of real-world affairs, should be borne in mind. In general, laboratory evidence is useful for determining the interactions among particular sets of variables very precisely, but under more or less idealized conditions. The principal weakness that attaches to the experimental results is a function of the very idealization of operating conditions that gives them great accuracy. If those conditions are not closely approximated anywhere in the environment, the theory created within the laboratory may have no applications and even very limited heuristic value. Natural-state experiments avoid that problem, but at cost, for they open the way to attributing specific effects to the elements of the theory that are actually due to factors outside the theory. Additionally, reliance on natural-state experimentation tends to limit the inquirers' ability to specify the conditions of application, hence may lead to serious errors in estimates of reliability.

The discussion of theories can be concluded with a brief summary of a few points of special concern to those seeking to apply or to justify them. First, for reasons that should by now be clear, the primary importance of identifying purpose as clearly and precisely as possible requires special emphasis. Second, reconceptualization, changing the basic conceptual apparatus used to deal with a set of phenomena, may be essential. Third, the "N of Instances" fallacy, the assumption that confidence can in all cases be increased simply by increasing the number of observations made, must be avoided. Here it may be useful to recall the Indian tribe that required one member to rise each day before the sun appeared and recite a prayer in the belief that the sun would not rise if the ceremony were not performed. No matter how often the juxtaposition of events continued without exception, that could not establish a causal link between the prayer and the rising sun. In a somewhat different vein, major exceptions to established rules and failures in application should be recorded along with successes. Finally, imaginative instantiation, that cherished darling of the philosophers, counts for nothing as evidence, and should be abandoned. There is nothing wrong with the use of imagination, but the fact that a situation not covered by a particular theory can be imagined has no significance—there must be a real case.

FULFILLING NORMATIVE REQUIREMENTS

Creating and justifying the apparatus needed for fulfilling the normative requirements for directing human actions on defensible grounds (creating decision or policy models), is by far the most difficult part of the intellectual enterprise. It is also the area in which current traditions, in both ethics and policymaking, are least useful and must usually be either augmented or replaced entirely. Two primary instruments are required: first, a set of concepts that identify all of the normatively significant dimensions of the outcomes available for choice through action; and second, a priority or preference-ordering, properly justified, that can be used to select the preferred outcome among those available in a particular choice. Neither is widely available at the present time, and each is complex and difficult to produce and justify.

Most of the major assumptions that must be made before a justification for a preference can be created have already been examined. The central focus is the conditions of life in each of the available outcomes of those persons affected by the action or choice. It can be assumed, for reasons already noted, that in a limited but very important sense, one human life is the equal of any other, meaning that departures from equality of weighting must be justified. The quality of individual life, which is the focus of argument in normative decisions, is a function of two major factors: the content of the natural environment and current human capacity to alter that environment, including the quality of both the scientific and the ethical knowledge available to informed opinion. Actions or choices, which are analytically identical and may be performed by individuals or by collectivities, provide the necessary link between human capacity and resources and the quality of life of the population. Action is therefore used as the central focus of the analytic/critical apparatus, meaning that the elements included in the intellectual structure are determined by reference to the requirements for directing actions on a defensible grounds.

Given an actor with some capacity to produce change in the environment voluntarily, choice is unavoidable. Without an actor, the concept of choice would be absurd; without some capacity that can be exercised voluntarily, it would be meaningless. The result of action, and the indicator of action, is a world that is different than it would have been had capacity been exercised differently. It follows that action is precisely equivalent to choice. The object of choice, the thing that is chosen, is the full content of one of the outcomes available through the exercise of capacity.

To direct actions, both empirical and normative knowledge are required: first, the actor or critic must know what *can* be done, must be able to project the normatively significant content of the options from which a choice can be made; second, some basis is needed for deciding what *should* be done, what choice to make from among a specified set of outcomes. The empirical requirements have already been considered; discussion of the normative requirements begins with the conceptual apparatus needed to structure the content of the options and then proceeds to the development and justification of priorities.

Justification will focus on the consequences of action for some human population. In principle, criticism or justification of actions could be based on any of the three major elements in an action: the actor, the action, or the set of consequences flowing from the action, or some combination of all three. In practice, only the consequences of action provide an adequate basis for decision. Justification by reference to the actor (*argumentum ad hominem*) has long since been discredited; criticism based on assessment of actions fails because the same action can produce radically different consequences when applied to different situations, yet the consequences cannot be ignored without risking self-contradiction or even absurdity. Choices can, however, be justified on the basis of a comparison of the content of the available outcomes, carried out in terms of past experience, duly organized and extrapolated. Note particularly that the focus of criticism is the action or the choice and not the actor and that the actor's intentions are irrelevant to criticism of the action, although they may figure heavily in criticism of the actor.

Given a focus on consequences, the first task in reasoned and defensible choice is to project the content of the outcomes, the set of consequences to be expected from each of the actions available to the actor, plus the outcome to be expected if capacity is not exercised. Defensible choice requires a systematic comparison of the content of the outcomes, focused on the conditions of life of the population that each contains. Each outcome is best construed as a film clip of the future, open-ended and increasingly uncertain as it moves further away from the present. Human actions usually trigger a chain of consequences or effects; in principle, the full set must be taken into account so far as it can be anticipated, given time, resources, and so on. Further, human actors, whether individual or collective, usually have a range of actions available, each dealing with a different part of the environment, and a "choice among choices," made in precisely the same way as any other choice, is actually required in every particular case.

The outcome to be expected if no action is taken can be projected using either a forecast or a theory; causally linked theories are needed to project the effects of action. The outcomes must be attainable; the technology, resources, and so on needed to apply the theories must be available. And since the concepts used to make the theoretical projections of outcomes will not always capture their normatively significant dimensions, some additional theoretical mechanism may be needed to translate them into an acceptable set of normative variables.

Normative Concepts/Variables

The crux of the problem of creating an adequate set of normative concepts can be underscored in a very simple way: assume that a choice must be made between living one of two lives: what information is then needed before a decision can be made and justified? The question cannot be answered in the abstract, for it will depend heavily on the kind and amount of information that is available at the time of decision. In the absence of *any* information about the two projected lives, no meaningful choice is possible, though a decision can be made—by tossing a coin, for example. The problem is not to decide in abstract terms what would be adequate for reasoned choice generally, but to determine the best choice given the information actually available when the choice is made (which does not exclude the possibility of choosing to delay the choice until more data are available). Thus, one life might appear much less desirable than another if it was known that it was unlikely to last more than a few years while nothing presently known indicated an early demise for the second. But if that information were not available to the chooser(s), then it would be irrelevant to the decision. In practical terms, the question is not, "What information should be demanded if everything conceivable could be made available?" but "What is most relevant and significant from the information that *is* available at the time of a decision?" The normative variables are designed to supply that information.

Given the assumptions already made, the information produced by applying the normative variables will refer to some aspects of individual life, to those aspects that influence its quality or relative desirability. However, that does not imply a need to identify the characteristic of a human trait or attribute that makes it normative. In practice, *any* aspect of a human life may be considered significant, depending on circumstances, on the other attributes or characteristics of the life in question. In effect, the significance of particular bits of information cannot be assessed in isolation; some basis for comparison is essential. Furthermore, as noted earlier, choices are matters for judgment rather than decision rule, and the basis for judgment cannot be stipulated in wholly abstract terms. The discussion will therefore begin with the fundamental normative concept, the "quality of life," seeking to give it meaning, and allow the grounds for judgment to emerge from the context.

The Quality of Life

Comparisons, whether they refer to the outcomes available for choice, or any other construct, require a continuum that can be identified and in some way measured. In normative affairs, the basic continuum used to determine the relative preferability of outcomes is the quality of an individual life. But each life is a complex configuration of features and the differences between life states can be minuscule yet overwhelming or very large yet insignificant. Most of the problems encountered in efforts to create an adequate set of normative concepts, and a justification for preferences, are due to the peculiar character of the concept "quality of life." Yet without some such basic concept it is impossible to proceed and there is no defensible alternative available. Happily, a precise analogue can be found in the much more fully developed discipline of medicine. There, the concept "state of health," which is widely used by physicians to compare overall health conditions of the same individual, or the relative states of health of two or more persons, presents precisely the same conceptual problems for its users. Physicians have succeeded at least partly in resolving their conceptual dilemma, and medical practice can serve as a model and supply illustrations for dealing with the conceptual problems encountered in efforts to develop and apply an ethic that requires an assessment of life quality.

Four major types of difficulties arise out of the characteristics of the fundamental normative construct, the quality of individual life. They rule out the use of certain standard "scientific" procedures in the process of making and justifying choices. The limitations are serious, for if the value of each normative variable could be measured reasonable well, and the particular values taken by each variable in each of the options could be determined, it would be possible in principle to devise a procedure for determining a value for each normative variable in each outcome. Developing a rule that could be used to calculate the value of the "quality of life" variable (which could serve as a basis for choice) would then be possible at least in principle.

Unfortunately, the character of the overall normative variable (the quality of individual life) does not permit that kind of measurement. The effect of changing the value of a given normative variable must be measured in terms of its impact on the life as a whole. That turns out to be impossible.

The reason is irrefragable: the quality of an individual life is not completely captured in any finite set of variables, hence there can be no standard unit for measuring overall quality. It follows that no rule is possible for calculating the value of the quality of a life from the values taken by any specific set of normative variables. Comparisons of the quality of life, like comparisons of the "state of health," can be produced and justified, and a way of doing so is suggested below, but they cannot be based upon direct measurements. That limit has the effect of ruling out such techniques as cost-benefit analysis or utility measurements or estimates as a basis for making justifiable normative decisions.

A second type of problem that emerges out of efforts to apply normative concepts to human affairs is a function of the observer's perspective, the distance between observer and life being observed—usefully labeled the "microscope-telescope" problem. Its importance is particularly great in the management of collective affairs but it affects individual choices as well. The heart of the problem is accessibility, for the aspects of life that are available to an observer vary with distance. The "life" that appears to close and intimate observers may not be accessible to the observer at a distance, and in some respects at least, proximity can obscure features of a life that are readily seen from afar. The difference is not a matter of bias or prejudice but of what is actually visible given the position of the observer. For that reason, if a decision is made about the kind of information needed for making a choice, that will often determine where the information should be gathered, and to some extent where the decision should be made. In effect, the kind of data demanded for making normative decisions will influence the information-gathering and decision-making apparatus in place in a given society, and conversely, the system in place will influence, perhaps adversely, the quality of the decisions that can actually be made.

A third handicap on the development of adequate normative concepts is the number of functions they are required to perform, for each function tends to require a concept of a slightly different character. Normative concepts are commonly used for five major purposes. The first is to locate areas where change is needed on normative grounds. A second, equally important, is to identify the fortunate and unfortunate in society, and thus provide the working models for avoidance and emulation used by society's members, as well as a base for developing the collective ethic. Third, the normative variables serve as basic continua for comparing outcomes in reasoned decisions. Fourth, they provide the basic constructs used to inventory the society as part of the overall apparatus needed to direct public policymaking. Finally, they are needed to determine the effects of individual and collective action, to serve as a basis for the kind of monitoring system needed to improve the quality of public policymaking. Concepts useful for performing one of these functions may be quite useless or even counterproductive for another. Thus concepts that are perfectly valid as "early warning devices" can have disastrous effects if used as an action base, where they are likely to lead to actions that are equivalent to repairing or replacing a warning light instead of attacking the problem that caused it to go on. The way in which homelessness and drug addition have been treated in contemporary American society illustrates the error and its potential effects particularly well.

The final and in some ways most difficult problem to deal with in normative conceptualization arises from the need to treat human life holistically. In any choice, each outcome must be treated as an indivisible whole. It is easy to forget that individual lives must also be treated as wholes. What is compared in choice is the remainder of the "journey" that constitutes a human life as it appears in two or more different film clips, beginning at the point where action is taken and extended as far as time, knowledge, and resources permit. Various well-established human attributes serve to complicate the process. First, there is great diversity among individual lives; human populations are homogeneous only in very limited, and often trivial, respects. Second, life has duration as well as intensity and breadth, yet most of the available conceptual apparatus deals with life over the short run, or even cross-sectionally (in snapshot terms). There is a need for concepts that will more accurately state conditions of life handled at present by the use of adjectives such as "permanent" or "temporary." Third, human life has both subjective and objective dimensions, and information about the latter can come only from the individual involved. How quality can be controlled under those circumstances is a difficult yet unavoidable problem. To ignore subjectivity would be absurd and unacceptable; to depend on it too much creates the opportunity for the "happy hog" to flourish immune to criticism. Fourth, life has a social as well as an individual dimension; no human can survive in total isolation. Finally, life can be intellectualized, projected in its entirety, out of experience; it need not be lived in an eternal present. That intellectual capacity is a potential danger, of course, for imagination and the intellect can conjure a world in which all things are possible while in the world in which the species must live and die that is decidedly not the case. However, that same intellectual capacity may also be the instrument of salvation for the species, since it makes possible the development of the kinds of tools needed for creating a defensible normative system.

Two other points need be noted only briefly. First, the set of normative variables in use should be as comprehensive as possible, for omissions cannot be remedied but surplus information is eliminated more or less automatically when comparisons are made. Unfortunately, there are few if any criteria currently available for judging the relative comprehensiveness of alternative sets of normative variables and little or no effort is currently being made to establish them. Second, the normative concepts used to structure outcomes, which identify the primary factors that influence the relative preferability of different conditions of life, are linked to and justified by reference to, the conception of "the quality of individual life" that has come to be accepted, usually uncritically, within the society or culture—they are usually part of the mores and folkways of society. That tends to make them far more difficult to alter, or improve, than might otherwise be the case.

The Structure of the Normative Variables

In abstract terms, an adequate normative variable is a complex structure, and its use involves some fairly complicated processes; in everyday affairs, both are readily managed. The most effective way to demonstrate both the complexity and the ease with which it is usually managed, is to trace the evolution of one normative variable, viewed structurally. The primary function of the apparatus is to transform the immediate effects of action, the initial change that action produces, into a value for some normative variable. That requires a genuine theory, a set of variables together with rules linking their values, and an assumed causal relation. The reason for that requirement will be apparent as the structure evolves.

The normative variables refer to attributes of an individual life. At any point in time, an individual life can be described, incompletely but adequately, by stating the values of some finite set of variables (not necessarily variables that have normative importance). The structure of that initial descriptive account can be depicted in the following way, assuming that the value of each variable is set by observation:

$$[V_1, V_2, V_3, V_4 \ldots V_n]$$

Description

The square brackets indicate that the content of the description is an open set, a selection, and cannot be calculated. In effect, no rules of interaction or rules of selection are included in a descriptive account, though some basis for selection is clearly essential.

Input Variables. Actions affect human lives in one of two ways: they can either produce a change in the value of one of the life's attribute variables, or they can prevent such a change from occurring when otherwise it would be expected. An actor may strike another person, and thus induce change directly by the action, or the actor may prevent someone else from striking the person, and thus prevent a change from taking place. In either case, the world is then different than it would otherwise be, and the formal requirements for action have been satisfied. Whatever the effect produced, if actions are to have any impact on the life, the value of at least one of the variables used to describe the person must be altered. The variable(s) whose values are altered directly by action need not be "normative" in any intrinsic sense; a pinprick, properly placed, can cause death, or it can have virtually no effect on the person. Those variables whose values are altered directly by action can therefore be separated from the rest of the descriptive account and labeled *Input* variables *(IV)*, producing the following structure:

$$[IV_1, IV_2, IV_3 \ldots IV_n] \qquad [V_1, V_2, V_3 \ldots V_n]$$
$$\textit{Inputs} \qquad\qquad \textit{Description}$$

A theory is needed to connect the action taken to the initial change in the value of an Input variable; another theory is required to link the change in the value of the Input variable to a change in the value of the normative variable; and a third theory would be required to link the value of that variable to the value of the variable "quality of life" if it were possible to create such a linkage. Those theories are contained in the rules incorporated into the structure.

Buffer Variables. The impact of an action on an individual's life is a function of two factors: the nature of the initial change induced by an action and the person's other relevant characteristics. Knowing what action has been taken, or the initial change induced by it, is not enough; a blow to the head that would stun a small and frail person might have no effect whatever on a large and muscular individual, for example. The apparatus must be able to transform a change in the value of an Input variable into a change in the value of some normative variable, otherwise it makes no contribution to the effort to produce and justify choices. The mediating effect of other individual attributes must be taken into account. The function of these Buffer variables will vary depending on the combination of attributes that characterize the particular individual, but the apparatus can in principle be generalized, as the effect of a monetary fine of a given magnitude can be generalized for various income levels. Such Buffer variables will therefore be included in the original descriptive account of the person.

Separating the Buffer variables from the remainder of the descriptive account produces an analytic apparatus that now takes on the following appearance:

$$[IV_1, IV_2 \ldots IV_n] \qquad [BV_1, BV_2 \ldots BV_n] \qquad [V_1\ V_2 \ldots V_n]$$
$$\textit{Inputs} \qquad\qquad \textit{Buffers} \qquad\qquad \textit{Description}$$

To this point, the apparatus remains mainly descriptive but interaction rules are needed to link the external action to the initial change in the value of one or more of the Input variables, and to identify real and potential "Buffer" variables.

Separating the Buffer variables, and grouping them to show the way in which they influence the impact of an initial change on the individual's quality of life, creates an invaluable feature of the overall apparatus. The values of a set of Buffer variables can be specified in such a way that they identify a class of persons all of whom will be affected in the same way normatively by the same action, thus fulfilling one major element in the set of requirements for directing actions on defensible grounds, particularly for the conduct of collective affairs. That aspect of the functioning of the Buffer variables is also particularly useful for creating the kind of population inventory needed both for making collective decisions or for monitoring the effects of collective actions.

Measuring the Value of a Normative Variable. The value taken by a normative variable depends on the amount of change induced in the Input variables and the values taken by the relevant Buffer variables. Rules are therefore needed that will link the values of the three variables. In some cases, such rules can be supplied, but in other cases (such as "state of health") they lie beyond human capacity.

The rules need not be arithmetical; such relative terms as "more" or "less" are often enough for decision. In other cases, a set of "cutoff" points, values of the normative variables that are considered grossly unacceptable, other things equal, will suffice as a basis for choice. The structure of an apparatus able to measure the value of a normative variable (to the extent that it is measurable) can now be diagrammed more fully. The surplus descriptive variables, those not employed in the calculations, can be dropped from the equation, leaving the following structure:

$$([IV_1 \ IV_2 \ . \ . \ . \ IV_n] \qquad [BV_1 \ BV_2 \ . \ . \ . \ BV_n] \qquad [R_1 \ R_2 \ . \ . \ . \ R_n])$$

$$\text{\textit{Inputs}} \qquad\qquad\qquad \text{\textit{Buffers}} \qquad\qquad\qquad \text{\textit{Rules}}$$

The parentheses around the full set of variables and rules indicate that the value of the overall normative variable can now be calculated, given a specification of the amount of change that has taken place, using the rules of interaction.

Measuring the Quality of Life. Significant human actions may affect a number of normative variables simultaneously; the analytic framework must be able to take all such changes into account. One solution to the problem would be an overlay, a superset in which each of the normative variables appears as a unit, as an Input variable in the set used to measure the value of the Quality of Life variable. The resulting apparatus, if it could be created, would then have the following structure:

$$([NV_1 \; NV_2 \ldots NV_n] \qquad [R_1 \; R_2 \ldots R_n])$$

Measuring the quality of an individual life

Unfortunately, that kind of conceptual apparatus lies beyond human capacity. The "quality of life," like the "state of health," is not amenable to direct measurement. The concept has meaning and usefulness, but its value cannot be measured or calculated. A different approach to comparison and justification of preferences is essential.

Preferences and Priorities: Justification

Analytically, action or choice can begin at one of two points: (1) with an actor who has some capacity to change the environment and must decide how that capacity should be exercised; or more commonly, (2) with a situation in the environment that requires change in terms of some accepted normative criteria. In either case, a five-step procedure is required to provide a justification for the subsequent action. First, the actor who will actually function in the environment must be identified, for capacity may vary with the person, even if the action is a function of an office or status. Second, the full set of outcomes available to the actor, including the consequences of inaction, are projected as fully as time and resources allow, and their probability of occurrence, the reliability of the theoretical apparatus used to make the projections, estimated. Third, the content of those outcomes, specified using an adequate set of normative variables, is compared systematically in a context grounded in past experience and a *preference* is established, a solution is produced to the particular choice (the choice among available outcomes may be judged a matter of indifference given the accepted ethic). Fourth, the solution to the particular choice, the preference, is generalized to create a *priority,* an instrument in the form "Prefer outcome *a* to outcomes *b,c,d . . . n.*" Fifth, that priority is applied, identifying the preferred outcome. A policy or action program can then be created that is expected to produce that outcome with some degree of reliability.

The problems encountered in steps one and two are common to all forms of inquiry, empirical and normative, and the way in which they can be resolved have already been discussed adequately. The crucial point in justification occurs at step three, in the effort to produce a defensible solution to the particular choice problem. Generalizing and applying that solution to future cases, and even creating the action program or policy needed for such applications, can be regarded as fairly routine matters. The discussion will therefore concentrate on the justification of preferences, and the apparatus required for that purpose.

Limits and Possibilities. Before any justification can be created, or evaluated, the criteria to be applied to the justification must be established. There must be agreement first on the set of assumptions comprising the accepted theory of knowledge. Beyond those fundamentals, though related to them, will lie a further set of assumptions relating to the nature of the inquiry and the expectations to be fulfilled relating to the form and content of competent argument. The need to clarify those underlying assumptions is particularly important for inductive inquiries, for they cannot be conducted in a vacuum. Unless some body of acceptable assumptions is available to serve as a point of departure, the enterprise cannot begin. The source of these assumptions, and even their quality, is less important than their enabling function. A normative focus serves to reinforce the requirement even further, for both the criteria employed within the physical sciences and the way in which those criteria are generated, which tend in most intellectual discussions to be taken for granted rather than articulated, are not really adequate for normative justification and must be augmented.

The reason why scientific canons of reasoning are inadequate for use in normative argument is found in the differences between the kinds of conclusions to be justified in physical science and in ethics, particularly ethics of the kind required for directing human actions. Scientists seek to justify propositions in the form "What is the case?" or "What is likely to be the case under stipulated conditions?" Such propositions have a *testable* meaning; their implications need only be compared with the results of action or observation to provide an adequate test of the content. The central question in normative affairs, "Which outcome should be preferred in a given set?" is not testable in that sense. That is, the results of acting on normative propositions do not answer the question: "Have the preferred results been achieved?" Something further is required. A different kind of argument or criticism is therefore essential for supporting such conclusions.

How, then, to provide a justification for statements of preference, for normative conclusions? In general terms, applicable to all forms of inquiry, the answer is fairly simple: by argument and the exercise of judgment. But the peculiar character of normative propositions means that the kinds of arguments and judgments that are used in empirical inquiries will not suffice for normative justification. Further, there are other handicaps to be overcome, of which the untestability of normative conclusions is only one special case. Some of those handicaps are shared by the physical sciences: determining the actor's capacity, projecting the outcomes of action and estimating their probability of occurrence, and generalizing the results of a solution to a particular choice problem—all create the same kinds of obstacles for both empirical and normative inquirers. Both science and ethics are inductive inquiries, they share certain limitations that inhere in that process, particularly if the term "inductive" is taken to indicate the direction of contingency between specific and general propositions rather than referring to a method for producing conclusions. Within an inductively generated knowledge system, generalized statements are contingent upon particular statements, and if they conflict, it is the general that must yield. Most important of all, no inductive system can be created in a void; there must be an ongoing and at least partly successful knowledge base in place before induction is possible. Even trial-and-error techniques will not function unless error can be identified.

One special handicap that constrains normative inquiry has already been touched upon; the "measurement" problem effectively rules out relying upon tests of the kind employed in the justification of empirical propositions. The nature of the overall continuum used to make choices (the quality of an individual life) imposes three additional limits on the normative inquirer that are worth underscoring. First, no standard unit can be produced for assessing the relative desirability of a human life, and that effectively rules out the use of such concepts as "utility" in a decision-making apparatus. Second, life cannot be treated as a single variable whose value can be measured indirectly by inference from its constituent elements, in the same sense that the value (not the selling price) of a painting cannot be calculated or measured by a rule from the qualities of its parts. Third, human lives are not wholly interchangeable, and their distinctiveness must be captured in the critical apparatus. The limits are well illustrated by the concept "state of health" as it appears in contemporary medicine. A state of health that would be considered as a disaster in one case could be regarded as a triumph in another without inconsistency. In effect, the relative character of normative judgments, and their justifications, means that an external referent must be stipulated before assessment is possible. In normative affairs, a conception of what a human life *could* be, and even more important *should not* be (as reflected in the benchmarks), within a given society must be created. That construction may be grounded in affective reactions but it is produced and justified intellectually and not affectively. Moreover, since it is created out of past experience, systematic justification of criticism will necessarily include reference to that body of experience.

Argument, Evidence, and Judgment. As in empirical inquiry, adequate justification of normative conclusions depends on argument, and that in turn implies the use of judgment and supporting evidence, which depends ultimately on the accepted theory of knowledge. Technically, argument that is meant to justify accepting a set of particular assumptions, whether empirical or normative in content, requires prior acceptance of a very complex set of more general, and to some extent interlocking, assumptions. Those basic assumptions, taken collectively, make up what is usefully labeled a "discipline." Less general than the theory of knowledge, it provides the immediate context that makes evaluation or criticism of conclusions possible in principle. The "discipline" need not be academic or scholarly, but use of that label (in quotes, to indicate the special meaning attached to it) serves to indicate its general character perhaps better than any other term. The discipline will consist of the sets of assumptions and practices, the body of information and knowledge, and the appropriate set of canons of inquiry, evidence, and argument, that are currently accepted by the group that makes up the "fully-informed and competent" set of persons concerned with a given set of phenomena (what is usually referred to as "those in the field"). Typical examples are found in the body of training and experience acquired by a physician or an agronomist, or the kind of training plus experience that marks a skilled shoemaker or fisherman. Unfortunately, as already noted on several occasions, there is at present no adequate discipline directed to the kind of inquiry that concerns us here (applied ethics). The field is now in a premeasurement state, to be outgrown in due course if possible. However, some elements of the needed apparatus are available and they provide a point of departure from which an adequate discipline can, and in fact must, be constructed.

The function of a discipline in the justification of preferences is most clearly seen in the context of a real choice. If a choice must be made and justified between two automobiles, or two pairs of shoes, it is obvious that simple comparison will produce nothing more than a descriptive account of similarities or differences. Evaluation of the content of the choice requires a further piece of apparatus: without some conception of what the content could be, or would be if it were either highly desirable or grossly unacceptable, there can be no grounds for justifying the assessment. Justification of a preference for one of two states of human life requires reference to an equivalent apparatus. In effect, the various states that human lives have occupied in the past must have been ordered at least partially, and the ordering justified (accepted by informed opinion) before any preference can be justified. The structure is fundamentally an intellectual product, but firmly grounded in past experience and judgment, in effect, summarizing both.

To put the problem somewhat differently, some means must be found for both accepting the content of a discipline and correcting or improving that content over time out of experience while using and relying on it. A very brief quotation from an old friend and colleague, Norton E. Long, will serve to illustrate the kind of activity that is involved and suggest some of the elements of a solution.

We are not bemused by the fact that a hammer is an instrument devised in action for the purposes of action, and improved in action for purposes of action that themselves improve with the improved possibilities the hammer's improvement opens up. . . . The improver of hammers—quite undogmatically unconcerned with metaphysical impossibilities . . . goes on in a humanly meaningful way to improve his hammer. . . . And men by their practice agree that he has made an improvement.[4]

Most of the basic prerequisites to justifying preferences (without falling into circularity) given an adequate discipline, are stated or implied in the extract.

First, an improver of hammers (or critic of such improvements) must have a purpose to be achieved through action or use; something must need hammering before improvements in hammers can be made. Second, an instrument expected to fulfill the purpose in hand must be available, a hammer (or a recognizable need for a hammer) must be in place. Third, a "discipline" is required that summarizes and generalizes the knowledge available relating to hammering, including at a minimum: (a) an overall construction of what hammering is about, (b) data that tell us what has been hammered in the past with what instrument to what effect, (c) an ordered set of evaluations of assessments of those results, including a set of benchmarks indicating unacceptable as well as highly desirable qualities or attributes that can be applied to them, and (d) a set of epistemological/ methodological criteria to be used in subsequent argument. The crucial elements in the discipline include both the set of criteria that have been used to argue and justify improvements in the past and the results produced by accepting and applying those criteria. Those results will include an integrated priority system that orders the conditions of the world created by hammering according to that set of criteria. That, unfortunately, is what is most lacking at present in applied ethics, and it makes the task of creating additional priorities much more difficult and hazardous than would otherwise be the case. Finally, there must be a number of informed and competent persons who accept and employ the discipline, a group of hammerers who are self-consciously concerned with hammering and seek to improve it.

If these conditions are transposed into the normative realm, five major requirements emerge as essential for justification of preferences: (1) a clear purpose (maintaining and improving the human condition) and a commitment to pursue that purpose in real cases; (2) a set of normative instruments (normative variables and priorities) together with a generalized summation of the results obtained by accepting and applying them; (3) a set of criteria for dealing with methodological/epistemological questions, including standards of evidence and argument; (4) an overall construction of what a human life can be to serve as a base for arguing the adequacy or relative significance of particular normative variables, and the cogency of proposed evidence; and (5) a body of informed opinion and/or practitioners to sit in judgment on claims to have justified or improved the existing ethic, including claims to have improved the capacity to assess such claims. Every justification that is produced is conditional upon a discipline of this kind; the quality of the justification is a function of the quality of the discipline. For that reason, present-day ethics is unlikely to improve its usefulness for directing actions so long as it continues along its present route, for little if any effort is presently being expended on these questions. The principal danger inherent in the foregoing construction of the nature of the justification that can be offered for a preference is, of course, slipping into circularity. That problem, however, turns out to be manageable.

Avoiding Circularity. The absolute need to begin with an established system of priorities, however inadequate it may be, in order to justify a preference, seriously increases the danger of circular reasoning. The danger can, however, be avoided without unduly complicating the apparatus employed in justification. For the overall apparatus (the discipline) is comprised of a number of different elements, each to some extent independent of the others, and the whole is controlled by the underlying theory of knowledge. In the process of justifying a preference, these elements will be combined and recombined in various ways that tend to rule out the likelihood of circularity remaining in the system unnoticed. The danger is lessened still more by the need to begin the justification process with a specific, real-world case, which contains some or all of the natural-state constraints that inhibit lapses into circularity.

At a minimum, a normative discipline adequate for justifying preferences will include: (1) a set of normative concepts; (2) an integrated set of priorities; (3) an intellectualized construction of what a human life can be, based on what it has been in the past but including extrapolations onto the future; (4) a set of benchmarks that identify the unacceptable and highly desirable conditions of life as they have appeared in the past; and (5) a number of methodological premises, particularly premises that relate to the purposes of inquiry and the canons of evidence and argument accepted within the field. There will also be a body of organized past experience, both particular and generalized, relating to the conditions of life that have appeared in the past, subjective reactions to those conditions, and subsequent judgments of their relative preferability, suitably conditioned by intellectual considerations.

Four aspects of the discipline are particularly important for maintaining and improving its quality while avoiding circularity: the adequacy of the conceptual apparatus and priority system, the internal consistency of the whole, the relation between the discipline and the content of past experience, and the methodological acceptability of the canons of inquiry it contains. Applying the discipline to a particular case combines these elements in different mixtures and that provides the needed opportunities for inconsistencies to surface. Collectively, since their basis in experience will differ at least to some extent, an examination of the relations between those elements approximates a text of the whole apparatus. Thus the validity of the conception of human potential accepted within the discipline depends on its agreement with past experience; the particular case to which that cumulative judgment is applied is, however, to some extent independent of both past experience and the concept of human potential. One can therefore serve as at least a partial check on the other.

The content of a particular choice is examined first by reference to the accepted set of priorities and their accompanying benchmarks, looking for grossly unacceptable human situations that can be eliminated forthwith, other things equal. In the process, the concept of human potential included in the discipline will be checked automatically against both past experience and the content of the particular case. The possibility of redefining the content of both past experience and the particular case, of reconceptualizing the whole problem, appears at that point in the analysis. Of course, a reconceptualization will not be carried out or even considered fully, on every occasion, but if there are gross or obvious errors or inconsistencies within the apparatus applied to the case, the procedure should bring them to the actor or critic's attention. In addition, the presence of a community of informed and competent scholars concerned with the improvement of the discipline should serve to reduce still further the likelihood of inadvertent circularity so long as the results of their labors are being applied regularly and systematically to the conduct of real-world affairs.

The level of consistency achieved between the priority system, the benchmarks, and the overall construction of human potential (which serves as the fundamental integrating apparatus for the overall discipline) is a particularly important focus for criticism, since it tends to be highly sensitive to the kind of probing that occurs at each application to a real case. Each effort to locate and justify a preference provides an opportunity to identify inconsistencies among those elements.

In more general terms, the validity of each of the elements in a justification is checked by multifactor comparisons linking a present case and the body of cumulated experience. The adequacy of concepts, priorities, and benchmarks is determined by their relation to the content of past experience and the overall construction of human life. That overall construction, on the other hand, is tested against past experience, and against the results achieved by using generalized past experience to deal with the particular case. The benchmarks, which are generated out of past experience with conditions judged to be either disasters or great successes by currently accepted standards, can also be checked against the overall construction of human potential, as well as the particulars of the case in hand.

Such checks or tests are hardly on a par with the kind of test that is possible with respect to empirical knowledge, but they do tend to promote the development of a coherent basis for action, and to reduce the danger of creating or perpetuating a self-fulfilling ordinance. It is worth noting that self-conscious efforts to test the quality of the discipline, and protect it against circularity, fulfill one of the necessary preconditions to improving the capacity of the body of "informed and competent" critics within the field. The procedure is not very orderly, and success is uncertain, but applied self-consciously and with integrity it offers reasonable grounds for optimism with respect to future improvements. The principal difficulty at present is the relative shortage of persons actively concerned with such questions and the almost complete lack of an organized and coherent discipline to serve as a focus for efforts to assess and improve the available capacity for assessment.

Given an ongoing discipline, and a body of informed and competent persons concerned with justification of preferences, development can proceed in a fairly systematic way. The aim of an argument to support a preference is to show as clearly as possible that the content of the discipline accepted by the individual who puts it forward justifies the judgment made. To that end, the argument begins with the conclusion to be justified. If there is a disagreement about its acceptability, the assumptions used to reach it, empirical, normative, and methodological, are exposed systematically. Both the content of the disciplines accepted by those engaged in discussion and the underlying theories of knowledge each accepts are examined for points of acceptability. Even if there is no disagreement about conclusions, the same procedure is followed, pushing back the supporting argument to expose as many layers of assumptions as possible. Agreement on conclusions is not an adequate basis for assuming agreement in judgment. Meaningful agreement requires that conclusions be based on more or less the same body of fundamental assumptions before two or more persons can be said to agree. The best justification possible is reached when the consensus of informed and competent opinion appears. Its persuasiveness is a function of the level of development attained by the field. It would be pointless to try to judge an agrument that appears in a poorly developed field such as applied ethics using standards borrowed from chemistry or some other highly developed field of study.

Simplifications. A range of simplifications make the task of justifying preferences somewhat less onerous than might otherwise be the case. First, no more is needed than the capacity to deal with real problems; imaginary problems, like imaginary evidence, can be ignored. Second, there is no need to impose a preference-ordering on all of the options available for choice; no more is required than identification of the preferred outcome— the remaining options can be left unorganized. Further, the assessment of the justification must be realistic; there is no point in asking for a level of justification that the current discipline cannot produce. And the two fundamental substantive assumptions already made (that human life is the basic unit of value and that one life is, *qua* life, the equal of any other) suffice as a starting point for future development. Moreover, the process of establishing a variable as normative solves the problem of which values of that variable should be preferred. That is, the argument needed to show that health is an important aspect of life must show that good health should be preferred to poor health, other things equal.

That characteristic of the normative variables greatly simplifies the justification of preferences in which only one human life is involved. Experience can be expected to suggest in fairly short order which kinds of life conditions are unacceptable and that will usually suffice for dealing with single-person choices—consider how easy it is to argue in favor of deafness rather than blindness, assuming that one must be chosen. When more than one person is involved, the task is again much simplified by a process that can be labeled "conflation," by aggregating all of the attributes of humans found in each outcome onto a single person or small group of persons. In combination with the equality assumption, conflation serves to simplify very complex choices in a useful and productive way. Obviously, such choices are not thereby made easy in the literal sense (choosing pain and misery is not easy even in those cases where it cannot be avoided), but the apparatus needed to deal with the problem can be made more manageable.

Because the priority system must be ordered transitively or lose its usefulness for directing actions, every choice can be broken into a number of two-outcome choices, thus avoiding the need to deal with the full set simultaneously. That is, given a set of n outcomes, the actor or critic need only select a pair, compare them, and if possible establish a preference for one. The "loser" can then be abandoned and the "winner" compared to another of the available outcomes, following the same procedure. In due course, the process will decide the preferred outcome, or lead to an impasse in which some or all outcomes are equally acceptable or equally trivial.

Reducing choices to dyads serves the additional purpose of facilitating the identification of the benchmarks needed to separate the trivial or unimportant from both the unacceptable conditions of life and from the highly desirable conditions of life. As outcomes and conditions of life are compared, and the results registered, the less desirable conditions that are rejected will tend to cluster at the bottom of an integrated priority system. Conversely, the outcomes regularly preferred should in due course emerge at the top of such an ordered structure. The elements in the apparatus can be connected through common or shared life states, or by introducing a hypothetical state into the ordering, producing an integrated overall normative structure in which the undesirable conditions of life are clustered at one end of the continuum and the highly desired states of life are grouped at the other. The benchmarks that are appropriate given capacity (it would be pointless to set benchmarks that could not be implemented) can then be selected and an argument produced to justify them. The analytic simplicity of the solution is not always matched in real-world affairs, but the principle involved is clear enough.

Beyond the assumption that one human life is equal in worth to any other, which in practice has enormous power to influence choice if applied rigorously, particularly in collective affairs, one additional substantive principle can be adduced in general terms. It follows from the ongoing and irreversible character of individual life. Regarded as something that exists in nonrecurring time, life cannot be replaced, and in some cases at least, it cannot be offset or "balanced." Put differently, some aspects of life are nonnegotiable. One does not raise children to serve as a supply of spare parts. Some conditions may be preferred to others considered even worse but they cannot be counterbalanced by other gains. If that principle is accepted, the need to avoid such nonretrievable reductions in the quality of individual lives will tend to control the justification of preferences where they appear. The principle can be asserted as a very simple rule: *minimize misery*. The "Utilitarian" precept is in effect inverted; minimizing harm replaces maximizing good. That does not rule out causing temporary harm to a person in order to produce greater benefits over the long run, or sacrificing one individual's betterment for the betterment of the conditions of life of others. But it does suggest the importance of beginning an examination of the options on the assumption that the first aim is to avoid causing irreversible and serious damage to some, whatever the benefits to others may be: assuming that an overall strategy of minimizing misery is essential.

Other minor simplifications available within the context of the approach need only be summarized. First, the problem of dealing with intergenerational change, with the tendency for priorities to lose their validity as conditions in society change, is managed with surprising ease within the critical apparatus. If human life is accepted as the basic unit of significance, the problem vanishes. All that is required is to attend to the conditions of life of those now living, for that will include at least three or four generations, and their potential life span is well in excess of existing projective capacity. Further, decisions made using the critical apparatus should not be expected to hold forever; all that can be hoped for is the best decision possible at the time when the decision is made. The need for successive decisions, if only to test the initial judgment, is built into the approach.

The apparatus also deals readily and easily with such problems as the psychological aberrations that appear in reported experience. The information needed to discount bizarre or unacceptable accounts of experience is produced automatically by extending the attributes of the individual doing the reporting, as must be done. Such built-in procedures also help to avoid most of the difficulties associated with efforts to avoid punishing the innocent and rewarding the guilty or separating support for a sound choice made for valid reasons from "doing the right thing for the wrong reasons."

Finally, the elimination of personal bias from justifications, which is in principle a horrendous task, can be accomplished by a surprisingly simple procedure: the identity of the persons affected by an action is suppressed *in justification.* Nothing of substance is lost, for all of the relations that must be known in order to project the effects of action can be retained. The attributes or characteristics of the individuals affected by the action can be kept intact. So long as the proper names of those involved are eliminated from the actual justification provided for a preference or priority, personal bias is effectively eliminated from the supporting argument.

What is perhaps most surprising about the way in which the problem of justification can be resolved in principle is the extent to which it turns out to be an intellectual function. In the present state of human development, the influence of affective reactions is at best marginal, whatever it may have been in earlier times. Indeed, one of the more interesting questions to be raised in an ethics that is concerned with directing action is "What kinds of questions should be left for decision of the basis of affective reactions?" Tentatively, but quite strongly, the answer seems to be "very few." The intellect provides an acceptable or defensible way around the measurement problem, and the other kinds of handicaps that affect normative inquiry, by reason of its peculiar character. Similarly, the overall conception of human potential, of what human life can be under a range of circumstances (which is essential for justification of preferences) can be created and justified intellectually in strong enough terms to provide a basis for the evasion. What is even more surprising is the extent to which that procedure has become a commonplace in other aspects of choice. It comports well, for example, with normal practice in a host of everyday choices, ranging from selecting a pair of shoes or an automobile to deciding the kinds of action that great powers should take in world affairs.

THE SOCIAL CONTEXT

For all practical purposes, every human action takes place in a social context that profoundly influences both the kind of normative system that can be developed and the manner in which it is applied. Taken in conjunction with the existing national state system, the implications of the overall social context for normative development are quite profound and can only be touched upon briefly here.

That society plays a crucial role in normative affairs is commonplace, but like many such commonplaces, its implications are too seldom explored systematically. Assuming that humans living in isolation would perforce practice extreme selfishness, frequent human interactions serve to render that basis for action, and for justification of preferences, impossible to maintain. In that context, social organizations are generated out of the need for a normative system that rises above pure selfishness, for they make possible (in principle, at least) dependable enforcement of an unselfish normative system that would be too risky to practice for any individual absent the kinds of guarantees that society makes possible. Of course, there is no inherent necessity for them to do so, and in fact, that result only rarely occurs. In most cases, social organization serves to buttress selective selfishness. Nevertheless, their potential remains as perhaps the most important element in the future development of every human normative system. Furthermore, the interactions of organizations are subject to or controlled by the same relational logic as the interactions of individuals. In both cases, that logic leads ultimately to the creation of sovereign organizations, of entities that claim and enforce supreme authority, in principle at least, over particular territories, including the all-important power to set the limits of their own authority or jurisdiction.

For the short run, perhaps the most important normative aspect of social organizations is the imperative that forces them to differentiate members from nonmembers in ways that are significant, particularly for members. In practical terms, the national states provide the boundaries that control or limit the development of normative systems. In principle, that apparatus provides a means for enforcing or reifying the equality principle. Unfortunately, it also provides a very powerful apparatus for violating it. The conclusion to which one is driven by the logic of present-day social-political organization, given the international system in place, is intellectually intriguing, but rather discouraging in human, or perhaps better, humanistic terms.

If (1) the ultimate purpose of the human enterprise is to maintain and improve the conditions of life of the human populations within the limits of available capacity; and if (2) that purpose is to be fulfilled through human actions, directed by an appropriate, corrigible, intellectual apparatus, and performed in . . . a . . . social context, . . . and if (3) suggested ways of directing human actions, and judging the results, have to be justified using the criteria and procedures set forth . . . , then the most important task facing humanity at present is not to produce "better" or "more moral" individuals but to learn how to use the power and authority of the governments of the various national states in normatively defensible ways, to convert these governments into effective normative instruments.[5]

A detailed discussion of the implications of that set of judgments or conclusions would require us to move far beyond the limits imposed by the purposes of the present volume and must therefore be eschewed.

NOTES

1. See Robert Bierstedt, "Nominal and Real Definitions in Sociological Theory," in L. Gross, ed., *Symposium on Sociological Theory* (Harper and Row, 1959).

2. For typical examples, see Carl G. Hempel, *Aspects of Scientific Explanation and Other Essays in the Philosophy of Science* (The Free Press, 1965); Ernest Na-

gel, *The Structure of Science: Problems in the Logic of Scientific Explanation* (Harcourt, Brace, and World, 1961); or Karl R. Popper, *The Logic of Scientific Discovery* (Science Editions, 1961).

3. John Stuart Mill, *A System of Logic,* Book VI (Methuen, no date).

4. Norton E. Long, "Foreward," in Eugene J. Meehan, *Value Judgment and Social Science: Structures and Processes* (Dorsey Press, 1969).

5. Eugene J. Meehan, *Ethics for Policymaking* (Greenwood Press, 1990), p. 201.

3

Cognitive Skill Testing

From a strictly analytic perspective, the approach to cognitive education and training proposed here is based on a straightforward and comparatively uncontentious set of assumptions and relations. The primary assumption is normative: the function of knowledge is to maintain or improve the conditions of life of *some* human population. Knowledge is therefore identified with the intellectual apparatus needed to perform that function, which has the effect of equating knowledge with the various kinds of patterns that can be imposed upon or matched to past human experience and then used to direct actions to the achievement of the overall purpose—or, more commonly, to attain one or more of the subordinate purposes through which the overall purpose is fulfilled. Those patterns include, in addition to descriptions, forecasts, and theories, the preference-orderings or priorities imposed on the different sets of conditions of life that are available to a particular actor at a given time and place as well as the policies used to attain the preferred outcome. Since action serves as the essential link between knowledge and real-world conditions, the knowledge requirements for achieving human purposes can also be specified in terms of the requirements for directing human actions on defensible or corrigible grounds. The individual's capacity to acquire, assess, and apply such knowledge (cognitive skill or competence) is assumed, *ceteris paribus*, to be the primary determinant of the quality of intellectual performance. Measured levels of cognitive skill are assumed to be linked, through human actions, to levels of real-world achievement.

The overall approach is captured in, and integrated by, the theory of knowledge set forth in Chapter 2. That theoretical structure is amenable to two basic tests, each contingent upon the availability of an external or independent performance criterion. First, if real-world performance can be evaluated at least to the extent of separating exceptional achievers/performers from others whose performance is less than outstanding, then any valid measure of cognitive skill, any test that can be inferred and/or extrapolated from the theory of knowledge, should account for the differences in achievement among individuals and serve as a predictor of future levels of achievement, other things equal. The second test of the validity of the proposed theory of knowledge is to derive or extrapolate a program of education or training and apply it. The program should produce an improvement in cognitive skill as measured by a valid test and ultimately an improvement in real-world performance, measured by external criteria.

The effort to create and apply a measure of cognitive skill is sketched in this chapter, with particular attention to the results obtained from testing carried out in Guatemala and Costa Rica. The inquiry did not try to identify *all* of the constituent elements of cognitive skill; that was neither necessary nor possible. Instead, the primary goal was to create a test of cognitive skill, a way of measuring it, with sufficient diagnostic and predictive power to account for differences in cognitive performance that could be identified using external criteria. Further, the study did not seek to learn how either particular cognitive skills or the overall complex of skills was actually acquired in real cases, nor did it try to identify those elements that were fostered by socialization processes, those engendered by formal or informal education or by work experience, and so on. Such questions are clearly important for obtaining the information needed to design education programs that take fullest advantage of the potential available in existing institutions and practices, but the resources needed for an enterprise of that magnitude simply were not available. A well-defined relation between certain kinds of university curricula and cognitive skill levels appears in the findings, but it should be treated with caution, for such relations were not isolated systematically from the effects of other factors such as intelligence or specific curriculum content. The various educational/training programs developed from the theory of knowledge and tested in the United States and elsewhere will be examined in Chapter 5.

EVOLUTION OF THE APPROACH

Viewed historically, the analytic clarity of the approach to cognitive testing and training is somewhat misleading, for it ignores the changes that took place in both theory and measuring instruments as the study progressed. That is, both the theory set forth in Chapter 2 and the test found in Appendix 3-A, changed considerably as experience cumulated. Historically, the inquiry into cognitive skill, the effort to measure it and then improve it by suitable education or training, began with an everyday problem: how to account for different levels of real-world performance or achievement? The set of assumptions on which the activity in question was proceeding proved inadequate for the task. Trying first to account for, and then to modify, that differential performance, both in the particular case and more generally, provided the purpose for the initial set of inquiries. Over time, every aspect of the inquiry benefitted substantially from that focus on a real-world problem. The theory of knowledge improved because testing against real cases was forced; the measuring instrument improved for the same reason; and both the initial development of the various programs for increasing cognitive skill and subsequent improvements in their performance were possible only because of the real-world phenomenon standing external to the apparatus as a check on validity and reliability.

The Problem

The concept "cognitive skill" or "cognitive competence" was developed in the late 1960s out of a study of the impact of leadership training for Latin American nationals intended to foster development, either nationally or locally, in Central America, sponsored by the U.S. Agency For International Development (AID).[1] The key assumption in the training, commonplace in the development literature of the time, was that a change in individual attitudes from what was termed a "traditional" to a "development" orientation would in due course produce greater levels of individual participation in community affairs, and such participation would lead to local and/or national development.

A careful examination of the performance of those who had been subjected to a training program designed to produce such attitudinal changes found that: (1) the requisite attitudes were present, at least in verbal form when the training ended; (2) participation in community affairs did increase; and (3) the direct and indirect benefits to individual trainees were substantial. However, (1) the attitudes to be fostered were actually present at the outset of training—because of the criteria and procedures employed in selecting candidates for training; (2) the set of preferences or priorities to which the trainees had been exposed tended to remain at the verbal level, and were little related to actual performance (suggesting that the training tended to reinforce a normative structure at the verbal level, but did little to further its application); and (3) most important of all, the results actually produced in the environment after trainees returned to their home locales fell far short of expectations in most cases. However, *there were exceptions*—some of the trainees did outstanding work.

Such differential performance was inexplicable given the assumptions on which training was based: the trainees were uniformly well meaning, highly motivated and even enthusiastic, and extremely active; there were sufficient resources available to warrant at least limited expectations of improvement. Yet in most cases, the level of performance was poor. In those few cases where achievement was outstanding, other factors were clearly at work. Comparison of those who succeeded and those who did not should in principle provide a way of accounting for differences in performance. As it turned out, those differences could not be accounted for in terms of education, training, resources, attitudes, IQ scores, or effort. It was clear that given the goal of fostering local and national development (and thus indirectly of maintaining and improving the human condition for some population), the emphasis on attitudes, even if it were linked to support for particular norms or preferences, was badly misplaced.

How, then, to account for performance differences? An answer was important, for learning the source of such differences should at least allow predictions of success or failure in future performances, and thereby provide the necessary leverage point for improving the efficiency of the education program. A study of the body of data collected during the course of the initial set of interviews with program alumni (which were taped almost without exception), uncovered one major difference between those who were relatively successful in their efforts to improve conditions within their community and those who were not: the successful tended to take what was initially dubbed an "engineering" approach to action meant to improve local conditions while the latter did not. That approach was not a matter of attitudes or intensities but of practices and procedures; the successful attacked their problem in a cognitively different way than those who were less productive.

Initially, no connection was made between the theory of knowledge (which was then stated in quite different terms from the version set forth in Chapter 2) and the engineering approach to development. Early efforts to improve performance were based on then-current theories of national development accepted within AID. At some point, the data produced by the initial survey of trainees were linked to the theory of knowledge. In effect, the problem was somehow redefined to focus on explaining the differences in real-world performance. The concept of intellectual or cognitive skill was created as part of the effort to provide that explanation. The theory (as then stated), if viewed in practical terms, amounted to a statement of the minimum necessary conditions for successful performance, and therefore suggested both a reason for the failure and a possible remedy. On that perspective, the first task was to determine if the elements incorporated into the theory could in fact account for the differences in performance. Accordingly, four points were inferred (or extrapolated) from the theory and incorporated into the basic questionnaire used in the study. They summed to asking whether differences in performance could be accounted for by differences in capacity for developing and applying patterns to experience. A preliminary survey suggested that the new focus was a much more powerful explanatory tool than a focus on attitudes; that led to a more extended test of the usefulness of the theory of knowledge in the inquiry.

As a first step, the questionnaire used to survey trainees graduating from the AID-sponsored leadership program was extended to include information about four additional points, selected because they could be related theoretically to the individual's ability to locate generalized patterns in past experience and use those patterns self-consciously to deal with future problems. Each individual was questioned in ways intended to produce information relating to: (1) the extent of individual awareness of or sensitivity to temporal aspects of experience (to the effects of past events on present conditions and to the future effects of present actions); (2) the individual's propensity to break complex tasks into simpler components; (3) the individual's tendency to employ complex, multiple-factor rather than simple, single-factor causal patterns as a basis for action; and (4) the individual's ability to recognize and avoid the more common of the informal fallacies. It was assumed, correctly as it turned out, that the relevant environmental conditions were roughly the same, and that attitudes and values were stable across the population. Index numbers were therefore constructed from the responses for a construct now labeled "cognitive skill" or "cognitive competence." They proved able to account for differences in individual accomplishments within the community with remarkable accuracy. Indeed, the ability of the theory to account for the differences in performance using such crude measures was so good that AID authorized a systematic effort to isolate and identify the factors at work more precisely, in the belief that it would provide a basis for developing a training program that could be expected to lead to improvements in performance.

A second questionnaire was therefore produced, this time designed to measure the individual's cognitive skill more precisely.[2] The need to isolate cognitive skill from other potentially relevant influences on performance posed a formidable design problem. At a minimum: (1) attitudes and information had to be stabilized for an adequate sample population; (2) the educational and occupational backgrounds of the individuals had to be sufficiently alike to justify the assumption that they could not account for differential performance; (3) within the population, the differences in participation and achievement had to be large enough to allow isolation of the effect of differences in cognitive ability; and (4) the substance of the skills involved had to be analyzed or elaborated enough to show differences that could in principle be reduced by appropriate education or training.

The most appropriate tool available, given the purpose at hand, was an elite study. Ideally a careful comparison of matched pairs of highly educated, urbanized individuals (Guatemalans in this case) whose work performance could be assessed with reasonable accuracy by peer groups, and who could be expected to share a basic set of attitudes and "values," but whose performance differed significantly, should produce the needed data. As might be expected, that turned out to be impractical. However, an elite group was isolated whose members could be divided into two basic subgroups: those who were performing their chosen work in an outstanding manner, and those engaged in the same occupations, had similar educational and socioeconomic backgrounds, but whose accomplishments were significantly less noteworthy. Some 200 Guatemalans (ages 25–45) in a range of different fields, and with varying levels of accomplishment (determined reputationally by a peer group review board familiar with their work) were identified. Interviewers from the same elite group were provided by the local agency cooperating in the research program, thus minimizing the risk of deliberate efforts to mislead for political or ideological reasons. Other risks involved in sampling based on reputation and peer group review, which are fairly well known, were hedged as fully as circumstances allowed. Members of the group that made the selection and did the interviewing were known to one another, and the process was open and informal. Neither the American nor the Guatemalan government was involved in the selection, thus avoiding the danger of an official bias or of political influence.

Identification of high-level achievers, which had been expected to pose difficulties in sampling, turned out to be relatively uncontroversial; the panel agreed on the selection of outstanding achievers with little dissent or argument. The most serious problem encountered in sampling was with sample size: when the list of high-level achievers reached some 60 persons, the resources of the selection group were exhausted, and efforts to extend the list by using other sources proved futile. Hence the data relating to high-level achievers are based on interviews with 55 persons. They were matched to about 100 others whose achievements were not, so far as the selection committee was aware, outstanding. As it turned out, two or three members of the control group were actually outstanding achievers as well, but the number was not large enough to influence the kinds of group-to-group comparisons required by the research design. Interestingly enough, members of that small subgroup were identified first by the cognitive skill test; the identification was subsequently confirmed by consulting persons who knew their work well.

Stabilizing Information and Norms

Successful isolation of the relation between cognitive skill and real-world performance quality required a systematic effort to stabilize information levels and norms, which made for a lengthy questionnaire. By using questions that focused on community affairs of a general nature, a fairly adequate body of relevant information was generated across the full sample.

Nearly everyone was well-informed, articulate, and closely tied to the Guatemalan information network (radio, press, television, and so on). At the aggregate level, the assumption of a common information base was readily justified.

The effort to stabilize norms or values focused on a set of ten continua or dichotomies supplied by AID; they were derived from the development literature of the day, augmented by AID's own experience. The same continua had been employed in the earlier study of the impact of training, hence all of the survey results were comparable along these dimensions. The ten continua were used to separate what was called a "development orientation" from a "traditional orientation," on the assumption that those configurations of attitudes were linked to social and economic development—indeed, they were widely believed to be necessary or even sufficient conditions for development to occur. The earlier finding, that differences in norms were relatively insignificant across the whole of Guatemalan society, held equally well for this sample.

The ten dichotomies can be expressed as simple "either-or" choices, provided it is clearly understood that in practice such preferences were usually hedged or qualified, particularly by the high-level achievers.

1. Conceptualization of social problems in collective, generalized terms (development) versus conceptualization in personal, familial, and specific terms (traditional).

2. Emphasis or primary focus in assessments of events on collective achievement versus emphasis on individual achievement.

3. Relying on the collectivity to serve as the primary instrument of social change versus relying on family or individual.

4. Active participation in community affairs, coupled with efforts to influence them versus acquiescence in or indifference to community matters.

5. Reliance on social institutions for achieving social goals versus reliance on leaders or specific persons.

6. Welcoming social change, and being optimistic about its effects versus fear of and resistance to such changes.

7. Valuing discussion and argument as a way of clarifying points at issue versus repression of argument and conflict and acquiescence to authority.

8. Focusing primarily upon the present and the future versus focusing almost exclusively upon the past.

9. Basing legitimacy on performance or achievement versus assigning authority on the basis of history, ascribed status, or associations.

10. Willingness to take risks in order to speed rates of social change versus a preference for safety and stability, whatever the effects on levels of collective achievement or progress.

As might be expected, the developmental side of these dichotomies was the choice of the overwhelming majority of the population surveyed. Indeed, even in the national survey conducted earlier, it had proved virtually impossible to find a tradition-oriented person, defined in these terms.

Indicators of Cognitive Skill

The four-element construction of cognitive skill used in the preliminary study was elaborated considerably in the new questionnaire, primarily by extrapolation from the theory of knowledge, modified and supplemented by the results obtained from a preliminary survey (see Appendix 3-B for details). The theory could generate a very large number of potential indicators of cognitive skill; experience with real-world achievers provided the information needed to determine an optimal selection. One major focus was the level of patterning skill demonstrated by the interviewee as indicated by the number of elements or steps in the pattern, the sequencing of cause-effect relations, and the use of dynamic as well as static patterns. Other important dimensions of cognitive performance incorporated into the test included:

1. Temporal sensitivity, indicated by awareness of the influence of the past on the present and the effect of the present on the future.

2. Experimental outlook, particularly evidence relating to ability to learn from experience, or the general reaction to failure.

3. Orientation to active intervention, measured by the extent to which the interviewee focused on events subject to human control, by the use made of social organizations in proposed interventions, by the abstract/concrete nature of the conceptual apparatus used to deal with the questions, and by the complexity or sophistication of the intervention proposed—the direct or indirect character of the proposed action.

4. Quality of conceptualization, indicated by the kinds of concepts employed for dealing with problems.

5. The level of reality control and sophistication that appeared in both analysis of problems and suggestions for dealing with them.

6. Capacity to deal with counterfactuals, to respond to queries in the form: "What events in the past might have prevented/produced this outcome?" It was included initially because Nelson Goodman's studies had demonstrated that the only acceptable basis for dealing with counterfactuals was a valid theory. It was retained because item analysis suggested that it was by far the best single indicator of overall cognitive performance.[3]

Additional weighting was attached to such things as: (1) awareness of both costs and benefits of proposed actions, (2) reliance on concrete rather than symbolic actions, (3) use of roundabout chains of actions, and (4) skill at formal inference/calculation, measured by the ability to recognize some of the more common informal fallacies. An overall assessment of the extent to which the individual approached problems, whether individual or collective, from an engineering perspective was provided by each interviewer, allowing them an opportunity for them to pass along any information relating to cognitive capacity not covered by the interview schedule.

Index Numbers

The questions used to assess cognitive skill were open-ended; each response was coded along a number of different continua. Some responses were weighted slightly, on the advice of a small group of Guatemalan educators who collaborated in the study (see Appendix 3-C). Based on the responses to the questionnaire, three index numbers were prepared for each individual: the first measured development orientation, or development attitudes; the second measured levels of community participation, as reported by the person; the third was a crude measure of cognitive skill or competence.

Sample Population Characteristics

The results of the elite survey cannot be extrapolated to the population of Guatemala as a whole. The national sample used to study the impact of AID-sponsored training was well-distributed geographically, ethnically, and occupationally; the elite sample used to examine the relation between cognitive skill and real-world performance was in many respects quite different. Each comprised about 90 percent males and only 10 percent females; more than two-thirds of each group consisted of persons between the ages of 26 and 50—though the national sample included more older persons. There the major similarities end. All of the members of the elite group were Ladinos, for example, while the national sample, reflecting the overall ethnic composition of the population, comprised about 40 percent Indians. Further, all of the elite were urban dwellers, whereas 80 percent of the national sample lived in rural areas. Again, only about 10 percent of the national sample were employed within the professions and about half were farmers; among the elite, none was a farmer, about 20 percent were professionals, 15 percent were governmental administrators and another 15 percent were politicians, and about 10 percent of the total were employed in banking, another 10 percent in industry, and about 10 percent in arts and letters.

Two more specific attributes of the elite group, education and income, may be particularly relevant to the findings. First, only 8 percent of the group had not completed secondary school, over 80 percent had a college degree, and about 50 percent had completed some graduate training. Average income, as might be expected, was far higher than the national average of 50–80 quetzals per month. Less than 20 percent of the elite group earned fewer than 300 Q. per month, about half earned between 300 and 800 Q. per month, and the remainder earned more than 800 Q. monthly.

The connections into the information network were strong and plentiful. Virtually every member of the elite sample read one daily newspaper; many read two or more newspapers each day. About 70 percent of the total listened to news broadcasts daily. As might be expected, over 90 percent of the group was judged to be well-informed on local, national, and international affairs—about twice the percentage found in the national sample. The difference was reflected in the kinds of issues used as a focus for discussion by members of the two groups. Those in the national sample tended to deal with specific, particular questions; jobs, housing, roads, food, or education for example. Members of the elite group were more concerned with such general problems as political instability or violence, socioeconomic conditions, illiteracy, and the lack of national development. Use of different concepts to identify problems produced very important differences in the kinds of solutions proposed. Within the national sample, simplistic solutions to complex problems were the rule, and the extent to which education served as a panacea for all social/individual ills was remarkable. Members of the elite, while valuing education, were concerned primarily with improving its quality (for the most part in unspecified ways and for unspecified reasons) rather than relying on it as a *solution* to serious social problems.

Given such differences in fundamentals, the similarity of national sample and elite with respect to basic norms or values is little short of astonishing. Although the elite tended to deal with problems in social terms, and proposed solutions at a level unmatched within the general population, in most other respects the differences in norms or things valued were relatively minor. Both were remarkably traditional in value orientation. Thus, more than two-thirds of both samples felt that age confers authority, and that the young should seek the advice and consent of their elders. Both groups were opposed to disagreement and conflict (and discussion), whatever virtues they might have in principle. Both were overwhelmingly local rather than centrist in their preference for authority structures. Both preferred lowering risk and gain to increasing potential gains at a cost of increased risk. About half of each group preferred elimination of foreign influence from the country to attracting foreign investments; roughly the same proportions believed that society functioned as a zero-sum game. Extreme individualism and belief in reliance on private initiative was almost wholly absent from both groups.

The Questionnaire

The questionnaire dealing with cognitive skills again posed some difficult design problems. Both the solutions adopted and the reasons for accepting them need to be made clear. Since cognitive skill is a characteristic of the person that closely resembles "intelligence" in conceptual terms, it must be measured by reference to the products of thinking and the arguments used to support them. It was therefore essential that the person being interviewed have an opportunity to generate those products with as little cueing as possible, and the discussion should focus on areas in which the individual was relatively well-informed. After experimenting with various approaches to the problem, both the use of objective questions and forced responses and reliance on a hypothetical "problem situation" were rejected. Instead, the interviewee was in effect allowed to pose his or her own questions and then answer them. All responses were taped, or in a very few cases recorded by hand and reconstructed in detail as soon as the interview was completed. Only a few persons objected to the recording, happily, and the findings are based on literal transcriptions of the responses, duly translated into English, in all but four cases.

Each interview occupied about one full hour. Once the necessary background data had been supplied, the interviewee was asked to suggest two of the more serious problems facing the people and government of Guatemala. The interviewer (also a Guatemalan, and a member of the elite group) selected one question as a focus for the interview. A sequence of questions was then followed, without prompting; if no response was forthcoming, the interviewer went quickly to the next question:

1. Why do you think this problem is found in Guatemala today? Why did this happen, or happen in this particular way?

2. Do you think the problem could have been avoided? How? or Why not?

3. What do you think can be done about the problem right now?

4. Is there anything *you* can do about the problem?

5. Suppose your suggestion was tried but failed, what should be tried next?

6. Looking at Guatemalan history, what events in the past have most influenced present-day conditions?

7. Looking ahead, what events taking place in Guatemala today seem most likely to affect its future in important ways? Specify?

8. What would happen in Guatemala if imports and exports were suddenly halted? How would such actions affect you?

9. How would you go about choosing an assistant from among five applicants for the position? What questions would you ask? What tests, if any, would you use?

10. What two changes would you most like to see take place in Guatemala in the near future?

11. What is the worst thing that could happen in Guatemala in the next five years?

Coding the results was time-consuming but not particularly difficult. Two coders were used, working together and cross-checking each question, particularly in the initial stages of coding, or in cases that did not fit well into the patterns that developed as coding progressed. Intercoder reliability was generally excellent; in the event of disagreement, the matter was decided by the principal investigators, or the response was omitted.

Findings

The primary assumption tested by the study, that achievement, and to a lesser extent participation, is linked to high levels of cognitive skill as measured using the index, and not to a "development orientation" or a "modernizing attitude," was strongly supported by the findings. Achievement was measured in terms of national reputation, judged by a panel of peers; participation and cognitive skill were measured using information obtained by interview. The numerical indexes used to express both participation and cognitive skill should be treated with care; obviously, all comparisons refer only to the groups as a whole. Nevertheless, the value of cognitive skill in accounting for differences in real-world achievement was clear, as evidenced by the aggregate indexes shown in Table 3.1. For *all* persons interviewed, both individually and collectively, cognitive skill as measured by the test correlated positively and strongly with occupational achievement, positively with participation in community affairs, and slightly negatively with development attitudes or norms.

The relation between cognitive skill and overall performance appears even stronger if the data are organized in other ways. The 15 individuals with the highest cognitive skill levels (average 77) were *all* members of the high achievement group. But their mean participation score was only 24 and their attitudinal index average was 36, both slightly below group averages. None of the 15 persons with the lowest cognitive skill scores (20

Table 3.1
Aggregate Indexes

	Cog Skill	Participation	Attitudinal
Achievers	57	28	33
Control Group	46	24	36

as against 49) was a member of the high achievement group. The 18 highest scorers on the developmental attitude index (average 46) had an average cognitive skill measure of 48 (slightly below the mean for the whole population) and only 2 of the 18 were included in the list of 54 high-level achievers. On the other hand, the average cognitive skill index for all members of the sample with a participation score of 30 or more (overall average, 26) is 58, nearly 20 percent above the average for the whole group.

Bearing in mind the crudeness of the measures, the following propositions were agreed by the advisory group to be justified by the results (were the consensus of the body of informed opinion at the time):

1. High levels of cognitive skill are related directly and positively to participation and even more strongly to achievement but not to attitudes or values.

2. High scores on the attitudinal index are not accompanied by high levels of cognitive skill or achievement.

3. Participation correlates strongly with high-level achievement.

4. Low levels of cognitive skill, as measured by the index, correlate strongly but negatively with both achievement and participation.

The results indicated that a further refinement of the instrument used to measure cognitive skill was still needed. In particular, the subclass of skills that contribute to the overall index had to be identified more accurately if the test was to be used as a diagnostic tool for developing education and training that could be expected to lead to improved performance.

The survey provided other information useful for both improving the cognitive skill test and linking the concept to other aspects of human performance, thus laying the groundwork for future experimental programs aimed at cognitive improvement. Certain curricula, for example, were much more strongly linked than others to high levels of cognitive skill; those whose occupations required them to interact systematically and reciprocally with the environment, to intervene in the world on the assumption of a causal relation between action and outcome, tended also to have much higher scores on the cognitive skill index. Thus, engineers, almost without exception, scored higher than those trained in arts and humanities, even if the training provided the latter included formal logic. Similarly, physicians, agricultural experts, bankers, and economists performed better than artists, journalists, or members of the clergy. Such results suggest that a test of this character may in due course serve as a defensible base for measuring educational achievement and evaluating educational programs. It is certainly more useful and informative than such measures as budgetary data, teacher's salaries, teacher/pupil ratios, and tests validated inside the school system.

The relation between cognitive skill as measured by the test and other aspects of human experience or performance turned out as expected in some cases, but quite differently in others. Thus scores tended (as expected) to increase with age and experience but were (unexpectedly) less influenced by the *amount* than by the *kind* of education acquired. Attitudinal indexes, curiously enough, varied only slightly and unsystematically with age, suggesting that either the questionnaire had uncovered a cross-section of the accepted value system of the time and place or that differences between age groups are perhaps less than we had been led to believe. Further, cognitive skill was relatively unaffected by such things as the amount of traveling done by the person, by the democratic/authoritarian structure of the father's household, or by the extent to which the father was involved in community affairs.

One relation deserves special emphasis, if only because of the tendency in academic and governmental circles to place an inordinate emphasis on the individual's level of engagement in community programs (on "participation"). High levels of cognitive skill appeared frequently in persons who were little concerned with community programs and "participated" very little if at all, even though they were usually highly successful in their occupational efforts. The rhetoric of the times asserted rather dogmatically (and still insists) that a bias to private concerns had unfortunate implications for society as a whole; that presumption was not borne out by the data and should probably be examined further. It is still moot, for example, whether an underdeveloped nation would benefit more from the actions of individuals skillfully pursuing their own interests or from the actions of those same persons pursuing community interests. Much depends, obviously, on the kinds of interests pursued and the nature of the limiting conditions observed in the process. Put differently, cognitive skill seems neutral with respect to the type of beneficiary: the habits of thought that lead to success for the private entrepreneur are precisely the same as those that identify the productive civil servant. The principal difference lies in the substance of the norms applied to decisions.

Summarizing briefly, a basic set of thinking capacities or practices can be identified that recur almost without exception among those individuals who perform exceptionally well in the environment (and who score very well on the cognitive skill test). They tend, as individuals and as a group, to

1. focus on macro problems in human affairs, usually of a complex nature: import/export requirements, common market potentialities, the effects of social violence, and so on;

2. generate complex, multifactor, multistage explanations of current events, and to be acutely aware of the risks and limitations associated with their use;

3. deal with relatively long strings or sequences of interactions rather than simple one-step, or two-element, relations;

4. urge preliminary study, planning, data gathering, and rational cooperation when dealing with significant problems;

5. regard elites as the primary agents of social change, avoid "democratic" rhetoric, but assume that fairly extensive collaboration between members of the public and private agents is essential;

6. be acutely sensitive to costs, and tend to seek alternatives that serve to reduce costs while securing the desired outcome or change;

7. deal readily with counterfactuals, usually by analogical reasoning from history, hence with good reality control and plausibility;

8. be acutely aware of the influence of existing institutional arrangements, and often include the price of modifying them in their calculation of costs and benefits;

9. be suspicious and guarded in their relation with others;

10. regard experience, successful or not, as a learning opportunity rather than a dead end—and expect to fail occasionally;

11. limit nearly every generalized proposition employed by an appropriate caveat; and

12. stress individual responsibility rather than governmental or collective obligations.

By way of contrast, the composite portrait of the individual with very high scores on the attitudinal index is quite different. Indeed, there is a strong element of incompatibility between the two, in the sense that these traits are rarely if ever found among those with high levels of cognitive skill. In general, individuals with high attitudinal scores tend to

1. "express opinions" rather than argue;

2. rely heavily on slogans and catch-phrases rather than on evidence and reasoning, to deal in rhetoric rather than argument;

3. regard the general population, the "people," as the primary agent of social change;

4. focus almost exclusively on individuals and their needs, ignoring social features or institutional arrangements, in both the way they defined problems and their recommendations for dealing with them;

5. recommend actions that seem primarily symbolic, therefore more likely to generate particular kinds of affective reactions than to produce any particular outcome;

6. look to government rather than the individual for assistance with human problems, individual or collective;

7. cope poorly with counterfactual questions;

8. show little evidence of learning from experience—indeed, they rarely if ever cite past experience, whether favorable or not, as evidence to support pursuing a particular course of action, or eschewing it;

9. focus on the intentions of the actor, or the actions taken, rather than on a comparison of available options, when making or evaluating decisions;

10. be highly trustful of others, at least verbally; and

11. emphasize such vague generalities as "voting," "democracy," or "participation" as solutions to problems.

FROM ACCOUNTING FOR PERFORMANCE TO PREDICTING PERFORMANCE

The Guatemala exercise showed fairly clearly that a test derived from the theory of knowledge could account for significant differences in performance, with good reliability, other things equal. Item analysis, however, indicated that the test was relatively inefficient. A number of experimental modifications were made and tested, principally with University of Missouri–St. Louis undergraduates, and the results were subjected to further analysis. The final version of the test (Appendix 3-A) combines the major implications of the theory of knowledge with the results of an item analysis of real-world applications of the earlier version of the test. That is, the theory implied that certain capacities or skills are essential for acquiring, assessing, and applying knowledge; to determine which of them are actually good predictors of human performance required empirical testing. The continua studied in this phase of test development included, among others:

1. Temporal awareness/sensitivity. Several major subdivisions of the concept were distinguished:
   a. order of precedence in causal linkages
   b. relations between present actions and future conditions, which are essential for making defensible choices
   c. sensitivity to changes in relations over time, or changes in patterns with time
   d. awareness of past constraints on present/future choices or actions
   e. avoiding excessive concentration on antecedents to present events—the "origins" fallacy

2. Patterning, the imposition of calculable structures on experience, including, the following considerations:
   a. differentiating, and dealing with, both dynamic patterns in which the rules link changes in value of variables, and static patterns in which the rules specify the limits for values of a particular selection of variables
   b. awareness of the set of limiting conditions under which patterns can be expected to hold or function properly, as well as the role played by catalysts and impediments
   c. the use of a *ceteris paribus*, required because pattern fit is always imperfect
   d. the need for at least two elements linked by rule; the limits that apply to systems including feedback (cybernetic structures)

    e. single and multiple stage patterns (sequences of linked structures)

    f. linear and nonlinear change rules

    g. populating patterns from experience—diagnosis

    h. patterning experience—creating theories/forecasts/priorities

    i. common denominators; common factors in diverse situations

    j. developing rules of change for complex cases

    k. use of counterfactuals

    l. formal modeling

3. Analysis: static/dynamic; breaking structures into constituent parts; reducing complex processes to stages

4. Calculation: primarily in algebra, arithmetic, and Aristotelian logic

    a. project implications of combining assumptions and with observations or data; use of Venn diagrams

    b. avoiding the common formal and informal fallacies: division, composition, amphiboly, post hoc, question begging, and so on

    c. differentiating forced inference and compatibility

5. Use of counterfactuals: If X had been different what else would be (or would have been) different?

6. Experimental attitude:

    a. trial and error learning; regarding failure as positive evidence

    b. testing; differentiating test and illustration

7. Judgment: arguments to support; systematic criticism

8. Conceptualization:

    a. locate inadequacies

    b. reconceptualization, when needed

    c. normative variables, adequacy of

    d. concepts and indicators

    e. measurements

    f. aggregates: uses and limits

9. Reality control; linking assertions and argument to experience

10. Focus on symbol/referent—intension

11. Purposes for which knowledge needed; preconditions to achieving them

12. Social factors: influence of

13. Devising intervention strategies (policies)

14. Capacity for making choices; reliance on comparisons

15. Radical individualism in ethics

16. Transferability: ability to assess knowledge claims made in both the language of the special field of study and in everyday terms

THE AMENDED TEST OF COGNITIVE SKILL: TESTING IN COSTA RICA

The generalized test settled upon and used subsequently includes 16 items and explores a number of dimensions of cognitive skill (Appendix 3-B). In particular, it probes the individual's capacity to avoid logical errors, conceptual ability, choice-making procedures, experimental outlook, patterning ability, analytic skill, ability to handle counterfactuals, ability to deal with generalized patterns, and ability to relate present conditions to future outcomes systematically. The coding instructions, and the procedures used to weight responses and generate cognition skill indexes, can be found in Appendix 3-C.

The revised version of the test was tested by replicating the Guatemala study in Costa Rica, under the auspices of UNESCO and the Center for International Education at Indiana University, and with the cooperation of the Ministry of Education and the University of Costa Rica.[4] The primary aim was to verify the results obtained in Guatemala, though it was understood that the replication should provide the Ministry of Education with information useful for future planning and the University of Costa Rica with a base for improving its introductory curriculum. A sample was drawn from seniors in the secondary schools and from the national university, suitably stratified to show the effects of curriculum differences. The results were expected to suggest areas where improvements were needed at both levels. The Department of Educational Research at the Ministry of Education provided access to a sample of secondary schools; the Department of Human Sciences at the university recommended a set of curricula where information was thought likely to be particularly useful. The secondary schools sampled were located in Guanacasta, Limon, San Isidro, Puntarenas, Alajuela, Heredia, Cartago, and San Jose. The sample included large and small, rural and urban public schools but did not include any private secondary schools. At the university, students in the departments of Philologia, Agriculture, Economics, Social Work, Engineering, Social Science, Microbiology, Law, and two honors programs (History and Spanish) were sampled.

Two other groups were added to the list to facilitate comparisons with earlier testing in Guatemala: first, a group of high-level achievers from the same age group as the Guatemala elite sample, also selected by a peer group panel, was used to identify the upper levels of the new index and thus stabilize interpretation; second, because of Ministry of Education concerns, a special sample was drawn from students who had dropped out of secondary school. The same test was administered to a large group of undergraduates at the University of Missouri–St. Louis, and to the students in an English honors program at a New Jersey high school, among others.

The new test was translated into Spanish by Professor Maria E. B. de Wille, then vice-rector of the University of Costa Rica, and her colleagues, and administered by students from the university under Professor de Wille's supervision. Where the meaning of questions was the same in both cultures, a literal translation was made; in other cases (such as question 6), a parallel question with the same cultural significance and implications was framed. The results were coded by students at the University of Costa Rica in cooperation with an American graduate student (Thomas Sowash) who

Table 3.2
Mean Cognitive Skill Scores

All students	21.8
All high school students	20.0
All university students	27.8
College students excluding Honors	26.0
College honors students	32.0
High level achievers	36.6
High School drop outs	17.5
U.S. High School Honors, New Jersey	31.4
First year students, UMSL	27.9

had taken an active part in the analysis and restructuring of the test used in Guatemala. Coding was done directly to numerical code sheets from Spanish, thus eliminating the need to translate and making the data available to those in both language groups.

Test Results

The mean cognitive skill scores for the various groups tested, which are only *relatively* comparable to scores on the Guatemalan test because of the differences in content, are set out in Table 3.2. With the revised test and coding schedule, the maximum number of points possible on the cognitive skill index was 52; the best score actually registered was 49 points.

If the overall groups are disaggregated to show particular secondary schools and university departments, the results are as shown in Table 3.3. In brief, replicating the test produced almost exactly the same results as those obtained in Guatemala. The high-level achievers scored consistently and significantly better than any other group; indeed, had all of their test questionnaires been fully completed, the mean score for that group would have been around 40.2. To that extent, the initial assumption that cognitive skill as measured by the test is positively related to achievement in the environment was further reinforced.

The relation between cognitive skill levels and school curriculum was also the same in both cases. The one major discrepancy was the measured level of cognitive skill found in the group from the School of Agriculture. In Guatemala, that group scored extremely well; in Costa Rica, they did

Table 3.3
Indexes for Secondary Schools and University Departments, Costa Rica

Name	Number	Cog Skill	% under 20	% above 30
Liceo Rodrigo Facia	41	18.1	71	7
Liceo de Stenas	32	21.9	41	13
Liceo UNESCO	30	20.1	53	3
Liceo Esparta	51	21.5	47	16
Liceo de Vincent Lachner	27	16.1	85	--
San Luis Gonzaga	30	20.5	47	3
Liceo Jose Laquin Varga	26	19.3	62	12
Diurno de Limon	36	16.3	81	6
Diurno de Canas	31	20.8	45	6
Samuel Saeng	41	20.8	54	12
Regional de Flores	27	25.1	33	13
Liceo de Puriscal	22	16.9	68	5
La Union	32	24.1	37	25
H.S. Drop Outs	12	17.6	67	25
University Departments:				
Philologia	12	28.8	25	58
Agriculture	10	21.9	50	20
Economics	11	30.0	9	46
Social Work	12	18.7	67	--
Engineering	23	28.1	17	35
Social Science	7	26.4	29	43
Microbiology	5	26.0	20	40
Law	16	23.6	38	19
Honors, History	11	32.6	9	55
Honors, Spanish	9	28.2	11	33

poorly. The students who administered the tests, however, provided a simple and more or less persuasive explanation: *cherchez la femme!* The test was administered by a very pretty young woman student, which produced a considerable amount of horseplay and showing off and greatly decreased the seriousness with which the test was confronted. The results were reflected in the test scores.

With the connection between cognitive skill and real-world performance firmly established, the major implication of the results of testing was an urgent need to develop education or training targeted at improvement of cognitive performance. Cognitive skill levels among university students, in Missouri as in Costa Rica, were well below the levels achieved by high school students in the New Jersey honors program—not to say the scores associated with high-level achievement in real-world affairs.

The strong relation between school curriculum and cognitive skill levels also offers possibilities that deserve further exploration. That relation can be dramatized quite effectively by organizing the results to show the percentage of students in each group whose scores were below 20 points and those above 30 points. The cognitive weakness of students in Social Work, Law (and in Costa Rica, Agriculture) is particularly marked. In fact, in 6 of the 11 groups of university students, more than 20 percent of the total scored below 20 on the test. The variation within secondary schools was, as might be expected, even greater. The basic reference point is the scores made by high-level achievers, which lay in the 35–40 point range. When secondary school scores for seniors fall below 50 percent of that figure, that is surely cause for serious concern (see Table 3.3, columns 3 and 4).

The data in Table 3.3 support two more very important conclusions. First, the scores made by the group of high school dropouts conflict with the common assumption that only the weaker students leave school and seek employment. If the sample is at all representative, and it is of course very small, then the students who leave school without completing the curriculum seem to be a cross-section of all levels of competence. The test scores of the group as a whole are significantly higher than the means for the three weakest schools, and about 25 percent of the group achieved scores of 30 points or more, which is better than the mean of all but two of the secondary school groups. Such results suggest that the assumption be reexamined, especially in light of similar results obtained in a testing/training program conducted at the University of Missouri–St. Louis at a later date.

Finally, the value of the cognitive skill test as a predictor of future performance, with respect to intellectual or academic affairs at least, was very strongly (and unexpectedly) demonstrated in the data produced by the Costa Rican testing. Table 3.3 shows the differences in overall skill levels found among those attending the different secondary schools in the country. Two schools (Union and Flores) stand out as exceptional; seven schools have more than 50 percent of their students below the 20 point level. As it turned out, the scores were a very accurate predictor of success in the university, at both the aggregate and the individual level. In fact, the striking similarity between the two patterns led the university to undertake an experimental program aimed at improving cognitive performance, and in that way improving performance in university work. Similar successes in predicting high-level achievement, particularly in work-related training, were subsequently reported from a variety of other sites, ranging from a graduate program in Public Administration in Managua, Nicaragua,[5] through groups of nurses at local hospitals, to the training program at the St. Louis Police Academy.

From a training perspective, the test appeared as a diagnostic tool of considerable value, for it pinpointed both the weaknesses and the strengths found in the various parts of the sample, much facilitating development of an efficient selection of training foci. By showing how little difference there is between the response patterns of seniors at the university level and those in secondary school, the test suggested that university education has far less impact on cognitive skill development than had been expected—and that its influence is heavily concentrated in a few areas. In fact, the implication, supported by subsequent comparisons of first-year students and graduating seniors at several American universities, is that most of the benefits of university education are felt in two areas: (1) in the sheer range and volume of acquired information, which serves to increase reality control and awareness of the multiplicity of factors that can influence particular events; and (2) in the level of cognitive competence *built into* the curriculum in which the student is enrolled.

A comparison of student performance on particular questions supports that judgment strongly. Responses to the questions expected to be most affected by changes in cognitive skill tend not to be altered by university training. Questions 7, 8, 13, 25, 27, 32, 33, 34, and 49, for example, are good indicators of the kind of conceptual sophistication that is probably the best single indicator available of overall cognitive performance. In Costa Rica, the high school and university populations performed equally well on all of them, in the sense that in no case does one of those questions effectively differentiate the two groups. The questions that do separate secondary school seniors from university seniors refer to the effects of increased information (Questions 15, 26, 27, 30, 45, and 57) or to the ability to take into account a wider range of potential influences (Questions 6, 11, 19, 25, 31, and 35). University students do produce richer and more complex patterns of relations, as might be expected, and that in turn accounts for their greater sensitivity to the costs of alternative actions (Question 22). University students also enjoy a relative advantage with respect to capacity to identify or recognize logical errors, though both groups have difficulty with nonobvious examples. About twice as many university students as secondary school students identified the easiest of the logical errors, but on the one really difficult example, only one-third of the university students and fewer than one-tenth of the secondary school students located the fallacy. The questions were presented in illustrations, and not as formal or symbolic problems, hence what was tested was the capacity to apply logic rather than to engage in formal logical operations.

Diagnosis

A detailed breakdown of responses, stratified to differentiate secondary school and university students, was made in order to learn the major similarities and differences among the student groups. The similarities found are particularly important. For example, if students are given an opportunity to compare two concepts in terms of either the symbols used to designate them (words with similar physical patterns) or the empirical phenomena to which the concepts refer, nearly half of each group dealt with the symbol alone; some 20 percent of the total dealt with both; only about 33 percent of each group dealt solely with the referent. Yet the symbol is utterly irrelevant in any comparison of concepts, which suggests that earlier training, particularly in reading, tends to focus attention on the physical characteristics of the symbols being read rather than on the meanings or intensions of those symbols. A similar pattern appears in the tests administered to American university students at all levels, regardless of field of study. One major implication is a relatively weak capacity to follow a complex train of thought in writing, even under examination conditions when motivation and concern are presumably very high—an assumption borne out in all subsequent tests of American university students. Similarly, the individual's ability to form or to apply complex patterns involving a number of factors is likely to be restricted by that propensity, and again that tendency has appeared regularly in subsequent testing. In a related question dealing with the use of credentials or past performance as a basis for assessment of actors, about 33 percent of each group focused exclusively on performance, while more than 40 percent of each group was satisfied by references to credentials (Questions 14, 17).

Perhaps the most important evidence of the cognitive inadequacy of university training, whether in the United States or in Latin America, is found in the responses to the set of questions (8, 28, 29, 32) targeted very specifically at the individual's ability to perform the kinds of complex and sophisticated intellectual operations required for dealing with real-world affairs (directing actions or choices). Even here, there was little difference between the performance of high school and college seniors. On Question 8, which requires the use of analogy, only 14 percent of the high school students and 18 percent of the college students dealt with the problem adequately. Similarly, when faced with a problem that required the introduction of a major change in conceptualization before it could be resolved (Question 28), only 6 percent of the secondary students and 10 percent of those in the university performed the necessary operation. In contrast, about half of the high-level achievers produced a conceptual transformation when answering the question. Again, when asked to produce an intervention strategy, nearly all (95 percent) of the high school students and some 87 percent of the university students could do no better than create a simple incremental pattern, whereas some 40 percent of the high-level achievers created a nonincremental intervention. Moreover, about 95 percent of each student group missed the inversion required for an adequate response, whereas nearly 90 percent of the high-level achievers saw the problem in that way.

There is, in other words, little indication in the students' responses to show that university education, not to say secondary school education, produces much capacity to perform complex cognitive operations. Of course, individuals do develop such skills, and intelligence is perhaps the best available predictor of the likelihood that they will do so. But that returns us to the Harvard syndrome, which is certainly wasteful and probably normatively indefensible as well. Furthermore, by the time the student reaches the university, mental habits are already in large measure fixed, and that strongly suggests beginning cognitive training very early in the academic career, perhaps even before the child enters school. Learning when it can be done most effectively is a matter of first importance for future experimenting.

Other specific questions served to confirm these conclusions and provided further support for a concentrated effort to develop programs of training able to generate higher levels of cognitive skill. For example, students usually dealt holistically rather than analytically with even very complex problems (Questions 10, 41, 54), using broad, loose, concepts rather than narrow, specific ones (Questions 13, 28). In most cases, they relied on simple direct relations rather than roundabout connections (Question 50). There was little concern for long-range effects of present conditions or actions (Question 48); the structures applied to problems were usually static rather than dynamic (Question 18); there was little sign of sensitivity to the temporal aspect of problem solving (Question 55), or indeed to the normative or social dimensions of action generally. The picture that emerges from the test results is of a school population that is literally unable to deal with problems for which there is no prefabricated response, directly and closely analogous.

NOTES

1. Eugene J. Meehan, *Ethics for Policymaking* (Greenwood Press, 1990).
2. Roy C. Macridis and Eugene J. Meehan, *Attitudes, Cognition Skill, Partici-*

pation, and Achievement, A Report Submitted to the Agency for International Development, AID Contract ced-824, August 1970.

3. Nelson Goodman, *Fact, Fiction, and Forecast* (Bobbs-Merrill, 1965).

4. Eugene J. Meehan, *Cognitive Skill Testing in Costa Rica,* A Report to UNESCO, 1972.

5. Letter from Professor Michael Bernhart.

Appendix 3-A
Cognitive Skill Test:
Generalized Version

The test should be administered under the following time constraints:

Question 1–5: Thirty seconds each
Question 7: Two minutes
All other questions, one minute each.

Each question should be time controlled *separately*.

Questions 1–5 deal with the ability to identify logical errors in argument:

1. Composition fallacy
2. *Post hoc* fallacy
3. *Ad hominen* fallacy
4. Division fallacy
5. Appeal to authority

6. A comparison of two written symbols that are similar in appearance but have difference intensions. Example: What does a canal have in common with a candle?

7. Exemplification of choice procedures. Example: How would you go about choosing an assistant from among a number of applicants?

8. Experimental outlook. Example: How would you decide what to eat if shipwrecked on an island populated by plants and animals wholly outside your prior experience?

9. Capacity to generate causal chains from experience. Example: Stipulate a chain of events through which a minor accident can become a major disaster.

10. Conceptual facility. Example: A polar bear can be "seen" as food, fuel, an enemy, and so on. In that same sense, what are some of the ways in which you can "see" an automobile?

11. Ability to fit experience to a pattern. Example: As the temperature increases, the amount of clothing that people wear outside of their houses decreases. Give two other examples where the same rule applies.

12. Patterning/strategic development. Example: What advice would you give to someone trying to win a prize by putting together a jig-saw puzzle as quickly as possible?

13. Dealing with counterfactuals. Example: If you were not here to take this test, what two reasons might account for your absence?

14. Fitting patterns to experience. Example: A feedback system is any apparatus that causes an action to be reinforced (positive feedback) or suppressed (negative feedback). Give an example of each kind of feedback from your own experience.

15. Capacity to deal with second-order relations (changes in the rate of change). Example: If Jones earns $2.00 per hour the first month on a new job, $2.10 per hour the second month, $2.50 per hour the third month, and $3.30 per hour the fourth month, what change has taken place in his earnings?

16. Fitting experience to a pattern or rule. Example: If a dog is given food each time it sits up, it will usually sit up again when seeking food or when food is displayed. What pattern or rule is exemplified in that case?

Appendix 3-B
Skills Explored by Each Test
Question

1–5. Ability to avoid informal logical errors.

6. Focus on symbol/referent; specificity/diffuseness of conceptualization; direct/indirect linkages among concepts; focus on whole/parts of objects.

7. Conceptual fecundity; reality control; specificity/diffuseness of conceptualization; focus on pedigree/performance; use of attitudes; conception of relevance; focus on performance/credentials; temporal sensitivity.

8. Single-stage/multistage patterning and conceptualization; experimental outlook; reality control; awareness of costs; use of analogy; orientation to intervention; normative apparatus employed.

9. Conceptual sophistication/complexity; reality control; conceptual "distance" spanned; abstract/concrete focus; incrementalism/reconceptualization in handling problems; use of evidence (causal/coincidental dependence).

10. Active/passive relation to objects; adequacy of concepts/indicators; innovativeness; conceptual sophistication.

11. Ability to pattern/organize experience; recognition of pattern in example; propensity to use derivative/original illustrations; testability of suggestions; reality control; conception of significance.

12. Capacity to deal with static/dynamic structures; actor/performance focus; ability to develop roundabout connections among events; static/dynamic focus; use of second and third-order relations; holistic/partial focus on events.

13. Capacity to deal with situations requiring the use of counterfactuals; temporal distance incorporated into relations employed; conceptual sophistication; complexity of patterning.

14. Capacity to deal with relations over extended time periods; dynamic/static emphasis; complexity of patterning.

15. Ability to deal with second- and third-order linkages.

16. Ability to locate rule or pattern in experience; ability to match pattern to other experience.

Appendix 3-C
Coding and Weighting Instructions: Cognitive Skill Test

CODING INSTRUCTIONS;
COGNITIVE SKILL TEST

(Weightings used to calculate Cognitive
Skill Index are shown in parentheses)

1)   0)   agree
      1)   disagree (1)
      2)   no answer

2)   0)   agree
      1)   disagree (1)
      2)   no answer

3)   0)   agree   (1)
      1)   disagree
      2)   no answer

4)   0)   agree
      1)   disagree (1)
      2)   no answer

5)   0)   agree
      1)   disagree (1)
      2)   no answer

6)   Question 6: No of points in answer

      0)   none
      1)   one
      2)   two
      3)   three (1)
      4)   four   (2)
      5)   five   (2)
      6)   More than five (3)

7)   Question 6: Focus on symbol/referent

      0)   none or not answered
      1)   symbol only:letters, words, etc. (1)
      2)   referent only: refers to event (2)
      3)   both symbol and referent (3)

8)   Question 6: Specificity/diffuseness of focus

      0)   none/no answer
      1)   diffuse: general features only
      2)   specific: particular features (1)
      3)   mentions both specific and general
            aspects of each (1)

9)   Question 6: Direct/indirect conceptualization
                  (observables/inferences)

      0)   not answered
      1)   direct: geometric features, etc. (1)
      2)   indirect: purposes, uses, relations (2)
      3)   focus on symbol only

10)   Question 6: Conceptualization: focus on
                  whole or part

      0)   not answered/ not applicable
      1)   whole only -- overall features
      2)   parts or elements only (1)
      3)   both parts and features (2)

11)   Question 7: Conceptual - number of factors

      0)   not answered
      1)   one
      2)   two
      3)   three (1)
      4)   four (1)
      5)   five (2)
      6)   more than five (3)

12)   Question 7: Reality control: use of experts
      0)   not answered
      1)   no reference to expertise (need for)
      2)   clear reference to expertise (1)

13)   Question 7: Specificity/diffuseness of
                  conceptualization

      0)   not answered
      1)   broad, diffuse concepts employed
      2)   specific, narrow concepts employed (1)
      3)   both broad and narrow concepts used (2)
      4)   procedural concern only -- how choice
            made, not criteria

14) Question 7: focus on performance/pedigree

    0)   not answered/unclear
    1)   pedigree only (experience, etc.)
    2)   performance only (1)
    3)   both performance and pedigree (2)
    4)   procedural concerns only

15) Question 7: reality control -- relevance of factors

    0)   not answered
    1)   answered but not codeable
    2)   all factors relevant (2)
    3)   some relevant factors, some not (1)

16) Question 7: use of attitudinal concepts

    0)   not answered
    1)   attitudes included in answer (1)
    2)   no reference to attitudes

17) Question 7: Focus on performance/credentials

    0)   not answered
    1)   credentials only
    2)   includes performance test (1)
    3)   uses both credentials and performance

18) Question 7: temporal focus: static/dynamic

    0)   not answered
    1)   static only: list of factors, no change
    2)   dynamic: involving actions (1)

19) Question 8: conceptualization - # stages

    0)   not answered
    1)   single-stage only (eating, fishing etc)
    2)   multi-stage: watch... <u>then</u>... (2)

20) Question 8: temporal sensitivity -- time
                      pressure

    0)   not answered
    1)   no awareness of time factor
    2)   clear reference to time limits (1)

21) Question 8: Experimental attitude

    0)   not answered
    1)   no sensitivity to need to test
    2)   clear reference to testing (2)

22) Question 8: reality control --
                sensitivity to costs

    0)   not answered
    1)   no sign of cost consciousness
    2)   clear reference to costs/dangers (1)

23) Question 8: use of analogy

    0)   not answered, answer unclear
    1)   clear use of analogy (1)
    2)   no sign of analogous reasoning

24) Question 8: Orientation to intervention
    0)   not answered, unclear
    1)   no sign of intervention
    2)   evidence of intent to act (1)

25) Question 9: number of connections in chain

    0)   not answered
    1)   one-three links
    2)   four links (1)
    3)   five links (2)
    4)   six or more links (3)

26) Question 9: reality control - plausibility

    0)   not answered
    1)   vague/untestable response
    2)   plausible response (1)
    3)   utterly implausible response

27) Question 9: conceptualization, linkages

    0)   not answered;unclear answer
    1)   close, tight linkages (1)
    2)   large jumps, poor connections
    3)   mixture of loose and tight links

28) Question 9: Abstract/concrete focus

    0)   not answered
    1)   abstract focus, complex apparatus (1)
    2)   concrete focus, simple apparatus

29) Question 9: type of connecting links

    0)   not answered
    1)   incrementalism, no conceptual
          transformation
    2)   conceptual transformation (1)

30) Question 9: reality control, causality

     0)   not answered
     1)   relies on chance, accidentals
     2)   plausible causal relations (1)

31) Question 10: Conceptualization, # responses

     0)   not answered
     1)   one to three
     2)   four-five (1)
     3)   six (2)
     4)   More than six (3)

32) Question 10: active/passive structure

     0)   not answered
     1)   auto as object of human actions only
     2)   auto as subject that acts on humans
     3)   auto as both actor and object (1)

33) Question 10: relation concept and indicator

     0)   not answered
     1)   close linkage, strong theory
     2)   weak or loose relation (1)
     3)   both strong and weak relations used (2)

34) Question 10: conceptual sophistication

     0)   not answered
     1)   commonplace concepts; trivial or trite
     2)   innovative conceptualization (2)
     3)   both commonplace and innovative (1)

35) Question 12: analytic skill -- # rules

     0)   not answered
     1)   one-two
     2)   three-four (1)
     3)   five or more (2)

36) Question 12: focus on actor/performance

     0)   not answered
     1)   actor focus only (stay calm, etc)
     2)   performance focus (2)
     3)   both (1)

37) Question 12: analytic skill -- # of factors

     0)   not answered
     1)   single-factor structure
     2)   multi-factor structure (1)

38) Question 12: static/dynamic focus

    0)   not answered
    1)   static, no temporal ordering
    2)   dynamic -- order specified (1)

39) Question 12: analytic skill -- focus
     on performance?

    0)   not answered
    1)   surface, e.g, rules of sorting only
    2)   performance: strategy (1)
    3)   both surface and performance (2)

40) Question 12: Analytic skill

    0)   not answered
    1)   puzzle broken into elements (1)
    2)   puzzle taken as whole/entity
    3)   both

41) Question 12: focus on whole, parts

    0   not answered
    1)   focus on parts of puzzle
    2)   focus on whole puzzle
    3)   both (1)

42) Question 11: number of examples

    0)   not answered
    1)   one example only
    2)   two examples (1)

43) Question 11: use of experience

    0)   not answered
    1)   used personal experiences (1)
    2)   academic examples only
    3)   derived examples from question

44) Question 11: testability

    0)   not answered
    1)   untestable
    2)   testable response (1)

45) Question 11: reality control

     0)   not answered
     1)   answers realistic/correct   (2)
     2)   answers incorrect or uncertain
     3)   one correct, one incorrect (1)

46) Question 11: ability to use experience

     0)   not answered
     1)   trivial/derivative response
     2)   good response, used experience   (1)
     3)   excellent response   (2)

47) Question 13: number of responses

     0)   not answered
     1)   unrelated responses
     2)   one good response
     3)   two good responses (1)

48) Question 13: time span

     0)   not answered
     1)   events all recent
     2)   events all distant (2)
     3)   both time spans included (1)

49) Question 13: conceptualization

     0)   not answered
     1)   trivial conceptualization
     2)   unusual/sophisticated concepts (2)

50) Question 13: analytic skill

     0)   not answered
     1)   simple, or direct connection
     2)   complex, indirect, roundabout (2)

51) Question 14: analytic skill -- rule
                   derivation/application

     0)   not answered
     1)   inadequate response
     2)   adequate response (1)

52) Question 14: conceptualization

     0)   not answered
     1)   commonplaces
     2)   complex, unusual, (1)

53) Question 15: rule derivation

      0)   not answered
      1)   inadequate response
      2)   adequate response (2)

54) Question 16: analytic skill

      0)   not answered
      1)   broken into elements/stages (1)
      2)   no analysis

55) Question 16: temporality -- static/dynamic

      0)   not answered
      1)   no time sensitivity
      2)   clear concern for time (1)

56) Question 16: orientation to person/performance

      0)   not answered
      1)   focus on person (keep cool, etc)
      2)   focus on performance/strategy (1)
      3)   both (2)

57) Question 16: reality control

      0)   not answered
      1)   unacceptable solution
      2)   acceptable solution (1)
      3)   exceptional solution (2)

58) Question 16: action orientation

      0)   not answered
      1)   no sign of action
      2)   clear statement of purpose (1)

59) Question 16: active/passive orientation
      0)   not answered
      1)   active: goes to the environment (2)
      2)   passive: wait for help
      3)   uncertain or advocating
            preparatory activity

60-65 ID NUMBER of Testee

4

Cognitive Improvement

In the process of developing a valid measure of cognitive skill or performance, the critical problem is to find a way of testing the proposed measure, to generate evidence to support the claim that it truly measures cognitive skill. The solution adopted here, though imperfect, proved functional: a group of persons agreed by the community of informed observers to be high-level performers in real-world affairs was located and used as a testing ground for proposed measuring instruments. The results provided positive evidence for three assumptions: first, that cognitive skill as defined was a prime element in determining the quality of real-world performance; second, that the elements included in the proposed test of cognitive skill provided a valuable indication of individual strengths and weaknesses—that the test was diagnostically useful; and third, that the theory of knowledge used to define cognitive skill, and from which the test items were derived, was validated to the extent that was possible given the research design. Of these, the supporting evidence provided for the theory of knowledge proved the most significant by far in the long run.

INTRODUCTION: THE MEASUREMENT PROBLEM

The significance of the support gained for the theory of knowledge in the course of the testing emerges most clearly when the focus shifts from measuring cognitive skill to designing programs for improving it. For with respect to the improvement of intellectual performance, the approach used to evaluate the test is closed. Fitting patterns to the attributes of high-level achievers does not serve as a test of proposals for improving cognitive performance. As in normative affairs, we are left with the consensus of informed opinion as the ultimate basis for all such judgments. Therefore, the emphasis shifts necessarily to the set of criteria used to judge the relative level of performance in real-world affairs. Of course, even during the development of a measure for cognitive skill, it was assumed that such criteria were available within the various fields of inquiry, and would be agreed to some extent at least by the body of informed opinion. Otherwise it would have been impossible in principle to agree on the identity of the high-level achievers used in the study. But the criteria applied are seldom articulated very clearly, and cannot in any case be stated exhaustively. That makes them difficult to identify, even for those within a field. Paper and pencil tests of intellectual performance are easily developed, of course, but they are only surrogates and must in due course be validated by reference to external criteria regarded as acceptable for assessing cognitive performance. In sum, a set of criteria that can be used to assess the quality of real-world cognitive or intellectual performance is essential, yet such criteria are extremely difficult to locate and articulate, even in highly developed fields of inquiry. For that reason, a kind of indirect validation of programs of cognitive education, obtained by producing evidence for a theory of knowledge from testing based on the theory, and then using the theory to develop the education programs, is the best that can be managed under the circumstances.

The difficulties that emerge out of efforts to design and then justify education programs for improving cognitive performance are not due to the need to rely on vague and often complex assessment criteria alone. Indeed, the most formidable obstacle to progress is the need to wait for performance data that can serve as grounds for judgment, for that can take a number of years. The ultimate test of any program of cognitive training is found in the performance of those who have been trained. That performance must be assessed or evaluated, and the evidence required for judgment is usually produced very slowly at best. Obviously, compatibility with a theory of knowledge is not a substitute for assessment based on real-world performance. Such theories cannot provide the criteria used to assess the quality of individual performance without risking the creation of a self-fulfilling ordinance—that is the reason for regarding the external support obtained for the theory of knowledge through cognitive testing as so important. But in the absence of any direct test of the validity of a proposed program of education, relying on a powerful and well-integrated theory that has at least some relevant external support provides the best available point of departure for the enterprise. In those terms, the theory performs an invaluable function, for if there were no starting point whatever, the effort to improve cognitive performance would be forced to rely wholly on serendipity and chance, and both are notably unreliable.

Individual performance within the education system, which is both read-ily accessible to university faculty and presumably an intellectual enter-prise, may appear an appropriate alternative base for measuring cognitive skill. Educational performance quality, as measured by grades and degrees, is widely used for that purpose in present-day society. However, the results of cognitive skill testing undertaken in the United States and elsewhere show that academic performance is not related very strongly to the con-cept of cognitive skill as defined here. That intellectual skill is required for academic performance is beyond argument, but the set of skills adequate for getting good grades in school is not identical to the set of skills re-quired for using knowledge to deal effectively and efficiently in real-world affairs. In fact, the evidence suggests that the set of skills required for obtaining good grades in school is useful, and usable, primarily or even exclusively within an academic or scholastic context.

Even if that were not the case, the information needed to make a sound assessment of student performance *after* leaving the educational system (which is essential for adequate evaluation of that system) is likely to be difficult to obtain. An attempt made at the University of Missouri–St. Louis to follow the members of a large experimental class of students into the external world foundered on precisely that point. Very simple question-naires, reinforced by follow-up postcards, produced less than a 5 percent response only two years after the class ended—scarcely enough for a valid judgment of the effects of the experimental program. Further, several of the respondents complained about the difficulty of assessing their own per-formance, and several more asserted that they were being improperly as-sessed by others at their place of employment.

Until such time as a longitudinal study can be made that extends over an adequate time period (several years at least), the principal argument for the proposed programs for improving cognitive skill must assume the va-lidity of the theory of knowledge from which it is derived or extrapolated. In the present case, some supporting evidence for that theory (detailed in Chapter 3) was obtained from the cognitive skill testing program; the remainder comes from a number of years of teaching students how to use the theory as a critical tool. For that reason, the argument used to defend the education and training programs will verge unavoidably on circularity. That may cause some discomfort and unease, but no good alternative is available. If the theory is sound, as appears from the evidence collected thus far, then persons with the skills enjoined by the theory should, other things equal, improve their cognitive performance. At present, the relation between training and performance in real-world affairs rests on informal, and therefore uncertain, measures, but they are not wholly lacking in per-suasiveness.

That may seem too slight a basis for a fundamental set of education proposals, but it is worth noting in context that if no valid measure of real-world performance is available (which is now the case), *and* there is no well-established (and testable) theory to serve as a base for evaluating performance, there is no alternative to assuming that IQ is the dominant factor in performance. The assessment system, both within education and in society more generally, will then tend to be IQ driven. Given the results obtained by administering the cognitive skill test, that is another good reason for accepting the theory of knowledge as a point of departure for cognitive education or training. So long as the theory is applied in full awareness of the limited body of supporting evidence, and the user seeks data that will in due course validate the training directly (and thus serve to further strengthen or modify the theory) no harm, and much potential benefit, can be expected from the effort.

THEORY-BASED COGNITIVE EDUCATION

Because of the current situation with respect to the criteria available for assessing intellectual performance, the discussion to follow concentrates on the use made of the theory of knowledge in the development of education programs intended to improve intellectual or cognitive performance. When education programs are theory-based in this way, improvements are possible only with respect to the set of purposes for which the theory was designed, and therefore only by reference to or in terms of the initial normative assumption on which the theory depends. Those limits accepted, the theory functions by identifying the set of purposes that can be achieved through action and the set structures and processes necessary (and perhaps sufficient) to achieve them. That analytic framework provides a way of stating "What must be done?" and "What does doing it require?" whether the individual is thinking to purpose, or trying to assess the efforts of others engaged in the same enterprise.

Assuming the validity of the theory, absorbing it, and learning how to apply it can be expected to improve individual capacity to acquire, assess, and apply knowledge (to increase cognitive skill as defined) and to supply the needed criteria for assessing such improvements. Put differently, the basic requirements that must be fulfilled before the kind of knowledge required for directing actions on defensible grounds can be acquired, assessed, and applied can be determined only within such a theoretical or analytic framework. Performance in fulfilling each requirement should improve given suitable instruction and practice. The model for the overall enterprise is taken from sports, where performance improvement is generated routinely by informed practice based on a theory of play that is developed in precisely the same way as the theory of knowledge sketched in Chapter 2.

Types of Cognitive Training

Individual performance in real-world affairs, and cognitive performance in particular, is reasonably assumed to be a function of the extent to which cognitive skill or competence has been developed by the person. In principle, a properly educated individual can become self-teaching, can learn how to learn without external assistance. The appropriate goal for all cognitive training is to create or produce a self-teaching individual (in that limited sense). That implies an individual who (1) knows when learning has occurred, (2) knows what has been learned, and (3) can assess the quality, the uses, and the limitations to be observed in applying that knowledge. Such improved cognitive ability can in principle be extended to almost every area of individual performance; the analytic apparatus is not field or function specific.

Types of Training

Two fundamental approaches to education or training can be derived from, or supported by, the theory of knowledge. First, and most important, the student can be provided with an opportunity to absorb the theory and apply it to real-world situations or problems; second, the theory can be applied to specific real-world problems by someone competent in its uses and limitations, and the results used to instruct the student, usually through suitable exercises. In both cases, the two essential prerequisites to success are an instructor who is well-versed in the theory and its applications, and a student willing to practice systematically and carefully for an extended period of time.

Depending on the time and resources available, education or training can also foster a range of attitudes, habits, techniques, and practices that testing has indicated to be important contributory factors in overall intellectual performance. They include such things as: (1) an "experimental" outlook, (2) a commitment to seeking knowledge useful for furthering the human enterprise, (3) an understanding of the importance of testing in use, (4) an undogmatic and questioning attitude toward assumptions and evidence, (5) a willingness to tolerate uncertainty coupled with some capacity for withholding judgment if the evidence available is inadequate, (6) some capacity to regard forced actions or failures as learning opportunities, among others. Training can also assist with the development of good work habits, improve the individual's capacity to perform the various strategic and tactical judgments that must be made in the course of systematic inquiries, enhance the logical or mathematical skills that the individual deploys, and perhaps most important of all, foster the kind of writing and reading that sound argument or criticism demands.

Working Assumptions. The basic assumptions on which the approach to cognitive education depends are relatively uncontentious, though some of their more important implications tend to be overlooked. Two of those assumptions are prime: first, that cognitive performance is a function of a combination of both native endowment and training received and there is no reason at present to believe that the former is or must be dominant; second, that nearly everyone has enough native capacity to become a competent thinker/critic. Given the enormous capacity of the neural apparatus, and the relatively small part of the whole that is actually used in most cases, it is reasonable to assume that adequate training can in principle enable most people to perform competently. Again, a good analogue is found in sports, where a competent coach can enable almost anyone who is not severely handicapped to perform reasonably well, given time and effort.

Put differently, it is assumed that the human intellectual endowment is in most cases grossly underutilized. Inherited intellectual capacity varies widely, and the advantages that nature provides cannot be overcome completely, if only in the limited sense that not everyone can be trained to a level of performance equivalent to playing golf on the professional tour. Nevertheless, there remain good reasons to assume that for most of humanity the quality of their intellectual performance is primarily a function of education or training rather than natural endowment. At the margins of native ability there is a small group of persons so badly disabled that no amount of training can produce competence. At the other extreme, there *may* be another group so richly endowed by nature that any form of training will impede rather than further development, although that assumption is at best dubious. Of course, some individuals do acquire intellectual competence no matter how little help they are given and some of them may even be able to overcome the effects of incompetent instruction. But even such persons, to the extent they are found, can be expected to benefit significantly from competent cognitive education.

In general, sound training can be expected to improve performance among the less well endowed even more than among the talented, and that has proved to be the case in all of the experiments conducted thus far. More technically, the difference between the overall performance of the more and less talented should decrease and the overall performance curve should be skewed to a higher level and be more strongly peaked than before. If the distribution of performance skills after training merely reflected the initial distribution of natural ability, if the results fit a normal distribution curve, then the training has added little or nothing to cognitive capacity.

Of course, no education program can guarantee success. At a minimum, the student must be motivated, and the kinds of cognitive education outlined below were not designed to *create* motivation. Motivation must be assumed, and in some cases at least, that assumption will be incorrect. The problem is complicated by the frequency with which motivation is misdirected rather than wholly absent. The student who seeks only to obtain a good grade in a cognitive training course can, within limits, succeed, although the instructor can, and should, restrict that possibility by using examination questions that require the application of the analytic apparatus to real-world affairs. Experience in teaching such courses suggests that an adequate level of motivation is usually available, but it may be severely restricted by existing institutional arrangements and the folkways and mores of those being trained. The student who self-assigns as an intellectual incompetent, and then proceeds to become a self-fulfilling prophet, provides what is perhaps the most common case in point.

The universal availability of motivation is more clearly evident among the very young. Only rarely is there a motivation problem in the elementary schools; judicious praise and encouragement usually suffice to produce effort that is sustained with amazing tenacity. Somewhere, and for some reason, the impulse to active efforts to obtain an education is lost by a substantial part of the school population. The loss does not affect everyone equally, of course, and one of the more tragic sights in any public school is a group of motivated and teachable children who are rendered unteachable in practice because they have been merged with others who have lost the impulse to learn. Very little seems to be known about the phenomenon. Simply blaming peer group influence is only an unhelpful form of question-begging. Perhaps the most tenable policy available, judged by the results obtained here, is to concentrate on preventing the *loss* of motivation rather than seeking to induce it. Preventive medicine, in this case as in many others, seems a better strategy than seeking a remedy after the disease is acquired. However, if the problem remains for the present beyond resolution, that does not decrease its significance for education or training. If the psychologist's white rat refused to budge, operant conditioning could not succeed. For precisely the same reasons, the student who will not try is for all practical purposes unteachable, or incapable of learning. To make matters worse, failure will usually serve to reinforce such passive behavior once the pattern has been firmly established.

Summary and Implications. A variety of educational programs can be inferred or extrapolated from the basic theory of knowledge, some aimed at improving overall performance and others at the development of more specific skills. All of the cognitive skill training derived from the theory, however, will make use of one of two basic formats: either (1) the individual is taught the theory, or parts of it, and provided with opportunities to learn how to use it; or (2) the cognitive structures and processes required for the performance of specific tasks, or achievement of specified purposes, are derived from the theory and incorporated into a set of exercises intended to develop the needed skills (which may be either general or specific). In the latter case, the student need not internalize the content of the underlying theoretical apparatus or the rules that govern its application to specific cases. The creation of so-called expert systems can be regarded as a special case of producing the kind of apparatus used in the second type of training. Other things equal, there are good reasons for preferring the first mode of training to the second.

In the first mode of instruction, the student learns or internalizes the theory of knowledge and then learns how to translate real-world problems into theoretical terms (or metalanguage) for criticism or solution. That mode or approach can proceed in two different ways: first, the individual can be taught the theory in abstract form, then given an opportunity to learn its applications under competent supervision; alternatively, the student focuses on the production of critiques (of both his or her own work and the work of others), acquiring theory and applications together.

At a minimum, effective use of the theory requires the student to: (1) know the purposes that can be achieved through intellectual direction of actions; (2) recognize their reifications in the flow of real-world events; and (3) know the instruments and processes needed to achieve each of these purposes, together with the requirements for acceptability to be applied to each one. It is also helpful for the student to learn, and thus be able to avoid or work around, the limitations and abuses to which instruments, processes, and purposes are subject. Those conditions satisfied, the individual need only identify the purpose at hand within the analytic framework, transfer the requirements for fulfilling it to the world of observation, and apply them systematically. In the second mode of theory-based cognitive training, the theory is applied to a specific set of problems or activities by an instructor, producing exercises that can be used to improve individual performance within that problem area. The first approach must be used to train those who wish to become coaches, or self-coaching players, in any particular sport. The development of calisthenics for use in training those who wish to play specific positions in such games as football, or the creation of expert systems, serves to illustrate the second approach to cognitive training.

There are considerable advantages to be gained by actually transferring the theory of knowledge to the student, by introducing the student to the coaching language, or metalanguage, and providing opportunities to apply it under supervision. In some cases, such training is essential, as a football coach must impart the full theory of play, and not just a set of exercises, to anyone preparing to become a coach. Those who are engaged in teaching and/or research, for example, cannot function adequately without self-conscious awareness of "what is being done," of purposes sought and the means being employed to achieve them, and the criteria of adequacy to be applied to all such efforts, and that requires knowledge of the full theoretical apparatus. Further, regular use of theoretical terms or a metalanguage facilitates generalization of what has been learned as well as transfer of learning from one area to another; parallels, analogs, and similes usually appear, or are more readily seen, when the metalanguage is used rather than the "language of play." However, the time required to learn to use the apparatus can be extensive, and in many cases the whole apparatus is not required, or the density and precision of some portions of the whole can be reduced without serious danger. A good parallel is found in medicine, where the technician can be trained to perform specific functions without having to first absorb the whole of medical knowledge. The person who designs such specific programs must, of course, have a particularly good command of the underlying theory and its applications.

The main reason for recommending reliance on transfer of the full theory of knowledge, plus suitable training in its application or use (particularly as a critical tool for assessing knowledge claims), is theoretical but compelling. Humans are not simple logical machines; they can and do transcend logical limits. Further, human knowledge is not discovered or borrowed but created; every act of learning has an irreducible element of creativity incorporated into it. Finally, humans are not always aware of what they know or how they use their knowledge. Those, and other human attributes, justify an approach to education that is not feasible with other living creatures. Humans can be told the purpose of the training, and the reasons why it takes the form that it does, and that allows the person being trained to assist with the training, and even to improve it in the process of being trained. The theory of knowledge itself requires precisely that kind of intellectual performance for application, particularly for justifying preferences. Sharing purposes and procedures amounts to sharing the theory, or metalanguage, on which training depends. Knowing the theory can in principle convert the trainee from a rote assimilator to a partner in an ongoing experiment. The validity of that principle has for the most part been borne out by the results achieved in various experimental programs.

Even if the psychological and theoretical value for the trainee of acquiring the underlying theory of knowledge are ignored, there remain powerful reasons for preferring a mode of instruction in which the student is a fully informed partner. The theory of knowledge makes possible an accurate statement of the meaning of action, of "what is being done," and provides a link between actions taken and the necessary conditions for achieving purposes sought. If the theory becomes part of what is learned, it can serve to link exercises performed to purposes sought, through often complex layers of intervening purposes, and that is precisely the kind of apparatus that is needed to distinguish between information and *evidence*, between data that are significant with respect to the purpose at hand and those that are not. Without access to a theory of knowledge, meaningful testing and improvement of knowledge is out of the question—the student is reduced to depending on conventions or formulas applied by rote.

Of course, a theory of knowledge embedded in a discipline will also serve that purpose, and that accounts for the different levels of cognitive skill imparted by the various curricula. But so long as the theory remains implicit, it remains immune to correction—a danger often noted with respect to the training, or overtraining, of specialists. One virtue of the theory of knowledge employed here is that it is readily linked to everyday actions, and personal experience, which makes it relatively easy for the individual to test its validity and learn its uses and limitations without having to rely upon specialized knowledge in any particular field of inquiry. So long as the purposes sought in the environment can be identified within the boundaries of the theory, the critical apparatus can be applied with profit. That is, if the specifics of the real-world situation being addressed can be translated into the metalanguage used to state the elements of the theory, performance in that situation can be improved and the judgment that an improvement has been made can be defended.

Each of the two basic formats used to transfer the theory to the student can function at a number of levels of sophistication or complexity. Indeed, although the full potential of the theory of knowledge as a source for cognitive training remains relatively undeveloped, it is already clear that it can be applied through endless sets of variant patterns. Experience with efforts to achieve specific goals is needed to identify the selection that provides optimal learning. Much depends, obviously, on the purposes to be fulfilled, the nature of the group to be taught, the environmental conditions in which the class is held, among others. Three levels of education involving direct transfer of the theory have been tested experimentally in varying degree: they are examined in the next section in some detail, together with an experimental cognitive improvement program targeted at children who are just beginning elementary school.

THEORY-BASED EDUCATION: DIRECT TRANSFER

Experimental education programs intended to develop cognitive skill by transferring the theory of knowledge directly to the student have been developed and tested for various levels of age and academic achievement. That kind of instruction was first introduced in the 1970s as a course targeted at graduate students who intended to become either university faculty (teachers of teachers), policy analysts, or some other kind of research specialist. It was extended later to the training of university undergraduates and students in secondary schools. In due course, that forced an effort to develop materials and techniques that could be used with very large classes, if only to test the validity of the "democratic" assumption that an educated public capable of self-government is possible at least in principle. In both cases, the theory was transferred directly to the students and they were provided with opportunities to learn how to use it effectively under close supervision. Usually, the theory was developed from fundamentals as the class progressed, emphasizing the purposes sought, the reasons for seeking them, the kind of structures and processes required (the necessary and/or sufficient conditions for achieving them), the major pitfalls to be avoided, and, of course, the special problems encountered in application. However, both at my own university and elsewhere, an alternative mode of teaching emerged in which the central concern was to develop the student's critical capacity with respect to knowledge claims—the theory was acquired concurrently but subordinately.

Advanced Training for Graduates

For graduate students particularly, systematic elaboration of the apparatus, and of the justification for accepting and applying it, proved to be essential. The students' main concern, rightly, was with the validity of the theory of knowledge and the reasons and evidence that could be offered to support it. For those with a primary interest in research or policymaking, the major goal of such courses was, and is, the develop a set of criteria that could be used to assess proposals for, or the results of, a range of different kinds of inquiries, and to determine the limits, if any, on the use that could be made of the results. The fairly modest extension of the theory needed to link it to defensible policymaking was completed in the early 1970s (though not published until 1981). Cognitive skill training based on a direct transfer of the theory of knowledge to the student proved particularly valuable for those concerned with either public or private policymaking. Similar experimental classes were created for teachers, particularly those who were to take part in cognitive training programs at the primary and secondary school levels. Those courses focused mainly on the theory, but included discussion of its pedagogical implications, with particular attention to classroom procedure and methods of testing.

Over time, the context in which the theory was made available to graduate students has been modified substantially. In the early 1970s, the principal emphasis was placed on learning the theory and developing skill in analyzing and criticizing knowledge claims. That led to significant improvements in the students' ability to deal critically with the efforts of others, particularly with articles published in academic journals or the quality press, but it also fostered the students' propensity to memorize the apparatus without fully understanding or appreciating its limits as well as its applications. Further, the critical structure was not being used in the conduct of personal affairs. Emphasis therefore shifted to criticism, particularly of the use made of the products of inquiry in collective decisions and to the kinds of arguments used to justify them. The materials were subsequently codified and condensed, producing a far more efficient and effective text.

The results obtained from the course, judged primarily by reference to the final critique required of each student, improved substantially as a result of these changes. The requirements to be fulfilled by the final critique, which were made available at the first class meeting, included an assessment, in both substantive and methodological terms, of a major policy proposal. The student could select his or her own proposal, from either academic or governmental sources, so long as it was seriously intended and contained a specific action recommendation. The quality of the criticism is judged in terms of both completeness and adequacy/accuracy; the grade includes an assessment of the way the critique is organized and presented in addition to dealing with the validity of the judgments involved. In sum, the course examination includes a range of factors that are not included in the generalized test of cognitive skill; in particular, it quite properly requires an explicit, self-conscious use of the analytic/theoretical framework as a critical tool. Given the wider purposes set for the course, the cognitive skill test would be grossly inadequate as a basis for grading, although the students who completed the course performed very well on the test when it was administered to them.

Perhaps the most difficult problem to resolve in the development of the course of study for graduate students has been administrative: scheduling classes. Although the empirical parts of the theory of knowledge can be covered reasonably well in a single semester, neither the necessary practice in applying it, nor the kind of intensive study needed to internalize the normative apparatus, can be managed within that time frame. But in practical terms, scheduling two-semester courses in a tightly organized graduate program is extremely difficult for both students and faculty. Nevertheless, the test results indicate very clearly that the value of the critical apparatus for the student is greatly reduced unless a second semester is available for internalizing the theory and becoming familiar with its applications. Further, the impossibility of internalizing the materials properly tends understandably to force the student to regard the course as just another obstacle to be overcome rather than as a fundamental and personally beneficial skill to be mastered.

Training Literate Adults

Until such time as a regular program has been incorporated into the elementary and intermediate school curricula, the largest potential use for cognitive training is to increase the skill levels of literate adults, the major consumers of knowledge in society. The most effective channel available for reaching the bulk of that population is through the universities and the secondary or technical schools. The second stage of course development therefore focused on the design of a training program that could be used with literate adults, particularly those just beginning their undergraduate work at a university. The materials created for such courses were not meant solely for use in formal classrooms. Cognitive training can be supplied in almost any location, by a variety of techniques: lectures, books, television, self-teaching texts, and computerized instruction, among others. The critical skills involved are wholly general in nature, and apply equally well to family purchases at the local grocery or to the conduct of public affairs. So long as the purpose is to direct action, and the actor or critic accepts the need to provide the best justification possible for accepting the recommendations, the critical apparatus can be employed with profit. In everyday terms, cognitive skill training for adults is more properly concerned with problems of intellectual consumership, with expanding individual capacity to deal effectively with the kinds of knowledge claims and judgments encountered in everyday life, than with the special difficulties encountered in research intended to add to the existing knowledge supply.

Training directed to adults generally uses the same basic procedures employed in graduate training: the student is taught the theory of knowledge and given an opportunity to learn how to apply it to concrete, real-world cases. Only the kinds of cases used to exemplify applications need be different. The theory is presented directly, with only a minimal amount of detailed justification unless the students request further discussion of specific points. The goal is rapid and efficient internalization of the theory of knowledge, so that as much time as possible can be spent applying it and having the applications subjected to systematic criticism and review. The primary concern is for students to learn what purposes can be handled within the theory, the instruments and processes required to fulfill each purpose, and the limiting conditions to be satisfied by each instrument. Ancillary exercises are used to give the students an opportunity to improve their logical competence, at least to the point where they can avoid the more common errors in reasoning, as well as to organize an argument or critique in a systematic and maximally effective manner.

Focusing on Critiques

Training that concentrates on the use of the theory as a critical tool is effective so long as the student realizes that such methodological or analytic criticism is decisive only for *ruling out* knowledge claims, that it cannot establish them. Further, he or she must realize that the criteria on which knowledge claims are established or accepted are commonly developed within a particular field of inquiry and are embodied in a set of conventions that is acquired as part of disciplinary training. In most cases, the sets of assumptions on which such conventions depend are only partly articulated; and in almost every case, some questions relating to the adequacy of evidence or the relevance of particular data to a given knowledge claim are subject to dispute and cannot, for the moment at least, be resolved. The point that must be made clear is that no amount of generalized cognitive training can provide all of the information and/or the criteria needed for establishing knowledge claims in specific fields or areas. Conversely, agreement with the substance of experience is not by itself sufficient justification for accepting a claim to know either; knowledge claims must also satisfy analytic or methodological criteria. Further, if the goal is critical as against simple rote learning, the student must learn to distinguish between propositions that are testable in principle and those that are not, between weighing evidence and illustrating a point, and so on. All such questions have a methodological dimension and they cannot be decided by reference to experiential or substantive data alone.

The analytic characteristics of knowledge claims, and the methodological criteria such claims must satisfy, have been excluded deliberately from the test of cognitive skill. Absent systematic training in the analytic apparatus, including such questions would have depressed all of the scores and accomplished nothing. But adequate real-world assessment of cognitive performances is literally impossible unless it includes reference to epistemological/methodological criteria. Knowledge claims, or efforts to apply knowledge, like athletic performances, always have both a substantive and a methodological dimension. If either is omitted, the resulting critique will be prima facie inadequate. Since methodological criticism is rarely encountered, even in academic writings, that suggests the value of concentrating on systematic criticism (production of valid critiques) in cognitive training. In principle, the organization and development of critiques provides a solid entry point for developing cognitive skill among literate adults, so long as it is suitably augmented by transfer of the full theoretical apparatus in due course. Indeed, that focus has been used as a point of departure for a very successful honors program in political science at Pennsylvania State University.[1]

Systematic efforts to criticize knowledge claims and their various applications are an important part of the overall improvement process in any field of inquiry. That provides yet another reason for including a generalized format for dealing critically with efforts to develop and/or apply knowledge to real-world affairs in cognitive texts and training. Such a format is sketched briefly in the following pages.[2] Although it deals mainly with systematic criticism of materials written by others, it is readily adapted to self-criticism as well.

To begin, the meaning of a "critique" must be separated clearly from the everyday meaning of the term "criticize." A critique is not a string of negatives, intended as a response to the question "What is wrong with this paper or book?" Nor is it a simple summary or condensation of a book or paper. Instead, "critique" refers to an overall assessment or evaluation of an effort to create, apply, or gain acceptance for, a specific knowledge claim. Such assessments will normally include five major points: (1) a statement of the purpose of the author; (2) an evaluation of the significance of that purpose; (3) a judgment of the extent to which the purpose has been fulfilled; (4) an argument, including evidence from experience, from methodology, and from the actual written work, to support that conclusion; and (5) any additional commentary needed to complete the assessment—for example, references to organization, sources, language, and so on. Each of these points may occupy a number of pages, or a number of paragraphs; much depends on the amount of space available for criticism, as well as the overall significance of the writer's purpose. In principle, drastic restriction of the commentary is advisable, since that forces the critic to concentrate on the relative importance of each of the points actually raised.

The form and content of critiques, whether written or oral, depend mainly on the functions that a critique must perform. At one level of analysis, the critic must replicate the line of reasoning followed by the author, for argument and criticism of argument raise many of the same problems. At another level of analysis, however, the two tasks are quite different. The critic must state clearly, and justify, the kind of argument that the author should (in the critic's judgment) have made. This may or may not coincide with the argument actually put forward by the author.

The difference in perspective of author and critic is marked particularly by the form of exposition employed in each task—if only because of the different target populations addressed in each case. Writing involves one author and a reader. The author examines a body of evidence that may not be accessible to the reader and seeks to fulfill some valid intellectual purpose to the reader's satisfaction. Criticism serves to insert another level of analysis between the author and the critic's audience, and the writing must reflect that difference in perspectives.

The structure and content of written critiques is determined mainly by the relations between author (or, more precisely, author's purpose), subject matter, and critic's argument on the one hand; and critic, subject matter, author's purpose and argument, and critic's purpose and argument on the other. The critic's exposition must reflect the needs of the *critic's* readers with respect to the points that the critic seeks to make. In the process, however, the critic has the responsibility to expose the evidence, judgments, and supporting arguments on which the assessment depends to further criticism by the critic's readers. To simplify the task somewhat, the discussion can be limited to three participants: the author, the critic, and the critic's reader.

For both author and critic, the central focus is the author's purpose. The primary task of the author is to state the purpose of the argument as clearly as possible and justify its significance; the reader must also be told what, in the author's judgment, is required to fulfill that purpose. The author can then proceed to try to satisfy those requirements as fully and systematically as time and resources allow.

From the critic's perspective, the author's purpose must be stated in two contexts, one substantive and the other methodological. Although authors only rarely state the methodological assumptions on which their work depends, critics must do so explicitly, else the criticism cannot be adequate. The analytic frameworks employed by contemporary critics vary widely. The one used here, for example, allows the author to describe, predict, project the effects of action, choose, produce a policy, and so on; the selection is based on the intellectual requirements for fulfilling the overall normative purpose for which knowledge is sought. The author must be trying to create or apply knowledge able to fulfill one of those purposes, test it, or provide an argument for accepting or rejecting it, otherwise the analytic apparatus, and criticism based on it, cannot be applied. A number of the stipulated purposes will be combined in almost every piece of writing, which tends to make serious and systematic criticism a fairly complex, and tedious, activity. If the author's purpose cannot be determined in either substantive or methodological terms, as occurs surprisingly often, that is already a serious indictment of the quality of the performance. The critic can, in such cases, go on to examine *possible* purposes, particularly if payment is being made by the number of words contained in the critique, completing the evaluation of the writing by the use of such terms as "if that was the intention, the performance failed/succeeded"—providing the reader, of course, with reasoning and evidence to support that judgment.

Once the critic has determined the author's substantive and methodological purposes, the critic must inform the reader how important they are considered to be and what (in the *critic's* judgment) is required to fulfill them, say what the supporting argument must contain. That statement becomes the base for the critique and opens the way to subsequent criticism of the criticism.

Analytically, the critic can then proceed to judge the author's performance and to inform the reader whether, and to what extent, the author has succeeded or failed. A critique is a performance assessment of some author (who may also be the critic) but it must be carried out in terms that allow the critic's reader to assess the critic's performance as well. Those overlapping requirements play an important part in the actual structuring of the writing.

The remainder of the critique is devoted to arguing the case for the critic's evaluation. Reasons and evidence that are provided will refer to both substantive and methodological aspects of the writing being criticized. That is, the critic must deal with the relation between the assumptions made in the writing, whether explicitly or implicitly, and the *content* of human experience as well as the relation between the purposes sought (in analytic or methodological terms), the requirements for fulfilling them, and the content of the written material being critiqued. In effect, the critic must link what the author actually did to what the author should have done (in the critic's judgment) in order to fulfill the purpose set for the inquiry. Evidence relating to the substantive quality of the author's work will come from the critic's knowledge of the subject matter; evidence for its methodological acceptability is created by applying the critic's analytic framework or "theory of play."

Some of the implications that follow from this construction of the meaning of the critiques are worth enumerating:

1. An assessment of methodological adequacy *must* be included in the critique.

2. Methodological criticism can be carried out even if the critic knows little or nothing of the subject matter, but it can only provide reasons for disallowing the author's case—methodology cannot establish an argument.

3. Author and critic may disagree about the requirements for fulfilling the author's purpose, and that should be acknowledged—though the critic may seek to convince the reader that the author is mistaken. Indeed, the critic may take the view that the author succeeded in his or her own terms, but that the criteria applied by the author were not adequate.

4. The reasons for the critic's judgments must be summarized at the outset, since that initial statement of the critic's judgment provides the points to be supported by what follows. It also supplies the overall framework for the critique. That is, points are normally treated in the main body of the critique in the order in which they appear in the summary, which is usually organized so as to deal with the most signficant items first. To repeat, no criticism of a performance is valid unless reasons and evidence are produced to support it; if space is limited, that merely restricts the number of points that can be made.

5. The critic is fully responsible for the clarity, organization, and force of the criticism. The author's inadequacies, however plentiful, do not excuse the critic.

6. The order of presentation in an argument/critique must follow the basic pattern set forth in the section entitled "Advanced Training for Graduates." Until the judgment is known, the supporting argument cannot be assessed. Further, the critic has a responsibility to expose his or her criticism to further criticism from others, and that requires a clear statement of the judgment made and the grounds for making it. Agreement with a judgment or conclusion is not enough; genuine agreement must include specific reference to the supporting evidence and argument as well.

7. Criticism will normally include references to the manner in which the author has organized and presented the materials, the quality of the writing, and anything else about the written effort that adds to or detracts from the force of the argument.

8. A checklist can be created that will apply very broadly to any effort to supply the instruments needed for directing actions. It will include such points as: (a) the quality of the concepts, indicators, and measurements employed; (b) the adequacy of the definitions; (c) the normative base (and a justification for any departure from radical individualism); (d) the validity of any theories and forecasts employed; (e) the correctness of the calculations or inferences made; (e) the quality of the diagnoses and other judgments; (f) evidence of bias or prejudice, omissions, or quality of presentation; (g) and last but not least, praise for things done well and suggestions for improvement where that is possible and appropriate.

9. Critiques targeted at a policy recommendation form a special class of cases, for such recommendations must be supported by a very complex form of argument since it will deal with both empirical and normative knowledge or assumptions. A number of quite specific points must be covered before the recommendation can be accepted or considered adequate:

a. Has the actor been properly identified? If there is more than one actor with capacity to alter a situation, has that been taken into account? Are the estimates of capacity acceptable?

b. Have the outcomes been projected properly? Are the normative concepts used to state them adequate? Are the estimates of risk or uncertainty attached to each of the outcomes reasonable? Has the outcome of inaction been included in the choice?

c. Has the preference been established? Is it supported by reasons drawn from or based on experience? Do the reasons refer to the conditions of life of some human population? Has the collective dimension of individual life been included in the outcomes?

d. Has an action program (policy) been developed? Does the author focus on causes or on cures?

e. Has a monitoring system been installed? Linked to policymaking? Is the set of factors to be monitored adequate? Any provision for unexpected outcomes or side effects?

f. Is there evidence that the author is aware of any weaknesses in the apparatus, any sources of potential error? What has been "headed off at the pass?"

Creating and refining checklists of this kind plays an important role in adequate cognitive training, even for undergraduates and students in the secondary or technical schools.

Pedagogical Considerations: Theory-Based Education

As every teacher knows, the way in which materials are presented to the student, and the kinds of materials used in illustrations and exercises, can have a major bearing on the results produced. Experience indicates that some practices and procedures are particularly valuable in cognitive training targeted at literate adults. They refer mainly to the use of concrete cases in transferring the theory to the student, the kinds of cases employed, and some of the supplementary materials that can contribute greatly to success.

The first point has to do with the respective roles of abstract materials and concrete cases in the teaching of theories. The issue is tendentious, but experience teaching the theory of knowledge to adults suggests the wisdom of concentrating on the abstract structure and minimizing examples and illustrations until it has been internalized. The reason is found in the students' lack of familiarity with the kinds of analytic considerations involved. If there is a firm understanding of the underlying principles on which the abstract apparatus depends, as in the case of a professional football team faced with a coach wishing to introduce a new system of defense, instruction may profitably begin with examples and develop the underlying theory later. But with respect to cognition, or a theory of knowledge, there is rarely if ever a tradition to build upon, even with graduate students. Concrete examples are therefore hopelessly vague or ambiguous until the framework needed to give them meaning, or stabilize it, has been deployed. It is as pointless to introduce examples before the theory of knowledge has been grasped as to begin a course in automobile engine repair by examining a carburetor if the students have no idea of the way an internal combustion engine functions. Once the theory has been grasped, illustrations are essential for acquiring "recognition skill," the ability to "see" the abstract purpose or structure in real-life cases.

Second, the central concern in teaching such courses should be the development of sound habits; they play a much greater role in competent cognitive performance than bursts of insight or inspiration. Training should be based upon regular procedures and standard checklists; exercises should be designed to fix or reinforce them. Time trials that are sufficiently constrained to force the student to rely on habit and internalized procedures rather than "rethink" questions provide a good test of that aspect of performance. Here again, athletics provide the best models for emulation. Good habits are not substitutes for creativity, of course, but little is known about how to foster the latter, and the importance of habits in the conduct of complex affairs is well established. The enormous complexity of the structures and processes involved in reasoned criticism of serious knowledge claims underscores the importance of habit and procedures. Faced with real-world complexities, and lacking procedural means for simplifying them, the individual is extremely disadvantaged. At a minimum, well-grounded habits and procedures can ensure that an argument or problem is examined along all of its major dimensions. Inquirers tend to find the things they look for; the prime function of quality training is to increase the likelihood that they will look for the right things.

Third, training should make use of real cases, avoiding hypothetical, imaginary, or concocted problems. So far as possible, the cases should be part of the student's personal experience: suitable examples can usually be found in the educational system, community affairs, athletics, and so on. There are sound practical reasons for insisting strongly on the use of materials that refer to personal, or at least real-world, affairs. Most important, real cases are subject to all of the constraints that operate in the world of experience independent of the observer. Unexpected side effects are found only in real-world cases, where they are determined by observation rather than assumed—or ignored. In imagination, nothing is given and all things are possible; imagination must supply its own constraints. The goal in cognitive training is improved performance in the world as it is; learning how to deal with unexpected side effects, with successive failures in the face of an implacable and unfriendly environment, is an important part of cognitive skill. Imaginary cases tend to reduce or eliminate that dimension of experience.

Of course, imagination has a role to play in teaching. For limited purposes, such as clarification of meaning, examples generated within imagination, or taken from literature, are perfectly acceptable. Indeed, they may be essential, for no real-world case satisfies a formal structure perfectly. But the individual engaged in learning how to criticize and apply knowledge must deal with cases in which the constraints that characterize the situation as it appears in real experience are all present. They provide the necessary experience needed to learn the level of tolerance with imperfection essential for dealing with real cases, to experience the satisfactions, and the frustrations, involved in thinking to purpose under genuine and only partly known constraints, and perhaps most important of all, to become sensitized to the major limitations that established habits impose on the individual observer.

Fourth, those who provide cognitive training should avoid the use of technical terminology that blocks the introduction of real experience into class discussions. Perhaps the best illustration of the practice to be avoided is found in statistics courses. When propositions are stated in terms of the relations between a "dependent variable" and an "independent variable" without specifying their meaning, that procedure literally forces the user to either translate or rely on formal standards or conventions for criticizing the proposition made. At best, the practice greatly complicates the task of bringing past experience to bear on the relation asserted. For example, a statement that links advancing age to public behavior (all humans tend to walk more slowly and carefully as they age) will intersect with some body of experience for nearly everyone; that experience provides one essential test of the relations asserted. But if the sentence is translated into statistical jargon, and age becomes an "independent variable" while behavior becomes a "dependent variable," or vice versa, a complex set of operations is then needed to link personal experience to the proposition—and the likelihood that experience will be used as a test of validity is much reduced if not eliminated entirely. To use experience, the user must first translate the proposition *out of* the technical jargon into everyday language in which experience is stored. At a minimum, the process of translation increases the risk of mistaking meaning. The implication, clearly, is that such translations should be made by the person who produces the assertion and not the reader or critic.

Finally, cognitive training targeted at undergraduates or students in secondary school must be supplemented in at least two important areas: formal reasoning or logical inference, and writing. Only the most rudimentary kind of assistance can be provided in a single course, or even a two-semester sequence, but the basic principles of class logic (subject-predicate relations), suitably augmented by learning to use Venn diagrams, plus familiarization with the more common of the informal fallacies (or at least being made aware of them and provided with some opportunities to learn to recognize them in real-world contexts) should be transmitted to the students if at all possible. A few pages of material dealing with logic can contribute enormously to student awareness and competence. If there is time, a summary treatment of Mill's "methods" for isolating causal relations is useful, if only because it forms the basis for much of statistical reasoning and its limitations therefore need to be understood by almost everyone.

The problems that arise in writing are much harder to deal with, for a great deal of unlearning is usually required because the kind of reading and writing that is currently being taught in the educational system is seriously inadequate. There, writing is usually treated as a single, homogeneous activity, embodied in the kind of writing found in the literary tradition. But such writing is inadequate for producing competent argument. In literary writing, emphasis is usually placed on technical matters such as punctuation, sentence completeness, the rules of syntax, and so on, or on such esthetic criteria as sentence balance, style of writing, or word choice. The substance of the writing, the knowledge claim incorporated into written propositions, is for the most part ignored. Worse, some of the strategies of exposition that are taught in literary courses are inappropriate, or even seriously counterproductive, when applied to the kind of writing needed for serious criticism—keeping the writer in suspense rather than announcing conclusions at the outset, for example.

Experience teaching students to argue has produced an alternative approach to writing that is neither complete nor fully satisfactory, but can lead to significant improvements in performance when used in conjunction with systematic reading, editing, and required rewriting of the materials.

Stripped to essentials, "argumentative" writing is judged in terms of clarity of meaning and quality of reasoning; it focuses on use of evidence, order of presentation of materials, and so on. Widely touted writing principles can be abandoned if they do not contribute to the quality of the argument contained in the writing. Thus punctuation can be ignored if meaning is clear, and even the sentence can be sacrificed to the proposition if the student prefers to write in that manner and does it well.

The resulting conception of writing (and reading) is radically different from, and in some respects incompatible with, the kind of literary reading and writing that is taught in the schools. In reading, for example, the focus of concern is the kind of knowledge claim being made, the purpose of the writer; if no purpose is found, the reading can be abandoned. In writing, Rule Number One is "have something to say about the world in which we live," either directly or indirectly. The reader should not be expected, and indeed should not be allowed, to clarify or interpret the case being made by the author. If what is written is unclear or ambiguous, then nothing can or should be made of it. Reading should be done as literally and precisely as the limits of language and perception allow; writing should proceed on the assumption that the reading will be carried out in that manner. The bridging terms, or attention-getting phrases common in the literary genre of writing, like the "harrumphs" that begin meaningless conversations, are omitted. Denouments and surprises in reasoning are not allowed. The best argument possible proceeds to continuous head-nodding from informed and competent readers—who are also reading literally. The framework employed in the writing, the order of presentation of materials, is a function of the author's purpose; that purpose is a precise inversion of the situation faced by the critic. Such principles may seem sacrilegious, but the central concern must be the use of language to communicate or criticize an argument. Until that has been accomplished, other considerations are wholly irrelevant.

Course Format for Large Classes

Experimental cognitive training began as a one-semester, lecture-tutorial graduate course with a small enrollment. It was soon clear that two semesters were required to produce a significant improvement in cognitive skill; it was equally apparent that improving cognitive skills on any significant scale would require very large classes. Traditional classroom technology was inappropriate given the peculiar character of the materials. One solution to the problem, successfully applied to classes comprising more than 500 undergraduates, is best described as a "correspondence-course-in-residence," using classes that meet twice weekly for 75 minutes. Lectures were abandoned as a teaching method. Instead the text was organized into units of 10–12 pages in length, each dealing with one basic topic. (A sample unit is contained in Appendix 4-A.) A set of questions was attached to each unit that forced the student to both restudy the central points of the unit, and integrate the abstract structure with personal or vicarious experience. The questions were answered in writing and submitted at the beginning of each class session. The written answers were corrected, with respect to both substance and writing, an assessment was recorded, and the paper was returned at the beginning of the next class period. Class time was spent discussing points that emerged from reading the questions submitted to the prior class, dealing with the questions just handed in, and answering any other questions that arose.

Various other techinques were added as the course progressed. Students were encouraged to submit written questions, to be answered in class or privately in writing, but in fact that right was rarely if ever exercised. Tutorial assistance, using undergraduates who had completed the course earlier (and done well) was made available, and widely used. Specialized units were produced and distributed to each student as needed and subsequently added to the text if they proved useful. In fact, that procedure turned out to be the most effective way by far of producing a sound textbook for the course.

Use of the format usually depends on the availability of assistance with reading and correcting papers. A class of 500 students will generate more than 1,000 pages of written material each week! The experimental course was conducted without benefit of readers, resulting in temporary near-blindness for the author. Good results were obtained in subsequent courses by training undergraduates who have already completed the course to assist with tutorials and with paper correction. If the program is just beginning, a small-scale preliminary course can be offered and the better students recruited to assist with the large course. Those students can be enrolled in a special course for which regular credit is offered by the department. Once established, that procedure guarantees an adequate supply of readers, and the benefits to both readers and enrolled students are substantial. Even if no assistance is available, students should be required to write answers to the questions. If necessary, they can be exchanged in class, corrected, a grade recorded with appropriate comments, and the paper returned. By sampling each batch, the instructor can maintain quality control and pinpoint the problem areas that need further discussion in class.

A justification for using the correspondence-course-in-residence format can be found in both general principles and the specific experience gained teaching the course. To develop their critical capacity, students must learn to be systematic and rigorous; that tends to be a slow and tedious process requiring a reexamination of the knowledge claim being criticized several times. That already commends the practice of relying on written communication as far as possible: first, because students are not habituated to such sustained concern with a single piece of written material; second, because oral-based capacity to retain complex materials precisely is both limited and unreliable. No other form of communication is as precise, stable, and accessible as the written word. There are also significant advantages for the faculty member in the use of writing as the primary mode of communication or interaction with students. Student deficiencies are easily pinpointed; the focus of discussion in the classroom is readily and accurately obtained; and the areas of the text that need supplementing, as well as the adequacy of exercise materials supplied to the students, are tested regularly. For the student, regular writing, if read systematically and rigorously, promotes more careful intellectual performance in terms of work habits, quality of writing, and, eventually, quality of argument.

The major limits on the large-class technique encountered thus far have been room size, acoustical technology, and the willingness/ability of students to adapt to the needs of large class size. The latter point is far more important than may appear at first sight. For example, in smaller classes, question time usually cues a loosening of discipline; in very large classes, the kind of casual conversation that is permissible in small classes will produce an intolerable noise level, particularly for anyone with some measure of high-frequency hearing attenuation—a commonplace as faculty ages.

Experimental Results with Large Classes

An experimental course using the correspondence-school-in-residence technique was conducted at the University of Missouri–St. Louis during academic year 1971–72 with over 550 students enrolled. Three major errors were made in the experimental design. First, an introductory political science course was used for the experiment, selected because it provided access to a control group of some 250 students in another large class. However, the students expected a course in political science, and many were aggrieved about being used as guinea pigs. Second, the attitude of the instructor in the control class toward the experiment was not checked in advance. It turned out he regarded the experimental course as a nuisance, and that attitude was reflected in the scores on the cognitive skill test, somewhat grudgingly administered at the beginning of the course. The result was cognitive skill test scores that averaged less than 22 (a clear aberration) and were therefore useless. Happily, the absence of control data turned out to be irrelevant, for the experimental group did not improve significantly, taken as a whole, from a single semester's work. Indeed, it was clear by midsemester that one term was not enough to complete the basic course—selecting a one-semester format was the third major error in the experimental design. The test scores demonstrated the depth of the mistake: the mean score for the experimental class *dropped* from 29.8 to 25.9 after the first semester. And that result is not an aberration, for the group of students who continued through the second semester vol-

Table 4.1
Experimental Class Test Scores

Student	Cognitive skill scores			G.P.A.	
	9/71	12/71	4/72	1972	1973
1	31	30	36	1.9	2.1
2	37	28	41	2.1	2.3
3	33	20	45	1.1	2.1
4	27	37	39	1.3	2.3
5	24	31	37	2.3	2.6
6	41	28	43	2.9	3.4
7	28	27	38	2.7	2.7
8	34	33	40	3.3	3.3
9	37	34	41	3.6	3.2
10	41	36	42	1.9	2.1
11	24	--	48	3.3	3.5
12	37	32	53	2.5	3.1
13	25	28	34	2.0	1.7
14	26	28	40	1.8	1.8
15	19	16	26	1.8	2.7
16	35	31	40	3.4	3.4
17	29	24	47	2.7	2.5
18	28	34	41	2.8	3.1
19	28	23	35	2.5	2.4
20	17	23	30	2.3	1.9
21	36	26	47	3.4	3.4
22	26	21	33	2.4	2.9
23	26	29	30	1.7	1.6
24	22	32	44	2.9	3.3
25	25	29	29	2.0	1.8
26	20	23	18	2.5	2.0
27	36	--	42	2.0	2.2
28	14	28	34	1.8	1.7
29	30	31	37	3.6	3.2
30	26	35	41	3.8	3.5
31	27	25	39	2.0	2.2

Cognitive skill: Possible points 80

Range: 14-53
Mean: 9/71   28.5
Mean: 12/71   28.7
Mean: 4/72   37.8

untarily, and therefore can be assumed to have made a serious effort on the test, also dropped in two-thirds of all cases and increased only very slightly in the others.

The value of the training, once a second semester was added, is clear from the students' cognitive skill test scores (see Table 4.1). The mean score for the group that completed both semesters of the course rose from 28.5 in September 1971 to 37.8 in April 1972. Almost every student in the class improved, although some did poorly in terms of course grade. So far as could be determined from interviews with the members of the class, and from reports by student/tutors, the prime factor in improving cognitive skill as measured by the test was the amount of time spent working on the course materials. Neither native intelligence (as measured by American College Testing [ACT] scores) nor skill at "grade getting," whether in the secondary school or at the university (measured by grade point averages), correlated significantly with scores on the cognitive skill test—a very important finding anticipated or, perhaps better, hoped for, on theoretical grounds.

Because the university's record-keeping system had not yet been fully computerized, it was almost impossible to make systematic comparisons of the effects of particular patterns of previous course enrollment on cognitive skill development. But in the spring of 1973, one year after the experimental class ended, records were processed to see if there was a difference in the relative effectiveness of the two courses, using conventional academic criteria—retention in school (or negatively, drop-out rates) and grade point averages. The two groups were not identical in composition: the control group contained a larger percentage of juniors and seniors (17% as against 8%); the experimental class had a much larger portion of first year students (75% as against 54% in the control). In terms of grades, the percentage of A and B students entering the class (where such data are appropriate) was about the same (23% in control; 20% in the experimental group), but the experimental group contained nearly twice as many students with D averages (31% against 17%) and a correspondingly smaller group of average (C) students (48% as against 60%). The figures, obviously, are only approximations.

Even if the improvements in cognitive skill are ignored, the superiority of the experimental method of teaching large classes is clear, whether it is measured by attrition rates or by grade point averages. Of the 205 students enrolled in the control class, only 77 percent received a grade whereas 82 percent of the experimental group actually finished the course. And if seniors who left school prior to the spring of 1973 are eliminated, 75 percent of the control class and 83 percent of the experimental class remained in school as of that date. Stratified according to class standing, the experimental class had a better retention rate at all three levels of enrollment (first-, second-, and third-year students). The difference is particularly marked with respect to C and D students, for the retention rate with the experimental group was 10 percent better with D students and 17 percent better with C students. There were, however, some surprises: two-thirds of the A students in the experimental class had left school by the spring of 1973 (without graduating)—an unexpectedly large figure.

In general, the effect of cognitive training on grade point averages was marginal at best. Such effects as were produced tended to favor weaker students, those with C and D averages, and particularly those in the first two years of university training—which suggests that students who have established a successful school technology, indicated by grade-getting performance, are less influenced by suggestions, however helpful, than students who have not yet developed such techniques.

One other point that emerged from the testing is worth noting. The results of the experimental course clearly indicated that a substantial improvement in cognitive performance required two semesters of training. But a special test administered to a small group of majors in political science, economics, and sociology at a later date brought that conclusion into question. In the test, which required no knowledge of the analytic apparatus, questions were replicated in everyday language and in the technical language of the discipline. Even students who had completed only one semester of training did much better with problems stated in everyday language than students who had not been exposed to any of it. More importantly, a high level of skill acquired explicitly in a course of training carried over into everyday problem solving (for as long as it was retained) but cognitive skill acquired implicitly (through the discipline) did not. Again, that corresponds well to theoretical expectations but the number of students was so small (only 33 altogether) that any inferences drawn from the results must be treated with great caution. At a minimum, test results suggest that ancient and dishonorable academic panacea—the need for further inquiry into the impact of such cognitive training, and its duration, on everyday performance.

The most significant finding by far with respect to education generally is that cognitive skill as defined is *not* a primary determinant of college grades, and that high school or university grades are poor predictors of the kinds of cognitive skills that the course was meant to produce. That tends to reinforce the view of cynics (like the present author) who claim that the American educational system is today almost wholly divorced from real-world affairs—whether by intention or not is uncertain and perhaps irrelevant. The data also support the charge that high school and university grades alike depend far more on capacity for recall and verbal/testing skills than on the student's ability to learn, criticize, and apply knowledge systematically.

That judgment receives further support from a detailed analysis of a selection of standard textbooks used in elementary/intermediate schools, focused specifically on the validity of cognitive claims made in and for them. Assuming that a student is extremely unlikely to acquire what is not contained in either texts or teaching, and that the teacher is more or less bound to the textbook by the logic of the classroom, the results of the analysis are extremely critical. Summarily, although such texts have appropriated the language of cognition, their content is grossly inconsistent with their claims. For example, in two major sets of texts, widely used in the United States, fewer than 5 percent of the alleged exercises in inference-making actually involved an inference. Similarly, almost all of the references to causality actually referred to imagined motivation. The texts in physical science usually consisted of endless sets of formal definitions, some fairly straightforward expositions of scientific information and/or laws, and a very small amount of thoughtful discussion. The question, "What is to be learned from the text?" is assumed as self-evident; in no case was it stated clearly, either in the students' or the teachers' editions of the material. Social science texts, on the other hand, tended to place great emphasis on asking the students "why" events occur, but said nothing about the criteria to be applied to student responses. To compound the problem, the context often suggested that "why?" was actually an utterly inappropriate question, roughly equivalent to asking "Why is a cow?"

Finally, the experimental course in St. Louis also produced, as a side effect, some measure of corroboration for the assumption that cognitive skill is almost wholly unrelated to IQ scores. The correlation between ACT scores and cognitive skill scores was consistently and at all levels below .2, which is almost meaningless. Further, the course showed that cognitive skill can be raised to very good levels (comparatively) regardless of native intelligence given sustained effort. In this respect, cognitive skill seems to resemble physical conditioning. The absolute level that can be achieved is probably limited by natural endowment, but nearly everyone can be trained to a more-than-respectable level of skill. Given the link between cognitive skill scores and real-world performance found during the testing carried out in Guatemala, Costa Rica, and elsewhere, that is perhaps the best evidence available for assuming that the kind of educated population needed for meaningful self-government is possible at scale in principle at least—though it would be both expensive and difficult to produce.

USING THE THEORY INDIRECTLY:
ELEMENTARY EDUCATION

Under some circumstances, direct transfer of the theory of knowledge to the student is inappropriate, or even impossible. Two such situations are particularly important: first, those cases where skills of a very specific kind are needed or desired (as skill at developing and using classifications is essential for airport police) and there is neither time, resources, nor good reason to provide the kind of generalized training made possible by transferring the theory itself; second, in the education of children who have not yet gained command of the language and therefore cannot be expected to deal with the kinds of abstract concepts employed in the theory. In such cases, what can be called "inferential" training is used to achieve the desired improvements: the implications of the theory of knowledge are worked out for a particular class of situations and the results are used to train students in ways expected to produce improvements in cognitive performance, which may be either general or highly specific.

The experimental work completed thus far has concentrated almost entirely on development of materials useful for improving cognitive performance in children. The principle involved, however, is precisely the same if the target population consists of adults with special cognitive needs; only the focus of concern is different. In fact, it is easier to create a cognitive training program for a specific purpose than to create a generalized program for use with children. In the former case, the effects on those who have been trained, and therefore the criteria to be used to select or create the materials, are relatively easy to specify. The appropriate criteria for use with a generalized program of education targeted at very young children, on the other hand, are much more difficult to decide and justify.

Nevertheless, there are urgent reasons for developing a program of cognitive training suitable for preliterate children. For one thing, the results of experimental courses at the university level, as well as the testing conducted at the university and in secondary schools, suggested that cognitive training should begin as early as possible. By the time the student had completed secondary school, the various factors that influence performance (study habits, reading and writing skills, self-assessment of intellectual capacity, and overall conception of the intellectual/cognitive enterprise and how to succeed within it) were already firmly established. Indeed, they were so strongly entrenched that a considerable amount of "unlearning" was required, particularly of those who were highly successful in conventional educational activities, and that proved exceptionally difficult to achieve. An examination of learning conditions and curriculum at the secondary level indicated that it was already too late at that point. A brief study of preelementary school programs sufficed to show that cognitive training was poorly suited to the rest of the preschool program, for the primary goal there seemed to be the socialization of the child to live in the company of others in relative peace and harmony. The elementary school was therefore the most reasonable starting point available.

Obtaining access to an elementary school proved difficult, mainly because of the widespread belief among school administrators that such training was already available within the school (in the curriculum, in children's television, in childrens' books and toys, and so on). A careful study of the content of the curriculum, as reflected in the textbooks used, and of what was actually taught in the classroom (using data obtained by interviewing teachers) suggested otherwise. As it turned out, the teachers were more or less constrained to rely on the textbooks, and the textbooks themselves were grossly inadequate as sources of cognitive training. In fact they could in every case be discounted almost completely, and in some cases regarded as counterproductive.

Virtually all of the texts sampled, whether they were part of the regular curriculum or regarded as extracurricular activities that contributed to overall education, were targeted at literacy, simple calculation and socialization of the child to the company of others. At best some of the rudiments of conceptualization were included in the materials, but there was no evidence of a theoretical base, and few if any signs of awareness of the need for one. The texts showed little potential for developing what is here labeled cognitive skill among the children. Thus, as noted earlier, more than 95 percent of all instruction purportedly relating to the child's capacity to make inferences actually involved no inference. Exercises claiming to improve the student's "judgment" or "critical ability" were in nine of every ten cases so vague as to be untestable, and where their content was clear the results claimed were unlikely to occur given the content of the exercise. Discussions with teachers working in elementary schools confirmed the results of analysis in quite dramatic fashion. The kinds of structures, processes, and operations needed for systematic and reasoned criticism of action proposals appeared only randomly or accidentally in their daily work. Extensive testing, at the secondary school and university levels, of both incoming and outgoing students showed all too clearly that the critical tools were not being supplied at either of those points in the educational system.

Program Design

Generalized cognitive training aimed at literate adults can and should be based on a deliberate and self-conscious effort to transfer the theory of knowledge, though it should also include exercises that facilitate recognition of knowledge claims and skill in criticizing and applying them. With children or illiterate adults that procedure is impracticable; for adults who have urgent and specialized needs, it is unnecessary and excessively time-consuming. Instead, an approach to program design is employed for which a sound good analogue is again available in athletics, where the creation and application of exercises and calisthenics meant to improve performance are routine. The basis for criticism remains the underlying theory of play but the theory is applied by the coach who designs the exercises.

The fundamental assumption underlying cognitive training is that familiarizing the student with the structures and processes required for directing actions (even though they remain unlabeled), or providing opportunities to perform the actions required for dealing with particular intellectual problems, will increase the likelihood that individual performance will improve. Familiarity, in other words, is expected to breed competence. Of course, great care is needed in structuring such exercises, and the rule that holds for theories (install a monitoring system to check for unanticipated real-world side effects) is essential here as well. For when learning is based on emulation, "what has been learned" can be highly ambiguous and may have little or nothing to do with the intentions of the designer. A good illustration is provided by the reaction of one of my former students to the experience of taking part in a United Nations simulation. Asked what he had learned by serving as a courier for one of the major powers, he responded with a surprising "How to roller skate." It seems that couriers were equipped with skates to speed message deliveries; the student's main concern was to master what was, for him, a new and intriguing activity. As every teacher knows, and every teacher sometimes forgets, what is learned by the student is not always what the instructor intended to teach.

Because of these and other hazards associated with the design requirements, cognitive training at the elementary school level places fairly rigorous demands on the teacher. The exercises generated from the theory of knowledge are usually quite general and will therefore have to be modified to fit the experience of the particular class being taught. (See Appendix 4-B and 4-C for example.) Those who develop texts and exercises intended for use in such courses can and should specify as accurately as possible the skills, habits, and attitudes expected to be furthered by use of the instrument. But the teacher must understand what is intended before he or she can adapt exercises to particular circumstances or monitor their effectiveness. That implies both a solid grounding in the theory of knowledge plus the creativity needed to generate appropriate links to the experiences of the particular set of children being taught—which can be a serious handicap when trying to introduce such courses in schools with already heavily overloaded faculty.

A further burden is placed on the teacher by the shift in emphasis required by changing from conventional texts to materials intended to develop cognitive skill—very briefly, from an orientation to "teacher actions" to a "child learning" focus. That is, training must proceed by structuring learning opportunities for the child rather than imparting information or performing specified teaching operations. However good the design of the materials may be, they are always potentially ambiguous and learning is then problematic. For the child, learning is an act of creation that takes place within the child. The teacher must therefore restructure the activity or external situation until the required act of creation occurs, and be able to recognize and encourage the result when it appears. Cognitive skill is developed by the child and not imparted by the teacher, hence the teaching entails a substantial amount of cognitive skill on the teacher's part.

One teaching technique, neither new nor revolutionary, turned out to be particularly useful for cognitive training at the elementary level. Capturing the child in a "catch me if you can" situation, best exemplified in the "chase" that appears in so many television cartoons, seems to create a competitive and demanding relation that functions very effectively as an incentive. Most children will pursue endlessly if thus challenged, spurred only by praise, teasing, and occasional success. The major problem with the technique is to keep the competition focused properly and develop an attitude of mutual forebearance; neither teacher nor students can make excessive demands on the other without destroying its value. The use of time constraints on exercises serves to heighten the tension generated by the chase, though again the demands must be reasonable. Perhaps the most difficult problem encountered in the classroom flows from the need to "externalize" the child's focus of concern. Elementary school education places great emphasis on the relation between the student's self and the external world, especially the way in which the world affects the self and the way the self reacts to it. There is a powerful tendency to solipcism built into the materials. In cognitive training, the reference objects usually lie outside the self, in the external or objective world. The aim of the training is primarily to master the relations among those external elements, or between the self and the external environment. The knowledge produced serves to relate or structure the elements in ways that are usually independent of the observer. Within the context of conventional elementary school teaching, that requires a significant shift in emphasis away from the focus of concern of the other materials used at those levels.

The substance of the exercises used for cognitive training are derived from the theory of knowledge by the same process used to generate the test of cognitive skill or to create effective calisthenics for a particular activity in athletics. Within the theory, reasoned justification or criticism of actions, whether past or proposed for the future, proceeds by organizing experience into patterns that can be used to achieve specified purposes and, through them, an overriding goal (maintaining the conditions of life of some human population). That overall goal serves as a measure of the relative significance as well as achievement. Those patterns are tested and improved in use out of experience, and that usually requires self-conscious awareness of "what is being done," stated in terms of an analytic framework. For that reason, the teacher must play a major role in the criticism and improvement of knowledge claims generated in class. Any of the structures, processes, activities, or contributing attitudes and orientations involved in the development, criticism, and use of knowledge can be incorporated into the class. The relative value of different clusters of such foci is determined empirically and pragmatically, by reference to the overall purpose that guides and controls all intellectual activity. In elementary training, primary responsibility for assessing the selection actually made will rest ultimately, and unavoidably, with the teacher.

Without attempting to exhaust the possibilities, the importance of certain aspects of the theory of knowledge is so obvious that their inclusion in *any* training program is a necessity. Thus conceptualization, measurement, the organization of experience into patterns, locating patterns within experience, awareness of costs and benefits associated with the outcomes available for choice, and calculation or logical inference, among others, will certainly be primary concerns in any cognitive training program intended for use in elementary schools. Other aspects of performance that relate strongly to successful cognitive performance, and are amenable to improvement through practice, include such things as the accuracy of perception, capacity for recall, attention span, size of the gestalt that can be handled at one time, and so on. A slightly different line of analysis suggests that the student must learn to look ahead in time, relate events over time, accept assumptions tentatively, engage in trial and error learning, make use of feedback mechanisms, develop and test strategies, link human actions to specific outcomes, and so on almost ad infinitum. All such dimensions of "what is involved" in successful cognitive performance are grist for the cognitive trainer's mill. The point, of course, is that cognitive skill is not built in a day, or in a single academic year; it must cumulate over time, and be modified and reinforced as the child matures and its experience broadens. Further, what turns out to be essential for one group may prove unnecessary with another; success with one class cannot guarantee success with the next. In that context, cognitive training is probably best construed as a beginning effort to develop habits of thinking that will endure and function effectively for a lifetime.

The Elementary School Experiment

The experimental program carried out in St. Louis at the Bel Nor Elementary School focused on six major continua, corresponding roughly to the set of skills, habits, and abilities regarded as primary determinants of cognitive skill. They were: (1) a set of prerequisites considered essential for successful training; (2) conceptualization and measurement; (3) logical calculations of various kinds; (4) organization or patterning of experience and relating such patterns to further experience; (5) systematic comparison of the outcomes available for choice-seeking reasons for preference; and (6) attitudes, orientations, and strategies useful for systematic assessment or criticism of action proposals. The various kinds of exercises were dispersed throughout the course rather than concentrated; some exercises were designed to contribute to a number of different skills. Information about the relative importance of different aspects of the process remains inadequate; much more study is needed to determine where and when to concentrate. Further, if some kinds of training are obviously antecedent to others, the best order of presentation, given the overall purpose of improving cognitive performance, is still to be learned, and that requires further efforts to improve performance in real classes.

Preparatory Training. Elementary school classes were observed for several weeks before program design was undertaken, trying to determine student capacities and limitations, class behavior patterns, the nature of the experience that provided common ground for student discussions, and so on. The conclusions reached tentatively were then checked with a number of practicing teachers before being applied. It was quickly apparent that some of the basic habits and skills needed for program success could not be assumed and would have to be imparted in the course of the training. Two points, which may be linked or related, stood out as particularly important: concentration and accuracy of perception and memory. For if a child cannot be "reached" effectively, if its attention cannot be captured and held long enough to carry out an exercise, nothing can be learned; other things equal, the longer attention can be sustained, the greater the likelihood of success. Similarly, without some capacity for accurate perception, retention, and recall, the child can hardly be expected to perform effectively in the environment.

The importance of having children "prepared to be taught," in this fairly specific sense, was unmistakable even to an outsider. The first task in any form of education is to gain the child's attention. That accomplished, exercises can be created that will stretch the attention span and enlarge the size and scope of the conceptual apparatus to which the child attends. Experienced teachers have a supply of techniques for capturing attention in this way. My own favorite is to foster a competitive emulation session— have the children imitate hand movements, for example, or produce copies of abstract figures under time constraints. Hand motions are particularly useful because they can be varied in speed and complexity over time. Other exercises for deepening the span of attention are mazes of varying difficulty, and stories of varying length that contain errors of fact, or contradictions, and thus provide the child with an opportunity to "catch" the instructor—and be rewarded with mock anguish when they succeed.

Accurate aural and visual perception, as every elementary teacher knows, cannot be assumed. But most schools focus on the physically handicapped child, leaving the "normal" child as the responsibility of the individual teacher. As it turned out, the capacity to capture and reproduce visual patterns, or to absorb and act upon aural communications, can be improved dramatically by suitable exercises. The simplest point of departure is to require the children to reproduce abstract patterns or diagrams; aural accuracy is improved using games that require physical actions based on verbal instructions. Such logical constructions as "the same as" can be introduced in the process, leading to a discussion of measurements of various kinds, and the judgments on which measurement decisions rest. The difficulty of the exercises is controlled by varying the length of stories, modifying the kinds of errors to be located, or embedding them more deeply into the context of the story, by compressing the time allowed for action, and so on. Informal teacher reports suggested that the resulting improvements carried over extremely well into other aspects of the curriculum.

The most useful exercise for stretching the memory turned out to be a variant of the system used in World War II to train pilots in aircraft identification. Flash cards were prepared containing abstract designs of varying complexity. They ranged from simple black and white figures comprising three straight lines to patterns made up of five or more lines, some curved, and drawn in two or three colors. The cards were exposed to view for several seconds (in the beginning); a few minutes later, the children were shown three cards and asked to identify the card shown earlier. As training progressed, exposure times were shortened, the complexity of the visual stimulant was increased, the mnemonic was eliminated by asking the students to actually reproduce the design themselves, and the intervening time between exposure and reproduction was increased and complicated by introducing other activities. By the end of the first four-month training period, almost all of the children were able to reproduce a three-element, two-color structure after a 20-minute time lapse with 80–90 percent accuracy. Again, there was clear evidence of a carryover into other school activities such as reading, or carrying instructions home to the parents.

Persistence, a positive and continuing response to challenge or to frustration, also proved amenable to improvement in the relatively small number of cases in which it appeared as a problem. The primary technique was to take the child's negative assessments of its own capacity at face value and use it as grounds for excluding the child from the activities of the rest of the class—and waiting. Most of the children had clearly learned that a negative response (I can't) eventually produced assistance from parents, teachers, and other adults. But if the child was packed off to another part of the classroom (excluded from further activity) it invariably returned to the scene of the action and took up the chase (whether the same result would be obtained with older children is uncertain, and perhaps unlikely). Indeed, children invented complex arguments for allowing them to return to the regular class work. A little judicious verbal support managed the rest. The technique functioned even with first grade students who had "failed" or been held back for a second year. A special class was organized when their unwillingness to integrate into the new group became a serious impediment to class learning. Use of the exclusion technique soon resolved all but one of the problem cases.

Not surprisingly, the best way to generate persistence is to introduce the child to enjoyable activity (which can be almost anything, given the omnivorous character of children's tastes) in a challenging manner. The cognitive training course itself provides a good illustration of the point: although the classes were held during the last 40–45 minutes of the school day, when the children were presumably tired and ready for rest or play, persistence proved not to be a problem once the basic activity pattern was established and the children's interest was captured. The reinforcement that came from parent interest, which increased significantly soon after the experimental class began, doubtless contributed to the overall heightening of student interest.

Conceptualization and Measurement. Concepts are the basic structures used to organize human experience, the spectacles through which the world is observed. Conceptualization, and related activities such as the development of indicators and measures, is perhaps the most fundamental, and most critical, of all intellectual functions. Problems that are stated using inadequate or inappropriate concepts cannot be solved; and in many cases, problem solving requires prior reconceptualization. Indeed, most major advances in science have hinged on the creation of new conceptual frameworks, new ways of looking at the world and its content. Beyond the concepts themselves, there must be adequate indicators (which require linking theories) and sound measures. It is, after all, unhelpful to know that anyone suffering from "Xania" will die in a fortnight unless given salt in large quantities if the symptoms of "Xania" are not known and the meaning of "large quantities" cannot be established.

When working with young children, opportunities for conceptual improvement are somewhat limited (conceptual improvements usually result from analogous reasoning from experience and children do not usually have the varied experience needed to trigger them) and improvement itself is hard to measure. But children can be introduced to such processes as conceptual transformation (without naming it, obviously) and various aspects of their conceptual flexibility and fecundity can be increased. Thus a class asked to connect an everyday event such as a fire to a citywide disaster is likely to begin by extending the fire to more and more buildings, increasing magnitudes but retaining the same conceptualization. Pressed to do more, however, various conceptual changes will emerge during discussion, perhaps by linking the fire to the destruction of food stored in warehouses, and through that to other aspects of life affected indirectly by the fire. Once discussion of such relations begins, there is a marked tendency for the connections to become increasingly roundabout and complicated as the children compete in introducing new and more bizarre routes. A parallel exercise can be created by asking the children to examine a common object such as an automobile through a variety of conceptual frameworks. Once the notion that an automobile may be "seen" as wealth, an expense, a status symbol, and so on has been grasped, and the value of the alternatives discussed, the list will be extended quite rapidly, and sometimes in quite disconcerting directions. The process should, however, be linked in the discussion to such things as the price that can be obtained for the object if sold within a particular conceptualization, and so on. Again, the children can be asked to develop a conceptual framework that will group two or more disparate things, as fruit can include both apples and pears. When such exercises were posed as contests between instructor and children, or between different subsets of the class, that proved to be an enormously stimulating and productive exercise.

The relation between concepts and indicators can be explored and extended by using a range of familiar situations in home and at school. The key is a set of questions that begin "What is the meaning of . . ." and go on to ask about something well inside the child's experience. How to interpret a large number of student absences? How can one tell that a parent is angry, or about to punish the child? Children soon learn to supply good indicators for very complex concepts, to produce indicators able to make very fine distinctions among class members, and perhaps most important of all, to identify indicators whose value is suspect, that are considered likely to lead to mistaken interpretations.

Activities designed to improve measurement capacity are readily linked to the discussion of indicators. All measures should be developed by the class rather than adapted from current practice—so long as the children are able to count, the task is feasible. Therefore, asking "Which blackboard in the classroom is largest?" and "How can you be sure?" leads quickly to the development of potential measures and a discussion of their value for dealing with that kind of question. Clocks serve as an excellent starting point for discussing dynamic measures: the prize for developing such a measure should probably go to the youngster who thought of using the corner traffic light to "clock" or to compare student running speed without actually holding a race—the students were to be timed individually using the traffic light.

Patterning. Organization of human experience to create knowledge, and fulfill purposes, requires the creation, assessment, and application of patterns—the imposition of formal structures on things observed. Those patterns capture the recurring features of experience and thus provide a means for directing actions to achieving purposes in the world—and supply the reasons for doing so. One major purpose of cognitive training at any level, then, is to generate awareness of the patterns needed to achieve particular purposes and the characteristics that make them adequate—or, more precisely, that invalidate them. Too much of the knowledge incorporated into the folklore takes the form of oversimplified, single-factor, or single-stage patterns. Such structures attribute crime to poverty, automobile accidents to drinking, wayward children to broken families, and so on. A useful antidote to such simplisticism, easily incorporated into the kind of training provided at the elementary level, is to encourage children to think of exceptions to such relational rules, and to explore complex and roundabout means of achieving particular goals that can avoid or minimize the exceptions. The child who tries to create a favorable climate before approaching a parent with a tendentious request, perhaps by feigning injury, is performing at a higher cognitive, if not a higher normative, level than the child who makes the request directly. It is probably unwise to encourage the young to prevaricate, but a healthy impulse to that kind of "conniving" or scheming is, on purely cognitive grounds at least, highly desirable.

Endless aspects of patterning can be explored in cognitive training; again, much more information is needed about the relative effectiveness of different points of emphasis. At a minimum, the student can be made familiar with the uses and limitations of static and dynamic structures, two-factor and multifactor relations, two-stage and multistage processes, and so on. Children can learn the role played by catalytic agents in reactions, or learn that knowing the necessary conditions for a change to occur can be used to prevent the event—and they can learn to use such knowledge for their own purposes. The operation of positive and negative feedback systems can be explored and some of their everyday applications identified. At a much more sophisticated level, students can learn the difference between zero-sum and nonzero-sum games, and how to convert from one to the other. And even first grade students can understand and exemplify such complex constructions as the "Prisoner's dilemma," and grasp some of their implications for individual and collective actions. In a simpler vein, static wholes can be broken apart and recombined, dynamic processes can be analyzed into their various stages, and everyday uses can be found for such knowledge. Again, children can be sensitized to the temporal aspects of change, to rates of flow, frequencies, durations, and even second-order changes (changes in change rates) and learn to identify them, exemplify them, and most important of all, to use them to deal effectively with their own everyday activities.

Most exercises in patterning are concerned with two basic types of operations. First, experience is examined for recurring patterns, and rules of change are sought that will fit the dynamics of what has been observed; second, patterns are taken as a point of departure and exemplifications are sought in experience. Usually, the imposed logic will be arithmetical, algebriac, or some form of predicate logic (children in the first grade can manipulate Venn diagrams with considerable skill after a little practice). Such exercises can be supplemented by others in which the children are asked to identify classes after a partial enumeration of attributes (simple diagnosis); such activities can be used to illustrate the pitfalls as well as the possibilities inherent in the process very dramatically.

Since relating visual patterns to experience is an important element in much intellectual activity, the children should be taught the rudiments of graphing on a two-dimensional surface. Such structures can be used to tell stories, and stories can become the basis for further pattern formation and testing. Figure 4.1, for example, can be presented as a graph of the speed of a skier over time. At point X, the skier achieves maximum speed; at point Y, the skier hits a very large tree and speed drops to zero. The class can then be asked to produce graphs of the skier's speed under different conditions (going over a cliff, for example), or other aspects of the skier's existence (fear levels, or pain). They can also be asked to use the same graph (pattern) to deal with other relationships. Children enjoy such exercises, particularly if they generate embarrassment, or even pain and suf-

Figure 4.1
Two-Dimensional Graph

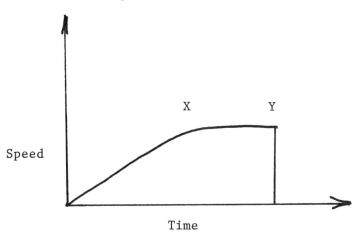

fering, for the persons involved, and become quite adept at inventing relations or information to fit patterns, or developing abstract patterns to depict given information.

Calculation, Including Probability. Calculation serves as the engine that drives the cognitive train, the dynamic element in the thinking system. That alone should suffice to justify beginning logical/mathematical instruction early and maintaining it until the student's repertoire contains everything he or she may foreseeably need in the future. The basic arithmetic program taught in the schools can be ignored (though not interfered with) by those concerned with cognitive training. It turns out to be useful, however, to discuss the basis for arithmetic since all children are familiar with its applications. Reducing the procedures to a single process—to counting, either forward or backward, in units or in groups—can encapsulate the whole of arithmetic, for decimals and fractions are simply devices for breaking units into parts that can also be counted. Such discussions can much facilitate the application of arithmetic to daily life—particularly if emphasis is placed on counting *units,* and insisting that the identity of the units counted must be clear. Further, if the teacher's reports are accurate, such practice contributes substantially to the children's ability to absorb new material in arithmetic.

In the experimental program, no logical instruction was added until the second grade, mainly out of respect for Piaget's canons about children and the use of logic. As it turned out, Piaget was grossly mistaken and logical instruction can and should be included in the first year of school. Most of the exercises actually used with second grade children were targeted at the basic concepts in Aristotelian or predicate logic, and illustrated by the use of Venn diagrams. Children very quickly grasped such notions as identity, difference, contradiction, and transitivity. The distinction between symbol and referrent was used to discuss the relation between logic and observation and proved quite useful for correcting, or even heading off, misapplications of arithmetic.

Students at the second grade level were also introduced to the basic notions of probability and risk, using ordinary dice, coins, and colored plastic balls to demonstrate meaning and implications. The concept of equiprobability was readily comprehended; the connection to distributions and probabilities was made with astonishing ease, using first a single die and then a pair. When the permutations projected for regular dice had been mastered, a pair of five-sided dice was constructed and the new probabilities were very quickly worked out in the class. To check comprehension, a game was developed in which the dice were used to distribute candy, and that provided the ultimate evidence of comprehension: the students tried to cheat. For example, if each row of students was assigned two numbers, and all students in any row whose numbers appeared on two successive throws of the dice received a piece of candy, there were almost immediate efforts to obtain unfair advantage in the assignment of numbers, and equally quick protests against them.

Sets of colored plastic balls and opaque cannisters provided a simple device for introducing such fundamental notions in logic as "all," "most," "some," and "none," and learning how to use them. It was established very quickly, for example, that "all" meant "each and every one without exception," and the implications were grasped immediately. Piaget not to the contrary, the children (age 6) performed basic logical operations with no sign of strain or uncertainty. That is, if the class was told that *none* of the balls in the cannister was green, they would assert with vigor that a given ball taken from the cannister was *not* green and provide solid reasoning to support their position. That is, the justification included explicitly the assertion that saying that "none of the balls was green" and saying that "a particular ball was *not* green," were only "two ways of saying the same thing"—their phrase for tautological.

Finally, a number of exercises were devised that made use of the skills developed in the discussions of probability. They required the students to infer from, or apply, general statements referring to their personal life experiences. The process was slow, for a linkage had to be established between a concrete situation and an abstract formula or rule, and that is very difficult for humans of any age. To illustrate, assume that a new dog enters the neighborhood. It is asserted that the dog bites. If that is all of the information available, should the student assume that the dog will try to bite him or her? What reason can be given to support or justify that assumption? What kind of statement relating to the color of the plastic balls does it resemble. What procedure was followed there? What happens if the same procedure is followed in the case of the dog? and so on. The process can then be reversed and the same situation used to explore the way in which general statements can be created and justified.

Attitudes and Orientations. The last major aspect of cognitive skill given special emphasis in the elementary school program was the development of a set of attitudes and orientations that are usefully labeled an "engineering" approach to the environment. Five specific factors were included in the training, each derived from the theory of knowledge but verified in the interviewing results obtained in Guatemala and elsewhere with high-level achievers.

1. *Orientation to intervention.* The individual who is to acquire and use cognitive skill to achieve a normative purpose in the environment must seek actively to promote improvements in the conditions of life of *some* population, either acting alone or in consort with others. One aim of training was therefore to reduce "wait and see" attitudes, the practice of treating life as purely a spectator sport, without producing recklessness. The children were encouraged to develop a healthy respect for the condition of "being alive" and to explore systematically, if in a limited way, some of the things that could improve or debilitate their present situation. The principal difficulty encountered was maintaining a decent level of reality control, keeping discussion within the bounds of real options or possibilities. Imagination appears to play an extremely important role in young children's thinking.

The second type of activity carried out in conjunction with development of an intervention orientation was to familiarize the child with multistage solutions to problems, with actions that create conditions intended to serve as a base for further actions, and so on. The training was intended to generate foresight, a habit of assessing future possibilities created both directly and indirectly by present actions. Such roundabout thinking is essential for the solution of a broad range of human problems, particularly in collective affairs.

2. *Experimental attitude.* Support for an orientation to intervention was sought mainly through systematic efforts to develop an "experimental" attitude, a willingness to act under conditions of uncertainty and use the results as a basis for justifying future actions. That attitude is a major element in the "engineering" outlook the training was meant to produce. It was most easily encouraged by focusing on problems taken from everyday life: trying to decide how to deal with a new toy, a new teacher, or a new kid on the block, for example, or by learning to learn from failure. It was fostered in more complex form by describing failures of various magnitudes and asking "What could be learned from them?" In the process, the students were also given an opportunity to learn the difference between a test and an illustration, and to determine to the minimum conditions of testability for different kinds of statements, as well as the conditions under

which different kinds of knowledge claims should be recognized—to recognize an adequately tested knowledge claim.

The heart of the experimental attitude is, of course, the propensity to look ahead in time to the consequences of present actions, including the decision to do nothing. One of the best devices available for this kind of training is the old Chinese game for two persons called NIM. Three piles of marbles (or sticks, or sets of lines on a sheet of paper) are used in the game; the piles contain five, six, and seven units, respectively. The rules are simple: the players take turns; at each turn, the player can take as many units as he or she wishes from any *one* of the piles. The object of the game is to force the other person to take the last unit from the board. Once mastered, the game can be used for a range of training purposes. It is excellent for teaching the student to anticipate future moves by the opponent before playing—to using "if . . . then" techniques. To provide opportunities to learn from failure, the instructor can begin with a pattern in which the first player is certain to lose (piles containing one, two, and three elements, for example) and have the student make the initial move. Once the game is complete, and the student has lost (publicly) the question is "What have you learned?" The first-order answer, which may take some prompting, is "Not to move first when faced with this combination." Further probing will in due course surface the need to "look ahead." The importance of looking ahead can be demonstrated by exhausting the options, then asking the students whether he or she would prefer to move first or second if faced with that condition, and why. Strategically, the information can be used to create situations in which that pattern is produced for the other player to deal with, which leads to other kinds of learning, and to other modes of strategic and tactical development.

3. *Withholding judgment.* By far the most difficult to produce of all of the attitudes needed for high-level cognitive performance is the ability to withhold judgment when the evidence is inadequate, or to recognize situations in which action cannot lead to learning. Part of the difficulty is a function of the sheer complexity of the construction required; partly it is an effect of early training in the schools. Technically, what is sometimes called "simple trial and error learning" requires a formidable set of known assumptions that can be corrected by the experience gained from the trial. The set of assumptions, and not the action, is the focus of testing and learning. Unfortunately, the point is not obvious, and not to children alone. In roulette, for example, it is widely assumed that knowledge of the odds provides grounds for betting; in fact, that is not the case. For *reasoned* or defensible wagering, the bettor must assume that a particular number or color will appear on the next turn of the wheel. It is the assumption that justifies wagering on that number. The mathematical odds indicate the likelihood that the assumption will be correct, and in the case of roulette, the information holds only over the long run. Whether the wager should

be made is determined by combining the likelihood of success with the rate of payment for the kind of wager involved. If an adequate assumption cannot be made, wagering cannot be justified. Since the mathematical odds refer only to the long run, there can be no justification for betting. Of course, people can, must, and do act in the absence of justification. But there is a difference between acting in ignorance and acting in awareness of ignorance; the latter leaves open the possibility of learning if only to identify situations from which nothing can be learned, and the former does not.

A range of techniques is available for developing awareness of the need to withhold judgment. Perhaps the most effective is also the most obvious: the student is provided with an inadequate knowledge base and asked for advice on how to proceed. A situation is described, for example, in which a young boy sees a house burning and hurries to call the fire department. He comes to a large and deep pond. There is no boat available; the boy cannot swim. Two paths around the pond are visible; one leads in each direction. Which way should the boy go? Why? Once discussion is under way, suitable impediments can be created on both paths, or it can be asserted that since the pond is frozen the boy could simply take a direct route (a not-too-subtle form of cheating likely to produce loud protests from the children). The immediate purpose of all such exercises is to add "withholding judgments" as one of the options in any choice situation, while noting that it need not preclude action. By and large, such instruction also runs counter to normal school pressures, which tend to force a response—not least because of competition for the teacher's attention. The distinction between suspending judgment and refusing to act can also be introduced and appropriate situations developed for each of those responses, and for discussing the way they relate in real-world affairs.

4. *Use of counterfactuals.* One of the best ways of developing theoretical capacity, and foresight, is to pose questions in counterfactual form: How would the present be different if the past had been different in some particular way? For children, such questions should relate to their own experience—that is, "What would be different in school today if your mother had kept you at home?" Such speculations involve the use of counterfactuals, and learning how to deal with them tends to produce invaluable habits of thinking in the student. There are two main reasons for stressing their use: first, it has been shown that an adequate solution to a counterfactual problem or question requires a valid theory, hence learning how to manage them is an important part of the theoretical enterprise; second, cognitive testing results suggest that the ability to deal with counterfactuals is the best single indicator of cognitive competence available. Since such questions are easily linked to everyday student experiences, they are a valuable, and readily accessible, training instrument.

5. *Development of policies.* A policy, or a "strategy," is a set of rules

of action that is expected to produce a preferred goal or outcome when applied. The aim of any policy is to achieve the preferred outcome with maximum efficiency, minimizing risk and optimizing costs. It follows that policies must be rooted in experience, used to anticipate and avoid or control future problems, and so on. Policies play a major role in the lives of both individuals and organizations. Development of competence in dealing with policies, of the capacity to assess them, is therefore an important part of cognitive training. At the elementary level, the range of available possibilities is somewhat limited. Exercises can be created around a variety of purposes relating to the school, the home, or the neighborhood, but they must be amenable to criticism on the basis of very limited experience— must be "obvious" to adult thinking. Thus efforts to develop a system for washing windows, or automobiles, call for a simple policy that is readily tested. Complicating the task, by asking for a division of labor between several groups, for example, calls for a more complex solution. The key to a valuable and productive exercise is the intructor's insistence that reasons be offered for expecting the policy or strategy to succeed. A simple activity, such as putting together a jigsaw puzzle, can provide a suitable base for almost endless discussion and testing.

EXPERIMENTAL RESULTS

The experimental course at the elementary level began in January 1975 with a single first grade class consisting of 30 students. It resumed in the autumn of 1976 in a second grade that contained about half of the original first grade group, and continued until the end of the 1976–77 school year. At that point, the school district conducted an evaluation of the program, interviewing all of the teachers and the parents of all students who had taken part. The evidence, though informal, was uniformly favorable: parents reported high levels of interest and much improved intellectual performance in conversations at home; teachers reported significant spillover effects in other parts of the curriculum; students indicated a strong liking for the course. The school district authorized continuation of the training, and the creation of a new program for training teachers to make use of the materials (not completed for lack of time and resources). Although the areas of improvement were not very accurately identified, both parents and teachers agreed that the effects on the children were highly desirable.

More objective data are also available to support the informal judgments of teachers and parents, and of the instructor. Children in the elementary school were at that time given the Metropolitan Learning Readiness Tests (MR) at the end of kindergarten and the Analysis of Learning Potential Test (ALP) at the end of the second grade. Both are standardized to national norms, expressed as percentiles. A comparison of student performance on these tests provides some indication of the effects of the ex-

Table 4.2
ALP and COMP Scores, Second Grades, Bel Nor, May 1975 and 1976

1975

School/teacher	# Students	ALP	COMP
Bel Nor total	77	60.47	61.38
Experimental	27	61.33	62.13
Teacher C	25	60.60	56.00
Teacher A	25	62.75	61.00

1976

School/Teacher	# Students	ALP	COMP
Normandy, total	532	50.45	- - - -
Bel Nor total	57	60.59	60.25
Experimental	19	66.25	66.00
Teacher A	20	58.00	55.50
Teacher B	16	57.50	59.50

perimental training, though it should be noted that those tests cover only a small part of the skills captured by the cognitive skill test, which is itself a weak measure of cognitive capacity. The numbers of students involved was very small; in 1975–76 the school had only 57 pupils enrolled in the second grade. Test scores for MR and ALP were available for only about half of the students; turnover rates were extremely high. Of the students for whom comparisons can be made, nine took no part in the experimental program, five received half a year of training, and five received a full year and a half of cognitive instruction.

The differences between the scores of students who took part in the experimental program and those who did not were striking. The gross differences in percentile rankings of the second grade students enrolled in the school are shown in Table 4.2. The scores of the members of the experimental group are about 14 points higher than those of the rest of the second grade students in the district, and some 10 points higher than the scores of the other second grade students in the same school. The data suggest that the differences were not due to native intelligence; the MR

Table 4.3

Change in Percentile Ranking, Second Grade, Bel Nor School, Classes of 1975 and 1976

<u>Class of 1975</u>

<u>Class</u>	MR May, 1973	COMP May, 1975	Change
Experimental			
All students	76.7	75.2	-1.5
Below 99th percentile	75.9	73.6	-2.3
Other second grades			
All students	86.7	80.0	-5.6
Below 99th percentile	83.3	76.4	-6.9

<u>Class of 1976</u>

Class/Teacher	MR May, 1974	COMP May, 1976	Change
Experimental			
All students	79.69	85.31	+ 5.62
Below 99th percentile	70.25	86.13	+ 15.88
Other second grades			
All students	67.93	71.20	+ 3.27
Below 99th percentile	65.86	69.20	+ 3.34

<u>Change by amount of Cognitive Training</u>

None	+2.9
one-half year	+4.2
One year or one and one-half years	+15.9

percentiles are lower in 1975–76 than in 1974–75, yet overall performance on the ALP was much better (66.3 compared to 60.5). Nor can the differences be attributed to teacher skill.

The clearest indication of the impact of the training on the skills measured by the standardized tests is found in the change in percentile ranking that took place between the end of kindergarten and the end of the second grade, as measured by the MR and the ALP respectively (Table 4.3). Students in the 99th percentile were eliminated, since the tests cannot measure improvements at that level. In two years, members of the experimental group improved their percentile ranking by nearly 16 percent; students who received no training improved by slightly more than 3 percent. The consistency of the changes, and the extent to which it is concentrated in the lower range of native abilities, is particularly heartening. Students who ranked *below* the 70th percentile increased their positions by 20, 23, 20, 23, and 5 percentage points in two years and there were no decreases. About half of the students in other classes who were below the 70th percentile on the MR test at the end of kindergarten actually lost ground on the ALP test two years later.

Materials were then prepared for use by one of the regular classroom teachers; the second experiment produced roughly the same kind and amount of improvement in performance. Further experiments were carried out with a small number of children (six) who were repeating the first grade, again with promising results. An effort to adapt the materials for a fifth grade class failed, mainly because the group was so large and heterogenous that it did not serve as a good teaching base—the same result appeared with respect to regular classroom instruction and the class was later broken into two parts. Unfortunately, professional commitments then intervened into what was admittedly a peripheral interest, and the experimental work had to be dropped.

NOTES

1. See Eugene J. Meehan, *The Thinking Game: A Guide to Effective Study* (Chatham House, 1988).

2. Discussion with Professor Larry Spence of the Department of Political Science, Penn State University.

Appendix 4-A
Sample Unit—University

CHOICE: INTRODUCTORY

Analytically, the quality of human life is a function of two major factors: the content of the natural environment, and human capacity for molding or shaping that environment. The natural environment sets limits to what can be accomplished, positive and negative. Rich farmland and vast mineral deposits represent a very different potential for life than icy tundras or barren deserts. To some extent, the limits that nature imposes can be evaded, and the possession of resources does not guarantee their use. The evasion depends on knowledge and technical capacity (which is also knowledge), including ethics, for both whose wants and needs and which wants and needs are satisfied depends on the way human efforts are directed and the way benefits are distributed within society.

The channel through which human knowledge is applied to the environment is the choice or action. It serves as the focus of the entire critical or analytic system. The various instruments developed in the text are those required to place human choices or actions on defensible and corrigible foundations. The form taken by each instrument, and the criteria of adequacy applied to it, are also determined by the requirements of defensible action. Thus an instrument able to project the effects of human action on the future is essential for reasoned choice and is therefore included here. It is labeled a "theory" because it corresponds fairly closely to the use of "theory" in physical science. But it is included here because the function it performs is essential for achieving the purposes for which knowledge is created. The remaining intellectual tools required for reasoned action will now be examined more closely, then brought together to show how they are actually used.

Human life is usefully conceived as an endless sequence of actions or choices. Empirical or scientific knowledge, the ability to predict and control events, is an essential prerequisite to defensible actions, but knowing what to expect, or how to produce and inhibit change, is not enough. That kind of capacity must be directed, applied in ways that are controlled by a normative or ethical apparatus. In the approach to ethics, or normative judgment, accepted here, actions are directed to maintaining and improving the human situation for some population. Three aspects of the choice process are particularly important in criticism. First, areas where action is needed on normative grounds, where the existing conditions of life are not acceptable, must be located. Second, the options available to the actor(s) concerned with the situation must be projected. Third, one of those options must be selected or preferred. Each function requires justification. The next step in the development of the analytic framework is to identify the kinds of knowledge required for reasoned choice, the kinds of instruments involved at each step, and determine how such knowledge can be produced, tested, and justified.

The overall procedure employed to generate predictions and ways of controlling events in the environment applies equally well to problems of choice or action. Human experience must be organized and generalized into patterns that can perform specified functions. Evidence obtained by applying those patterns can then provide reasons for modifying, improving, or rejecting them. In matters of choice, the critical base is provided by the human ability to react differentially to differences in the world, to prefer some situations to others. Those responses may have an affective base but they are likely to be conditioned intellectually before they can be justified. The details of the procedures required to justify preferences are explored here. The aim is to show the way in which human choices can be justified or criticized within the limits of human capacity. The focus is procedural and not substantive. That is, the goal is to clarify the way in which decisions can and should be made and not to make any particular decision.

Choice and Action

In everyday usage, the meanings of such terms as "choice," "decision," and "action" are not always clear; usage tends to be inconsistent. It is customary, for example, to speak of Smith's "choice" as either the set of options from which a choice must be made or the particular choice that has been made by Smith. Again, to "have no choice" means in some cases to be unable to act and in others to be able to act in only one way. The term "action" usually refers only to positive actions, although failure to act is sometimes included among "actions" in technical writings. The discussion therefore begins with a clarification of the meaning of basic terms as they appear in the critical framework.

The key to the meaning of action or choice as those terms are used here is an actor with the capacity to produce change. No action or choice can take place if there is no actor; if the actor has no capacity to effect change, there is again no action. An actor who has some capacity to produce change must *always* make a choice. Given capacity that can be exercised voluntarily, the actor is always faced with at least two options: failure to act, to exercise capacity, will produce one option; positive actions will produce one or more others. In that situation, action is inescapable. Put differently, capacity is both a necessary and a sufficient condition for choice. The result of action, and its indicator, is a world that is different from what it would have been had the actor exercised capacity differently. In that context, action and choice are identical, two terms that refer to the same thing.

That approach to choice allows us to concentrate on the set of outcomes or options that lie within the actor's capacity. The term "choice" can be used to refer to the full set of outcomes available to the actor or to the process of selecting one of those options. Preference will refer to the option selected; reasoned action serves to produce the preferred outcome. Criticism of a positive action and criticism of the intellectual processes by which a choice is made involve precisely the same set of considerations—they are analytically or critically identical.

An actor with the capacity to change the environment will be able to produce two or more outcomes if capacity can be exercised voluntarily. The results of action, the content of the outcomes, can be projected, in descriptive terms, by an appropriate set of theories. The projection will appear as the set of values expected to be taken by a given set of variables. Choice or action requires a preference for one set of values for those variables over another set of values for the same variables. An actor able to move a large stone, for example, can choose from among a number of different physical positions to place the stone. Those possibilities must be compared, seeking reasons for preferring one of them—those reasons serve as a justification for the preference. The same requirements must be fulfilled if the actor simply moves the stone to the preferred position and then offers a justification for the action. The substance of the justification will be precisely the same in either case. That is the sense in which choice and action can be collapsed analytically. It follows additionally that the consequences of action or choice can always be expressed in the general form "This set of values for that selection of variables *rather than* these other sets of values for the same variables." In symbolic terms, if there are two options, A and B, then the consequences of the choice or action can be stated "A *rather than* B." Preferences are based on comparison, and they are limited to the specific set of options available for choice.

The options available to an actor are the consequences to be expected from the actions lying within the actor's capacity at a given time and place. Because the outcomes always lie in the future, a theory is required to project their content. The projection will be stated in descriptive terms but it will not be a description—only an anticipated description. Because the content of the options is a function of the actor's capacity, it can be determined objectively. That is, capacity determines outcomes and is independent of the actor's awareness, intentions, and other subjective states. If one of the effects of war is a serious reduction in the supply of talented young persons, then that *is* a consequence of war; whether it was intended, recognized, sought after, or even taken into account by those who make such decisions, is irrelevant. Unless the object of inquiry is to criticize the actor, there is no need to inquire into awareness or motives. The focus of criticism is always the substance of the choice, the selection of one outcome in preference to specified others. The identity of the actor need be known only to determine the extent of capacity.

To avoid needless complications, criticism is limited strictly to actions and choices carried out by living humans. Dogs and cats may "choose" one food in preference to others, but they cannot generate the kinds of justification required for reasoned choices. True, dogs can be conditioned to select food that is more nutritious if less palatable than the alternatives, but in such cases, the "choice" is actually made by the person who does the conditioning. For similar reasons, acts of nature such as floods and hurricanes, although they produce very significant changes in the human situation, are not amenable to criticism. There is no element of human choice or direction in such events. Of course, the individual who knows that a hurricane is approaching but fails to warn the neighbors has made a choice that *is* open to criticism, but "condemning" hurricanes is only abusing language. When the actor cannot be identified, the available options cannot be determined, and criticism is impossible. That can lead to serious difficulties, as in dealing with such collective bodies as legislatures, where the alternatives may be difficult to determine because of the decision-making procedure employed. If each member of a collective body can only choose whether to vote for a measure, vote against it, or abstain, no individual makes the collective choice. That decision is made by aggregating individual choices and applying a formal rule. Actions of such collective bodies therefore come very close to being in the same class with floods and hurricanes—"acts of nature" of a peculiar kind.

The options included in a choice must be real and attainable. It would be merely silly to speak of "choosing" to fly by flapping the arms, or "choosing" not to die if that is the ultimate fate of all living things. Neither the necessary nor the impossible is a part of choice. Ideals and utopias can therefore play only a very limited role in human actions; if they cannot be achieved, they are not available for choice. Worse, if they cannot be achieved, there is no way to determine whether or not a particular action moves actor or society closer to or further away from the ideal. That is, if the route from city A to city B is unknown, there is no way to determine whether or not any particular step is a "step in the right direction." That requires knowledge of the complete route.

Finally, the objective here is to develop an approach to choice that refers to a significant form of human behavior and can be improved out of human experience. If choice occurs at every exercise of human capacity, real or potential, the significance of the focus could hardly be greater. If the quality of choosing and acting is to improve, instruments are required that can be justified out of experience and tested against experience. They must lie within human capacity. If reasoned choice or action depended on attributes available only in deities, humans could not make reasoned choices. Moreover, the approach to choice should allow commonplace materials (such as you or I), to become competent critics. No certain grounds for choice or action can be created, but systematic analysis should be able to produce a level of agreement more than adequate for an ongoing society seeking to improve normative performance, or for an individual with the same objective in mind.

The Critical Focus

Choices or actions involve three primary elements: an actor, a choice or action, and a set of consequences flowing from the action. In principle, criticism could focus on any one of those elements or on a combination of all three. In practice, choices *must* be criticized by reference to consequences.

Given a commitment to using human actions to improve the conditions of life of human populations, the strongest reason for insisting that choices be justified or criticized by reference to consequences is that the alternatives will not work. Efforts to justify choices by referring to either the characteristics of the actor or to the qualities of the action produce anomalies and inconsistencies that destroy their value. What is called *ad hominem* reasoning (argument addressed to the attributes of the person) is today rejected almost everywhere. The intentions of the actor are equally irrelevant to systematic criticism of choice because of the absence of any necessary relationship between intention and outcome. Humans frequently intend one outcome and produce another, or produce what is intended but for the wrong reasons. Worse, humans often act without knowing why they act, knowing what effects their actions are likely to have, or even without knowing they are producing an effect on themselves or on others.

The problem cannot be evaded by depending on the ethical characteristics of the individual actor. There is at present no agreed way to identify a "good" or "moral" person (or action), but even if that could be done, it would not provide an adequate basis for action. If all the actions performed by a "good" person had to be accepted, that would be tantamount to considering every operation performed by a "good" doctor to be successful—which is merely absurd. Since the effects of action cannot be ignored or avoided, even if they are not used as the principal basis for justification and criticism of action, focusing on the attributes of the person would lead unavoidably to anomalies and inconsistencies—either approving or disapproving precisely the same action, with precisely the same effects, because of the person involved. Efforts to judge outcomes on the basis of actions taken lead to the same result. Neither position is acceptable.

That leaves only one possible alternative: justifying or criticizing actions by reference to their consequences. Happily, an adequate critical procedure can be developed on that base. It depends on a systematic comparison of the content of the outcomes from which choices are made, carried out in the context of past experience with those outcomes. No more than a comparative rule of preference is needed: "Prefer A to B, C, or D," for example. In everyday affairs, judging actions by their consequences is common practice, although use of such justifications has been inhibited to some extent by the old homily that disparages it because "it implies that the end justifies the means." That is a curious kind of criticism, for if the outcome cannot justify efforts to achieve it, what else possibly could? The confusion lies in an improper inference attached to the old adage. Particular ends do not justify every and any means used to achieve them; that would be possible only if a doctrine of absolute ends were accepted, and that is not the case here. Instead, the "end," to the extent that one can speak of such things, is taken to *include* all of the effects of the means used to achieve it—and that effectively resolves the problem.

Comparison As the Basis for Preference

Every action or choice depends on the capacity to produce change. The difference produced, or the absence of a difference when it could have been produced by using capacity, provides the leverage needed to criticize the action. By comparing the outcomes that could have been produced by action, using an accepted normative system, reasons may be found in past experience for preferring one to the others. If not, then the choice is a matter of indifference given the accepted ethic. If reasons for preference are found and asserted, they become the focal point for subsequent argument, clarification, and potential improvement. Of course, not every human action is reasoned. What identifies a reasoned choice is the element of deliberate comparison of outcomes, the consideration given to the positive and negative aspects of the available alternatives. When a choice is reasoned, some justification for preference can be produced; that justification fulfills the necessary conditions for further improvement in the future.

The concept of a reasoned choice accepted here is very weak and easy to satisfy. Even the most perfunctory weighing of outcomes, and the most trivial of reasons for preference, satisfies the requirements. The quality of the reasoning can vary widely. Alternatives may be ignored; calculations may be mistaken; the theoretical apparatus may be flawed; the level of uncertainty attached to the projections may be overlooked, and so on. But the process of reasoning, of offering a justification for choosing a particular outcome from a set of known alternatives, opens the way to criticism of the argument, and that is all that can be expected or required. The individual who offers no justification for a choice is immune to systematic criticism but also without any capacity to convince others. Once reasons are proposed, their adequacy can be questioned, omissions can be identified, the implications of the choice explored, additions proposed, and so on. In the process, the justification can be strengthened, modified, or rejected. Whether in physical science or in normative argument, the processes required for improvement are set in motion when reasons are offered to support an assumption. The process of giving reasons allows the reasoning process itself to be improved.

For the rest, the development of normative knowledge follows the pattern already established with respect to empirical inquiries. The instruments needed to make choices are created as solutions to particular cases; such solutions, suitably generalized, become a solution for a class of cases exemplified in the particular. The instruments created need only compare the content of the options; there is no need for an external measure that can be applied to each outcome independently—that would be a much more formidable task. Over time, a system of priorities can be created that summarizes and rationalizes the solutions that have been produced for particular problems in the past, and the modifications introduced as a result of further experience. That structure, which is properly termed an individual's or society's *ethic*, can be examined for internal consistencies, and for implications, and thus generalized, and strengthened (or weakened) further. In a sense, society's mores reflect such generalized solutions to choice problems encountered earlier in history. The problem with mores is the tendency to ossification that goes with their sheltered or privileged status; criticism of the basic mores of society is usually a very difficult task.

As in theorizing, the procedures used to create solutions to choice problems cannot be formalized, but strategies of proven value can be developed for testing and improving such solutions once they have been proposed. The critic's task, like the chooser's task, is to examine choices systematically, in the context of past experience, seeking significant omissions, inconsistencies, and ambiguities, suggesting new aspects of the human situation that ought to be taken into account when choices are made, pointing to new possibilities that arise out of increased human capacity, and suggesting modifications in the apparatus presently in use. In each case, the reasons offered to support either actions or criticisms of action will link the choice to the analytic requirements for reasoned choice (will take into account the methodological dimensions of the problem), and to the substantive body of past experience. Both are essential.

EXERCISES

Review Questions

1. What are the two primary factors that influence the quality of individual life in modern society?

2. Explain why choice is defined by reference to an actor's capacity to produce change and not in terms of intentions or behavior.

3. Why are choices and actions analytically identical?

4. State the basic form in which the consequences of action or choice are expressed.

5. Why are the consequences of action, rather than the attributes of the actor or the actions, used as a basis for criticizing and justifying actions?

6. What advantages are gained by basing choices on a comparison of outcomes rather than on such external criteria as "goodness" or "justice?"

7. What are the identifying characteristics of a "reasoned" choice? Why is that definition regarded as "weak?" What implications follow from using such a weak conception of the term?

Discussion

1. If the conditions of human life are a function of the content of the natural environment and the knowledge available for dealing with it, under what conditions can a population optimize its potential?

2. Why is choice, as a process, so important in determining the quality of particular lives?

3. Discuss choice as a device for integrating empirical and normative knowledge.

Appendix 4-B
Sample Units—Elementary

GRADE 1, UNIT 1

Purposes: Increase perceptual accuracy (visual) memory extension

Time: 30–40 minutes

Materials: Set of four memory cards, two identical
Student work sheet
Crayon or pencils

Exercise 1

Draw an abstract figure on the blackboard, using a straightedge, such as the following:

Ask the class to copy it exactly. Allow time. Set aside temporarily. Ask what COPY means. Ask what IDENTICAL means (exactly the same).
NOW:

1. Draw the figure in the same pattern but much LARGER. Ask: Is that a good copy? Is it identical? Discuss. Why faulty? How to improve?

2. Draw the figure SMALLER. Ask questions as in 1.

3. Draw the figure to the right scale, but distort the elements. Have class criticize and correct.

4. Draw as accurately as possible, but freehand. Then ask if it is correct? How can it be checked?

5. Draw a square reference frame around the figure. Measure the distances from the frame to the figure, to show how it can be used to make more accurate measurements.

6. Add cross-hairs to the frame. Remeasure.

7. Discuss: The impossibility of making PERFECT copies. How to decide whether or not it's close enough? If time, discuss use of rulers, compasses, and so on.

The children can now be given the worksheet, which contains five patterns to be copied. Emphasize the need to make the copies as EXACT as possible. Allow as much time as possible, then collect and examine (return the next session).

Exercise 2

Select one of the identical cards. Explain that they will be shown one card, and asked to identify it later. Make it clear that you do not believe they will be capable of doing this. Then display the card for perhaps 10 seconds; turn face down on the desk. There is an arrow on the back to show the UP direction.

NOW: Return to Exercise 1. Collect papers. Discuss problems. Use perhaps five minutes on such activity.

NOW: display the three other cards and ask the students to identify the one that was displayed earlier. Each student can be asked to write the correct number on a piece of paper. Then identify the card. React strongly. The process should mark the beginning of an endless CHASE, if possible. If there is time, do another card; if not promise more in future.

GRADE 1, UNIT 14

Purposes:	Following verbal instructions
	Memory training
	Transitivity/consistency
Time:	20 minutes
Materials:	Exercise sheet
	Crayon/pencil
	Two cards: 2-element and 3-element

Exercise 1

Display *both* memory cards for about 10 seconds. Cover.

Exercise 2

Challenge class to complete the following exercise as accurately as possible:

Worksheet XX

_____

(Name)

1

2

3

4

5

----

1. Write name at top of exercise sheet.

2. In the square at the bottom right-hand corner of the page:

   place a cross in the upper right hand corner AND a circle in the center. (Wait then say STOP.)

3. In the square at the top right-hand corner of the page:

   place a cross in the center AND a small circle in the upper right hand corner.

4. In the square at the top left hand side of the page:

   place a cross in the upper right hand corner AND
   a cross in the upper right hand corner AND
   a circle in the bottom right-hand corner.

5. In the remaining square:

   place a circle in the top right-hand corner, AND
   a circle in the center AND
   a cross in the top left-hand corner.

Have the students exchange papers and go over the correct answers. Praise anyone who had a perfect paper, near-perfect paper, and so on.

Exercise 3

Explain that you are going to tell them some things about people they do not know; they must try to remember everything because you will ask them about it again. First:

   John is taller than Mary
   Mary is taller than Susan

Exercise 1

Have them draw the two figures on the back of the exercise sheet.

Exercise 2

Is John taller than Susan? What makes you think so? Review the information.

Exercise 2A (if time). "Arthur is wearing a red shirt. James' shirt is brown. Edward is wearing sneakers. Is Arthur taller than Edward?" (Withhold judgment.) Further data: "All persons wearing brown are taller than those who wear red. Now answer?" (Still not possible.)

Exercise 2B (if time). "Edward lives farther from school than Mary. Thomas lives one block closer to school than Francis. Mary passes Francis' house on the way to school. Who lives closest to school, Edward or Francis? (Ans: Francis.) Why do you think so?" If there is time, work the problem out on the blackboard. Or have the students chart the data.

These exercises may be elaborated almost ad infinitum if the students find them too easy, and if there is plenty of time.

5

Summary and Conclusions

Given the set of fundamental assumptions on which the approach to cognitive performance taken here depends, a range of conclusions can be justified from the theoretical and experimental work thus far completed. Most important, if cognitive skill is identified with individual capacity to acquire, assess, and apply knowledge of the kind required for directing actions on defensible grounds, and if the theory of knowledge set forth in Chapter 2 captures the essential preconditions for success, then cognitive skill or cognitive competence, which includes the ability to criticize claims to knowledge both methodologically and substantively as well as empirically and normatively, is an essential precondition to consistently successful real-world activity. That conclusion can be expected to hold for both individual and collective actors, regardless of the kind of activity involved or of the cultural, ethnic, racial, or other attributes of the actor. Very roughly, the sets of assumptions incorporated into the theory provide the foundation for the approach to testing and improving cognitive performance adopted for, or, more precisely, developed in the course of, the present inquiry. The apparatus is fairly clear and simple, wholly general in application, and because it is inductively based, can be tested against personal experience by anyone who wishes to do so.

The overall apparatus has been validated, tentatively and partially, through the major second-order assumptions implied or required by the theory of knowledge. Although both the test of cognitive skill and the programs for improving it remain in a relatively crude and undeveloped state, and much refinement and analysis remains to be done, the validity of the basic con-

cept of cognitive skill seems to be well established and the primary implications of the approach, taken as a whole, are clearly very important. Three
types of tests have been applied to the overall approach; in each case, the
results have been highly favorable. First, because the theory of knowledge
is inductively based, a test or measure of cognitive skill derived or extrapolated from it should both account for and predict high levels of individual
achievement consistently and accurately. Second, education programs based
on the theory should lead to reliable and significant improvements in cognitive skill, both as measured by the test and as reflected in real-world
performance. The first of these requirements has been met; the second has
not proved amenable to practical test and remains to be carried out at
scale over time. Third, the individual's capacity to deal critically and effectively with real-world knowledge claims should be greatly enhanced—assuming that a valid measure of performance can be created. The evidence
for the third point has been supplied by a variety of graduate and undergraduate classes, at my own university and elsewhere, in which the tests
employed were far more detailed and sophisticated than the generalized
test of cognitive skill. The two primary limiting conditions encountered
thus far in such cognitive education have been that instruction must be
performed by someone fully competent in the theory of knowledge; and
the student must make a serious effort to absorb and apply the analytic
apparatus.

With respect to individual cognitive skill, narrowly construed, a number
of significant conclusions can be drawn from the evidence and reasoning
set forth in Chapters 3 and 4. First, cognitive skill levels are virtually independent of IQ scores and grades-getting skills (as indicated by grades
actually obtained in either the university or in secondary school). Second,
critical capacity with respect to the application of knowledge (policymaking) can be developed to a very good level (compared to the skill levels
attained by high-level achievers in the environment), regardless of the individual's natural intellectual endowment, given reasonable expenditures
of time and effort on the student's part. Third, cognitive skill acquired
through the various experimental education programs was not field specific; it apparently carried over well, both into other fields of study and
into the conduct of personal affairs—though the evidence on the latter
point is both sketchy and anecdotal. Fourth, virtually everyone can be educated to an acceptable level of cognitive competence, and the materials
needed for such education are readily adapted to very large classes or to
computerized and other forms of self-instruction. It need hardly be added
that these findings are particularly important for any self-governing society
seeking to educate its citizenry to a level of competence adequate for controlling the conduct of collective affairs.

Somewhat more generally, three of the primary implications of the overall approach to the measurement and improvement of cognitive skill are

particularly important for improving the quality of intellectual consumership within society. First, it underscores in a very useful way the kinds of normative judgments required for the conduct of human affairs and their role in the acquisition, assessment, and application of knowledge. And it provides a way of introducing the student to the normative dimension of inquiry that is in large measure independent of any particular ethical system. So long as the commitment to justification is maintained, the source of the priorities actually applied to choices is irrelevant. Second, it tends to moderate the excessive emphasis on formal logical procedures that has characterized the philosophy of science, and to a lesser extent analytic philosophy, in the recent past. Third, it supplements or compensates for the restrictions placed on formal logical reasoning in inquiry by calling attention to the role that nonformalizable human judgments play in intellectual affairs and suggesting a way of evading their limitations. Fourth, it both requires and makes possible the kind of methdological criticism that is essential for adequate assessment of knowledge claims, and thus for improving the knowledge supply systematically and effectively.

The line of reasoning that supports those conclusions is as follows: if human actions can be criticized only by reference to purposes sought, then every system of thought, and every body of existing knowledge, rests on a commitment to some overriding or ultimate purpose to serve as an adjudication base in the event that purposes, or the means of attaining them, come into conflict. It follows that every body of knowledge that is meant to be both useful and corrigible or defensible out of human experience requires a commitment to some set of normative assumptions, as a commitment to justification from experience forces reliance on judgments. Of the normative assumptions required for the enterprise, two are particularly important yet relatively uncontroversial: first, the ultimate goal of every human action to be defended out of experience is to maintain or improve the conditions of life of *some* human population; second, in the limited sense of life *qua* life, one human life is equal in weight or worth to any other—that departures from equal weighting or treatment must be justified. Those two assumptions, plus their corollaries, provide an adequate point of departure for dealing effectively with most problems of choice.

Without minimizing, not to say eliminating, the importance of formal logic or mathematics in systematic inquiry, the approach to cognitive improvement does limit its role or function, partly by precise identification of its role or function in the development, assessment, and application of knowledge and partly by stressing the absolute need to rely on nonformal processes. Some apparatus able to calculate the implications of accepting certain sets of propositions, one or more of which are generalized in form, is essential for reasoned direction of action; directing actions on defensible grounds requires the application of a set of generalized assumptions that must be corrigible over time, and "application" without some capacity for logical calculation is simply impossible. Indeed, it is reasonable to construe knowledge as a special form of applied logic or mathematics. The critical point here is that the application of logic or mathematics to the world of experience is not itself a problem *within* logic but a problem in the *use of* logic, which is quite a different matter cognitively speaking. At some stage in the effort to justify knowledge claims of any sort, logical inference must be replaced by or supplemented with argument—the process of finding reasons for accepting a set of propositions that are persuasive to the body of informed opinion of the time, with all of the complications that implies. Argument is in effect a procedure or process in which those involved are forced to articulate the assumptions and evidence on which their position depends to the fullest extent possible, step by step. The limitations on the role of logic apply not only in normative affairs but in "scientific" inquiries as well. For that reason, among others, the approach implies that such disciplines as medicine, athletics, or agriculture provide a better emulation model for the intellectual enterprise than physics, astronomy, or chemistry—the so-called hard sciences.

Perhaps the most important conclusion to be drawn from the inquiry is also the most general: agreement on a set of fundamental assumptions, a theory of knowledge, of the kind set forth in Chapter 2, is one of the primary imperatives of intellectual life. Far more is involved than developing a mechanism for eliminating or reducing internal inconsistency. Without an agreement at the level of fundamental assumptions, criticism and improvement, or even argument in general, are effectively ruled out. For if there is no agreement on a set of fundamental assumptions, arguments cannot intersect, hence it is technically impossible to determine whether agreement or disagreement among the parties to the argument is genuine. The set of basic assumptions comprised in the theory of knowledge accepted by the individual are an integral part of *every* knowledge claim, and of every argument, whether or not they are identified by those involved. Put in slightly different terms, the significance of inconsistency in argument is well established; consistency in turn can be tested *only* through the set of generalized assumptions incorporated into the propositions whose consistency is in question. The theory of knowledge, in other words, serves as the essential *integrating* mechanism for the knowledge system as a whole; it provides the essential connections and assumptions needed for controlling the quality of the knowledge that is created and applied by those who accept it.

Within that general framework, the results obtained from the cognitive skill test can be regarded primarily as a way of legitimating, or establishing the validity and usefulness of, the concept of cognitive skill or competence. Such evidence also provides indirect support for the underlying theory of knowledge, but the theory can be defended by reference to a much stronger and more detailed body of evidence and reasoning. That is not to say that the theory of knowledge should be regarded as sacrosanct, or that it is part of a deductive enterprise; the structure is inductively based, and directly contingent upon the particulars of human experience. The additional evidence for the theory of knowledge comes primarily from its capacity to account for what has been accomplished where human accomplishments are well known and widely agreed (as in physical science), plus its potential for generating ways of improving performance in areas such as ethics or aesthetics as well as in the empirical disciplines. Most important of all, the theory is formulated in terms that permit individual testing against personal experience.

Construed very broadly, the approach to cognitive skill testing and improvement proposed in the text offers a possible solution to what is probably the most urgent problem in contemporary education: how best to prepare the youth to deal adequately and effectively with present and future problems, individual and collective, in an optimal way when the specific nature and content of those problems remain uncertain. The urgency of present need, whether it is expressed in terms of "problem solving," "creativity," or "critical thinking," is widely recognized. As cognitive competence is defined, only a tiny fraction of the human population, not excluding the well-educated members of the highly developed industrialized societies, can be considered adequately trained or educated. Even if analytic or methodological competence is left aside, most of the human population must be regarded as cognitive cripples. The extent of the problem tends to be masked within industrialized society by the availability of prefabricated responses to a wide range of situations within the culture—solutions to problems that can be withdrawn from the memory bank and applied more or less as conditioned responses. What is much more worrisome is the extent to which existing institutional arrangements are characterized by similar incompetence, and the evidence that suggests they are becoming gridlocked, incapable of improving themselves or of being improved by external forces. That is particularly true of the media, the political system, the educational system, and even some of the more highly developed of the physical sciences. As Professor James T. Bonnen notes in a recent paper, "the training and values of much of academic science are undermining the society's capacity for problem solving, while the need for such capacity grows more intense."[1] At the very least, the problem is far more serious in the 1990s than was the case when these studies first began in the late 1960s, if only because the need for competence is increasing almost exponentially, particularly for citizens of the self-governing industrial societies.

Systematic and critical examination of the quality of the intellectual activity that characterizes present-day industrialized society does not allow complacency or even optimism with respect to the future. There is little evidence of significant progress in recent decades in such important areas as intellectual consumership (capacity for criticizing knowledge claims), and there is some reason to think that present-day institutions actually inhibit improvement of the educational system. All of the objective criteria one can discover lead to pessimism. The quality of public discussion of public issues, whether in legislatures, in the bureaucracy, or in the media, remains extremely poor. The arguments produced by major figures in public life for matters of tremendous importance border on the ludicrous. The "vast wasteland" of television has been aptly titled so far as the quality of its cognitive content is concerned. The students in the secondary schools are for the most part cognitively incompetent; the university, so far as can be determined, adds little to cognitive skill or competence, though it does provide additional information and the opportunity for the highly intelligent and motivated to acquire cognitive skills (not necessarily those that are most needed, of course), sometimes despite the faculty and the curriculum.

In those terms, the theory of knowledge offers a base of resolving, if only temporarily, a number of long-standing disputes among educators about the nature and purpose of education—by providing a clear and unequivocal meaning for knowledge and a body of reasoning and evidence linking skill in the use of such knowledge to real-world performance. The theory cannot resolve the problem directly and substantively, but it can specify the kind of solution that is necessary and possible, and suggest ways of producing it. Last but not least, by showing why no final solution to such questions is possible, why *all* solutions are only temporary, it can help reduce the influence of dogmatism, and thus contribute to the elimination of outmoded and potentially dangerous nonsense from the body of assumptions currently accepted by the bulk of the society.

The apparatus thus far created, to repeat, requires a great deal of refinement and extension. Some of the more important of the required future inquiries relate to the nonscholastic effects of cognitive training and testing. In part, progress in those areas is likely to be contingent upon the development, or articulation, of criteria for assessing human intellectual performance that go well beyond what is available at the present time. A second fundamental requirement is for additional analysis of the substance of the generalized cognitive test to increase its diagnostic capacity and to create tighter links between the elements measured by the test and real-world individual requirements of particular kinds.

Beyond such relatively specific implications, there are various areas of human affairs where the approach to cognitive skill measurement and improvement, and the theory of knowledge from which they were derived, seem likely to have great potential value. Three in particular deserve careful attention: first, there is some reason to believe that mastering the theory of knowledge contributes to the enhancement of individual creativity, or at least increases the likelihood that it will appear;[2] second, the potential use of the apparatus for training teachers, and the teachers of teachers (not excluding those who "profess" at universities), needs careful exploration; and third, there is also some evidence to suggest that those who are provided with generalized cognitive education are thereby "readied" for additional training, particularly at the place of employment—that what might be called "general trainability" is increased.[3] Such points of emphasis are additional, of course, to further inquiry directed to ways of improving both cognitive testing and education or training in specific ways. Thus the duration of training effects, the relations between different kinds of cultural norms and the value of cognitive training, and the manner in which training can be reinforced institutionally, all deserve careful attention, among others.

NOTES

1. James T. Bonnen, "A Century of Science in Agriculture: Lessons for Policy Science," *American Journal of Agricultural Economics,* 68 (November–December 1986).

2. See, for example, Eugene J. Meehan, "Educating the Gifted to Use Their Gifts," *Gifted International,* 4, no. 2, (1987), and "Improving Critical Judgement in Science," in L. D. Gomez P., ed., *Creativity and Teaching of Science* (San Jose, Costa Rica: Consejo Nacional de Investigaciones Cientificas y Technologicas [CONICIT], 1983).

3. See Eugene J. Meehan, "Cross-Cultural Translation: Problems and Possibilities," in *Revista Internacionale de Philosophia,* forthcoming.

Bibliography

EVOLUTION OF THE THEORY OF KNOWLEDGE

Because of the centrality of the theory of knowledge in the argument, and because that theory has been modified significantly as a result of efforts to explore its implications for education, and to use it as a base for cognitive education and testing, a brief guide to the evolution of the theory and its applications in my own publications may prove helpful.

The point of departure in the early 1960s was a more or less conventional effort to apply then-current philosophy of science to the methodological/epistemological problems of the social sciences—published as *The Theory and Method of Political Science* (Dorsey Press, 1965), and supplemented by an application to contemporary political thought, published as *Contemporary Political Thought: A Critical Analysis* (Dorsey Press, 1967). Efforts to apply the conception of theory and theorizing implicit in the philosophy of science of the time very quickly surfaced its inadequacies, with respect to both empirical and normative inquiries. The modifications introduced into the empirical and normative aspects of the theory as a result of the failure of applications were published first as *Explanation in Social Science* (Dorsey Press, 1968) and *Value Judgment and Social Science* (Dorsey Press, 1969), then combined into a single volume: *The Foundations of Political Analysis: Empirical and Normative* (Dorsey Press, 1971).

The theory incorporated into the *Foundations of Political Analysis,* which now differed significantly from conventional philosophy of science, was tested fairly rigorously in the 1970s, first in education and then in the conduct of public affairs (policymaking). A graduate course based on the revised theory was taught regularly at the university level, and was monitored carefully. Further experimental classes, at both the university and elementary levels, were conducted in the early part of the 1970s. The use of the theory for improving performance in collective affairs was examined in two ways: first, as an aid to policymaking, in a close and mutually beneficial partnership with the Inter-American Foundation, a federal development agency located in the Washington, D.C. area; second, as a critical base, embodied in a sustained study of the national public housing program as it emerged in the city of St. Louis.

Very little of the material on the use of the theory in education has been published. A Spanish version of the unitized text meant for use in large classes was translated and published in 1976 by Editorial Trillas in Mexico City as *Introducción al Pensamiento Critico*. A second version was translated and published at the University of Costa Rica, together with a general introduction to the underlying rationale for the cognitive development program—the forerunner of this volume. Applications of the theory to governmental performance, and to policy analysis and criticism particularly, produced a considerable body of written materials, of which the more important were two studies of public housing policy: *Public Housing Policy: Myth Versus Reality*, published by the Center for Urban Studies at Rutgers University in 1975, and *The Quality of Federal Policymaking: Programmed Failure in Public Housing*, published in 1979 by the University of Missouri Press. The critical apparatus was also applied to the most highly regarded of the social sciences—economics—and the results published as *Economics and Policymaking: The Tragic Illusion* (Greenwood Press, 1982). The experience gained teaching graduate students produced a revised version of the earlier university-level text, published by Greenwood Press in 1981 as *Reasoned Argument in Social Science: Linking Research to Policy*. A much more efficient text for large classes of university-secondary school students appeared in 1988: *The Thinking Game: A Guide to Effective Study* (Chatham House).

The 1980s were spent trying to develop a more useful and usable alternative to the normative theories currently available in philosophy, or to the kind of cost-benefit analysis practiced by economists. The end result was a major revision of the traditional approach to normative practice, published as *Ethics for Policymaking: A Methodological Analysis* (Greenwood Press, 1990), and intended to demonstrate the kind of apparatus needed for directing human actions and suggest how it might be created and validated or argued.

BACKGROUND READING: A SELECTED LIST

Methodology and/or Reasoning

Aleksander, Igor, and Piers Burnett. *Thinking Machines: The Search for Artificial Intelligence*. Knopf, 1987.

Ascher, William. *Forecasting: An Appraisal for Policy-Makers and Planners*. Johns Hopkins University Press, 1978.

Ashby, W. Ross. *An Introduction to Cybernetics*. Science Editions, 1963.

Bailey, Norman A., and Stuart M. Feder. *Operational Conflict Analysis*. Public Affairs Press, 1973.

Ball, Terrence, ed. *Idioms of Inquiry*. New York University Press, 1987.

Beiner, Ronald. *Political Judgment*. University of Chicago Press, 1983.

Berlinski, David. *On Systems Analysis*. MIT Press, 1976.

Bernstein, Richard. *The Restructuring of Social and Political Theory*. Penn State University Press, 1978.

Bilsky, Manuel. *Patterns of Argument*. Holt, Rinehart, and Winston, 1963.

Blalock, Hubert M., Jr. *Social Statistics*. McGraw-Hill, 1960.

———. *Theory Construction-From Verbal to Mathematical Formulations*. Prentice-Hall, 1969.

Blalock, Hubert M., Jr., and Anna B. Blalock. *Methodology in Social Science*. McGraw-Hill, 1968.

Braithwaite, Richard B. *Scientific Explanation: A Study of the Function of Theory, Probability, and Law in Science*. Harper, 1953.

Braybrooke, David, ed. *Philosophical Problems of the Social Sciences*. Macmillan, 1965.

Braybrooke, David, and Charles E. Lindblom. *A Strategy of Decision: Policy Evaluation as a Social Process*. Free Press, 1970.

Brewer, Gary D., and Peter deLeon. *The Foundations of Policy Analysis*. Dorsey Press, 1983.

Brodbeck, May. *Readings in the Philosophy of Social Science*. Macmillan, 1968.

Brown, Harold I. *Observation and Objectivity*. Oxford University Press, 1987.

Buchanan, James M., and Robert D. Tollison, eds. *Theory of Public Choice: Political Applications of Economics*. University of Michigan Press, 1972.

Burk, Arthur W. *Choice, Causes, Reasons*. University of Chicago Press, 1979.

Calabresi, Guido, and Philip Bobbitt. *Tragic Choices*. W. W. Norton, 1978.

Carter, Lief H. *Reason in Law*. Little, Brown, 1979.

Cohen, I. B. *Revolution in Science*. Harvard University Press, 1985.

Cohen, Robert S., and Max Wartofsky. *Epistemology, Methodology, and the Social Sciences*. Kluwer Academic, 1983.

Cohn, A. G., and J. R. Thomas. *Artificial Intelligence and Its Applications*. Wiley, 1986.

Connolly, William E. *Political Theory and Modernity*. Basil Blackwell, 1987.

Dahlberg, Kenneth A. *New Directions for Agriculture and Agricultural Research*. Rowman and Allanheld, 1986.

Dallmayr, Fred R. *Twilight of Subjectivity: Contributions to a Post-Individualist Theory*. University of Massachusetts Press, 1981.

Derrida, J. *Positions*. University of Chicago Press, 1981.

Direnzo, Gordon J., ed. *Concepts, Theory and Explanation in the Behavioral Sciences*. Random House, 1966.

Dubin, Robert. *Theory Building*. Free Press, 1978.

Dunn, William. *Public Policy Analysis: An Introduction*. Prentice-Hall, 1981.

Eemeren, F. H. van, R. Grootendorst, and T. Kruiger. *The Study of Argumentation*. Irvington, 1984.

Evans, J. S. *Thinking and Reasoning*. Routledge and Kegan Paul, 1983.

Falco, Maria. *Truth and Meaning*. University Press of America, 1983.

Fay, Brian. *Critical Social Science*. Cornell University Press, 1987.

———. *Social Theory and Political Practice*. Allen and Unwin, 1975.

Feigl, Herbert, and May Brodbeck, eds. *Readings in the Philosophy of Science*. Appleton, Century, Crofts, 1953.

Feyerabend, P. *Against Method: Outline of An Anarchistic Theory of Knowledge*. New Left Books, 1975.

Fischer, F. *Politics, Values, and Public Policy: The Problem of Methodology.* West-view, 1980.

Fiske, Ronald W., and Richard A. Shweder, eds. *Metatheory in Social Science: Pluralisms and Subjectivities.* University of Chicago Press, 1985.

Flew, A.G.N. *Thinking About Social Thinking.* Basil Blackwell, 1985.

Ford, Nigel. *How Machines Think: A General Introduction to Artificial Intelligence.* Wiley, 1987.

Frankel, Charles, ed. *Controversies and Decisions: The Social Sciences and Public Policy.* Russell Sage Foundation, 1976.

Foucault, Michel. *The Foucault Reader.* Pantheon, 1984.

———. *The Order of Things.* Vintage, 1973.

———. *Power/Knowledge.* Marshall, Medham, Soper, 1980.

Gadamer, H. G. *Truth and Method.* Crossroads, 1985.

Gale, George. *Theory of Science: An Introduction to the History, Logic, and Philosophy of Science.* McGraw-Hill, 1979.

Geach, P. T. *Reason and Argument.* University of California Press, 1976.

Geertz, Clifford. *Local Knowledge.* Basic Books, 1983.

Gibson, Quentin. *The Logic of Social Enquiry.* Routledge and Kegan Paul, 1960.

Goodin, Robert E. *Political Theory and Public Policy.* University of Chicago Press, 1982.

Goodman, Nelson. *Fact, Fiction, and Forecast.* Bobbs-Merrill, 1965.

———. *Of Mind and Other Matters.* Harvard University Press, 1984.

Graham, George J. Jr. *Methodological Foundations for Political Analysis.* Wiley, 1971.

Habermas, Jurgen. *The Philosophic Discourse of Modernity.* MIT Press, 1987.

Hallam, John, and Chris Mellish, eds. *Advances in Artificial Intelligence: Processings of the 1987 AISB Conference.* Wiley, 1987.

Hayes, J. E. et al. *Machine Intelligence: The Logic and Acquisition of Knowledge.* Oxford University Press, 1988.

Hempel, Carl G. *Aspects of Scientific Explanation.* Free Press, 1965.

Hindless, Barry. *Philosophy and Methodology in the Social Sciences.* Humanities Press, 1977.

Hogarth, Robin M. *Judgement and Choice: The Psychology of Decision.* Wiley, 1980.

Holton, Gerald, and Robert S. Morison. *The Limits of Scientific Inquiry.* W. W. Norton, 1979.

Jarvis, I. C. *Thinking About Society.* Kluwer Academic, 1986.

Jencks, Charles. *What Is Post-Modernism?* St. Martin's Press, 1986.

Johnson-Laird, P. N. *Mental Models.* Harvard University Press, 1983.

Kahneman, D., P. Slovic, and A. Tversky. *Judgment Under Uncertainty: Heuristics and Biases.* Cambridge University Press, 1982.

Kaplan, Abraham. *The Conduct of Inquiry.* Chandler, 1964.

Kariel, Henry. *The Desperate Politics of Post-Modernism.* University of Massachussets Press, 1988.

Kuhn, Thomas S. *The Structure of Scientific Revolution,* rev. ed. University of Chicago Press, 1970.

Kyberg, Henry E. Jr., and Ernest Nagel, eds. *Induction: Some Current Issues.* Wesleyan University Press, 1963.

Lakatos, Imre, and Alan Musgrave, eds. *Criticism and the Growth of Knowledge.* Cambridge University Press, 1970.

Leatherdale, W. H. *The Role of Analogy, Models, and Metaphors in Science.* North Holland, 1974.

Levi, Edward H. *An Introduction to Legal Reasoning.* University of Chicago Press, 1949.

Lindblohm, C. E., and D. K. Cohen. *Usable Knowledge: Social Science and Social Problem-Solving.* Yale University Press, 1979.

Louch, A. R. *Explanation and Human Action.* University of California Press, 1966.

Lycan, William G. *Judgment and Justification.* Cambridge University Press, 1988.

Machlup, Fritz. *Methodology for Economics and Other Social Sciences.* Academic Press, 1978.

MacRae, Duncan, Jr. *Policy Indicators.* University of North Carolina Press, 1987.

———. *The Social Function of Social Science.* Yale University Press, 1976.

Margolis, Howard. *Patterns, Thinking, and Cognition: A Theory of Judgment.* University of Chicago Press, 1987.

Mayr, E. *The Growth of Biological Thought.* Harvard University Press, 1982.

Meehan, Eugene J. *Economics and Policymaking: The Tragic Illusion.* Greenwood Press, 1982.

———. *Ethics for Policymaking: A Methodological Analysis.* Greenwood Press, 1990.

———. *Reasoned Argument in Social Science: Linking Research to Policy.* Greenwood Press, 1981.

———. *The Thinking Game: A Guide to Effective Study.* Chatham House, 1988.

Mills, Glen E. *Reason in Controversy.* Allyn and Bacon, 1968.

Minsky, Marvin, and Seymour Papert. *Perceptrons: An Introduction to Computational Geometry.* MIT Press, 1979.

Mitchell, W.T.J., ed. *Against Theory.* University of Chicago Press, 1985.

———. *The Politics of Interpretation.* University of Chicago Press, 1983.

Mitroff, Ian A., and Ralph H. Kilmann. *Methodological Approaches to Social Science.* Jossey-Bass, 1978.

Mueller, Dennis C. *Public Choice.* Cambridge University Press, 1979.

Nagel, Ernest. *The Structure of Science: Problems in the Logic of Scientific Explanation.* Harcourt, Brace, and World, 1961.

Nagel, Ernest, et al. *Logic, Methodology, and Philosophy of Science.* Stanford University Press, 1962.

Nagel, Ernest, and Richard B. Brandt, eds. *Meaning and Knowledge: Systematic Readings in Epistemology.* Harcourt, Brace and World, 1965.

Nagel, Ernest, and James R. Newman. *Godel's Proof.* New York University Press, 1958.

Nagel, Stuart S. *Policy Studies and the Social Sciences.* Lexington Books, 1975.

Natanson, Maurice, ed. *Philosophy of the Social Sciences.* Random House, 1963.

Newell, Allen, and Herbert A. Simon. *Human Problem Solving.* Prentice-Hall, 1972.

Nisbett, Richard, and Lee Ross. *Human Inference: Strategies and Shortcomings of Social Judgment.* Prentice-Hall, 1980.

Olson, Mancur. *The Logic of Collective Action.* Harvard University Press, 1965.

Pappas, George S., and Marshall Swain, eds. *Essays on Knowledge and Justification.* Cornell University Press, 1978.

Paris, David C., and James F. Reynolds. *The Logic of Policy Inquiry*. Longman, 1983.

Polanyi, Michael. *Knowing and Being*. University of Chicago Press, 1969.

———. *Personal Knowledge*. University of Chicago Press, 1958.

Popper, Karl R. *Conjectures and Refutations: The Growth of Scientific Knowledge*. Harper and Row, 1968.

———. *The Logic of Scientific Discovery*. Science Editions, 1961.

———. *Objective Knowledge: An Evolutionary Approach*. Oxford University Press, 1972.

Putnam, Hilary. *Reason, Truth and History*. Cambridge University Press, 1981.

Quade, Edward. *Analysis for Public Decisions*. North Holland, 1982.

Quine, Willard Van Orman. *The Ways of Paradox and Other Essays*. Harvard University Press, 1976.

———. *Word and Object*. MIT Press, 1960.

Rajchmann, J., and C. West, eds. *Post-Analytic Philosophy*. Columbia University Press, 1985.

Rein, Martin. *Social Sciences and Public Policy*. Penguin, 1976.

Rescher, Nicholas. *Empirical Inquiry*. Rowman and Littlefield, 1982.

———. *The Limits of Science*. University of California Press, 1984.

———. *Methodological Pragmatism*. New York University Press, 1971.

Revlin, Russell, and Richard E. Mayer. *Human Reasoning*. V. H. Winston, 1978.

Ricci, David. *The Tragedy of Political Science*. Yale University Press, 1984.

Rieke, D., and Malcom O. Sillars. *Argumentation and the Decision-Making Process*. Wiley, 1975.

Riker, William H., and Peter C. Ordeshook. *An Introduction to Positive Political Theory*. Prentice-Hall, 1973.

Rock, I. *The Logic of Perception*. MIT Press, 1985.

Rorty, Richard. *Philosophy and the Mirror of Nature*. Princeton University Press, 1979.

Rosch, E., and C. B. Mervis, eds. *Cognition and Categorization*. Lawrence Erlbaum, 1978.

Rosen, Stanley. *The Limits of Analysis*. Yale, 1985.

Roth, Paul A. *Meaning and Method in the Social Sciences*. Cornell University Press, 1987.

Rudner, Richard S. *A Philosophy of Social Science*. Prentice-Hall, 1966.

Runciman, W. G. *Social Science and Political Theory*. Cambridge University Press, 1963.

Ryan, Alan, ed. *Philosophy of Social Explanation*. Oxford University Press, 1973.

Salmon, Wesley. *Foundations of Scientific Inference*. University of Pittsburgh Press, 1966.

Scheffler, Israel. *The Anatomy of Inquiry*. Knopf, 1963.

———. *Conditions of Knowledge: An Introduction to Epistemology and Education*. University of Chicago Press, 1983.

Schelling, Thomas C. *Choice and Consequence*. Harvard University Press, 1983.

Scriven, Michael. *The Logic of Evaluation*, 2d. ed. Edgepress, 1980.

Simon, Herbert A. *Models of Man*. Wiley, 1957.

———. *Reason in Human Affairs*. MIT Press, 1983.

Skinner, Quentin, ed. *The Return of Grand Theory in the Human Sciences*. Cambridge University Press, 1985.

Smith, John E. *Purpose and Thought: The Meaning of Pragmatism*. Yale University Press, 1978.

Spence, Larry. *The Politics of Social Knowledge*. Pennsylvania State University Press, 1978.

Stinchcombe, Arthur L. *Constructing Social Theories*. Harcourt, Brace, and World, 1968.

Suppes, Patrick. *The Structure of Scientific Theories*. University of Illinois Press, 1977.

Toulmin, Stephen. *Foresight and Understanding*. Harper and Row, 1961.

———. *Human Understanding*, Vol. I. Princeton University Press, 1972.

———. *The Philosophy of Science*. Harper and Row, 1960.

———. *The Uses of Argument*. Cambridge University Press, 1964.

Vaillancourt, Pauline M. *When Marxists Do Research*. Greenwood Press, 1986.

Weiss, Carol, ed. *Using Social Research in Public Policy-Making*. Lexington-Heath, 1977.

Weiss, Carol, and Michael Bucuvalis. *Social Science Research and Decision-Making*. Columbia University Press, 1980.

Ethics: Its Purposes, Meaning, and Character

Aiken, Henry D. *Reason and Conduct: New Bearings in Moral Philosophy*. Knopf, 1962.

Arrow, Kenneth J. *Social Choice and Individual Values*, 2d. ed. Yale University Press, 1963.

Barnsley, John H. *The Social Reality of Ethics: The Comparative Analysis of Moral Codes*. Routledge and Kegan Paul, 1972.

Barry, Brian. *A Liberal Theory of Justice*. Oxford University Press, 1973.

———. *A Treatise on Social Justice*. University of California Press, 1989.

Beardsmore, R. W. *Moral Reasoning*. Routledge and Kegan Paul, 1969.

Brandt, Richard B. *Ethical Theory: The Problems of Normative and Critical Ethics*. Prentice-Hall, 1959.

Brink, David O. *Moral Realism and the Foundations of Ethics*. Cambridge University Press, 1989.

Broad, C. D. *Five Types of Ethical Theory*. Littlefield, Adams, 1959.

Callahan, Daniel, and Bruce Jennings, eds. *Ethics, the Social Sciences, and Policy Analysis*. Plenum, 1983.

Colby, Anne, and Lawrence Kohlberg. *The Measurement of Moral Judgment*, Vol. I: *Theoretical Foundations and Research*. Cambridge University Press, 1987.

Danielsson, Sven. *Preference and Obligations: Studies in the Logic of Ethics*. Filosofiska Foreningen, Uppsala, Sweden, 1968.

Dewey, John. *Theory of the Moral Life*. Holt, Rinehart, and Winston, 1960.

Dunn, William N., ed. *Political Analysis: Perspectives, Concepts, and Methods*. JAI Press, 1986.

———. *Values, Ethics and the Practice of Policy Analysis*. Lexington Books, 1983.

Edel, Abraham. *Method in Ethical Theory*. Bobbs-Merrill, 1963.

Engelhardt, H. Tristram Jr., and Daniel Callahan, eds. *Science, Ethics and Medicine,* 3 vols. Hastings Center, 1976, 1977, 1978.

Findlay, J. N. *Axiological Ethics*. Macmillan, 1970.

Fleishman, Joel, and Bruce Payne. *Ethical Dilemmas and the Education of Policymakers*. Hastings Center, 1980.

Foot, Philippa. *Theories of Ethics*. Oxford University Press, 1967.

Frankena, William K. *Ethics*. Prentice-Hall, 1963.

Fried, Charles. *An Anatomy of Values*. Harvard University Press, 1970.

Gauthier, David P. *Moral Dealing: Contract, Ethics, and Reason*. Cornell University Press, 1990.

———. *Practical Reasoning*. Clarendon Press, 1963.

Gibbard, Allan. *Wise Choices, Apt Feelings: A Theory of Normative Judgment*. Harvard University Press, 1990.

Gouinlock, James, ed. *The Moral Writings of John Dewey*. Hafner Press, 1976.

Grassian, Victor. *Moral Reasoning: Ethical Theory and Some Contemporary Moral Problems*. Prentice-Hall, 1981.

Hancock, Roger N. *Twentieth Century Ethics*. Columbia University Press, 1974.

Hardin, Garrett. *Exploring New Ethics for Survival: The Voyage of the Spaceship Beagle*. Viking Press, 1968.

Hare, Richard M. *Essays in Ethical Theory*. Oxford University Press, 1989.

Harvard Educational Review. Reprint No. 13, "Stage Theories of Cognitive and Moral Development: Criticisms and Applications."

Kattsoff, Louis O. *Making Moral Decisions: An Existential Analysis*. Nijhoff, 1965.

Kemp, J. *Reason, Action, and Morality*. Humanities Press, 1964.

Kerner, George C. *The Revolution in Ethical Theory*. Oxford University Press, 1966.

Kohlberg, L. *Philosophy of Moral Development*. Harper, 1981.

Lamont, W. D. *Law and the Moral Order*. Aberdeen University Press, 1981.

Lewis, C. I. *Values and Imperatives: Studies in Ethics,* ed. John Langa. Stanford University Press, 1969.

MacIntyre, Alasdair. *After Virtue: A Study in Moral Theory*. University of Notre Dame Press, 1981.

Meehan, Eugene J. *Ethics for Policymaking: A Methodological Analysis*. Greenwood Press, 1990.

Moore, F.T.C. *The Psychological Basis of Morality*. Macmillan, 1978.

Moore, G. E. *Principia Ethica*. Cambridge University Press, 1903.

Najder, Zdzislaw. *Values and Evaluations*. Clarendon Press, 1975.

Newell, A., and H. Simon. *Human Problem Solving*. Prentice-Hall, 1972.

Polanyi, Michael. *Knowing and Being,* ed. Marjorie Grene. University of Chicago Press, 1969.

Raskin, Marcus G. *The Common Good: Its Politics, Policies, and Philosophy*. Routledge and Kegan Paul, 1986.

Rawls, John. *A Theory of Justice*. Belknap Press, 1971.

Reiman, Jeffrey H. *Justice and Modern Moral Philosophy*. Yale University Press, 1990.

Rescher, Nicholas. *An Introduction to Value Theory*. Prentice-Hall, 1969.

———, ed. *The Logic of Decision and Action*. University of Pittsburgh Press, 1967.

Richards, David A. J. *A Theory of Reasons for Action*. Clarendon Press, 1971.

Rokeach, Milton. *The Nature of Human Values*. Free Press, 1973.

Scheffler, Samuel. *The Rejection of Consequentialism*. Oxford University Press, 1982.

Sellars, Wilfrid, and John Hospers, eds. *Readings in Ethical Theory*, 2d. ed. Appleton, Century, Crofts, 1970.

Singer, Marcus G. *Generalization in Ethics*. Knopf, 1961.

Singer, Peter. *Practical Ethics*. Cambridge University Press, 1979.

Slote, M. *Beyond Optimizing: A Study of Rational Choice*. Harvard University Press, 1989.

———. *Common-Sense Morality and Consequentialism*. Routledge and Kegan Paul, 1985.

Smith, Adam. *The Theory of Moral Sentiments*, eds. D. D. Raphael and A. L. Macfie. Clarendon Press, 1976; first published in 1759.

Stocker, Michael. *Plural and Conflicting Values*. Clarendon Press, 1990.

Taylor, Paul W. *Normative Discourse*. Prentice-Hall, 1961.

Toulmin, Stephen. *The Place of Reason in Ethics*. Cambridge University Press, 1960.

von Wright, Georg Henrik. *The Logic of Preference*. Edinburgh University Press, 1963.

Wallace, G., and A.D.M. Walker, eds. *The Definition of Morality*. Methuen, 1970.

Wallsten, Thomas S., ed. *Cognitive Processes, Choice, and Decision Behavior*. Lawrence Erlbaum, 1980.

Warnock, G. J. *The Object of Morality*. Methuen, 1971.

Warnock, Mary. *Ethics Since 1900*, 2d. ed. Oxford University Press, 1966.

Wellman, Carl. *Morals and Ethics*. Scott, Foresman, 1975.

White, Morton. *What Is and What Ought to be Done: An Essay on Ethics and Epistemology*. Oxford University Press, 1981.

Winch, Peter. *Ethics and Action*. Routledge and Kegan Paul, 1972.

Wren, Thomas E. *The Moral Domain*. MIT Press, 1990.

Cognition and Related Topics

Anderson, John R., ed. *Cognitive Skills and Their Acquisition*. Lawrence Erlbaum, 1981.

Ashby, W. Ross. *Design for a Brain: The Origins of Adaptive Behavior*. Wiley, 1960.

Bloom, Floyd E., and Arlyne Lazerson. *Brain, Mind, and Behavior*, 2d. ed. W. H. Freeman, 1988.

Boulding, Kenneth E. *The Image: Knowledge in Life and Society*. University of Michigan Press, 1961.

Bruner, Jerome S. *Actual Minds, Possible Worlds*. Harvard University Press, 1987.

———. *Beyond Information Given*. W. W. Norton, 1973.

———. *Toward a Theory of Instruction*. Harvard University Press, 1966.

Bruner, Jerome S., J. J. Goodnow, and G. A. Austin. *A Study of Thinking*. Wiley, 1956.

Bruner, Jerome S., R. R. Oliver, and P. M. Greenfield. *Studies in Cognitive Growth*. Wiley, 1966.

Cole, Michael, J. Gay, J. Glick, and D. Sharp. *The Cultural Context of Learning and Thinking*. Basic Books, 1971.

Eemeren, F. H. van, R. Grootendorst, and T. Kruiger. *The Study of Argumentation*. Irvington, 1984.

Ennis R. H. "A Concept of Critical Thinking." *Harvard Educational Review* 32 (1962), 81–111.

———. "Conditional Logic and Primary School Children: A Developmental Study." *Interchange* 2, no. 2 (1971).

———. *Logic in Teaching*. Prentice-Hall, 1969.

Ennis, R. H., M. R. Finkelstein, E. L. Smith, and N. H. Wilson. *Conditional Logic and Children*. Cornell University, Department of Education, 1969.

Feldman, David H. *Beyond Universals in Cognitive Development*. Abley, 1980.

Feldman, Shel, ed. *Cognitive Consistency*. Academic Press, 1966.

Festinger, Leon. *A Theory of Cognitive Dissonance*. Stanford University Press, 1957.

Feyerabend, P. K. *Knowledge Without Foundations*. Oberlin Printing Co., 1952.

Flavell, J. H. *Cognitive Development*. Prentice-Hall, 1977.

Friedman, Sarah L. et al., eds. *The Brain, Cognition, and Education*. Academic Press, 1986.

Gagne, Robert M. *The Conditions of Learning*, 3d. ed. Holt, Rinehart, and Winston, 1977.

Giere, Ronald N. *Explaining Science: A Cognitive Approach*. University of Chicago Press, 1988.

Goldman, Alvin I. *Epistemology and Cognition*. Harvard University Press, 1988.

Gregg, L. W., ed. *Knowledge and Cognition*. Lawrence Erlbaum, 1974.

Grossberg, S., ed. *The Adaptive Brain*, Vol. I: *Cognitive Learning*. Elsevier, 1988.

Harper, Robert et al., eds. *The Cognitive Process*. Prentice-Hall, 1964.

Hart, Leslie A. *Human Brain and Human Learning*. Longman, 1983.

Harvard Educational Review. Reprint No. 13, "Stage Theories of Cognitive and Moral Development: Criticisms and Applications, 1978.

Hill, Claire C. *Problem-Solving: Learning and Teaching*. Francis Pinter, 1979.

Inhelder, Barbel, and J. Piaget. *The Early Growth of Logic in the Child: Classification and Seriation*. Harper and Row, 1964; first published in 1959.

———. *The Growth of Logical Thinking from Childhood to Adolescence*. Basic Books. 1958.

Jeffress, Lloyd A. *Cerebral Mechanisms in Behavior*. Wiley, 1951.

Jencks, Christopher et al. *Inequality*. Harper and Row, 1972.

Johnson-Laird, P. N. *The Computer and the Mind: An Introduction to Cognitive Science*. Harvard University Press, 1988.

Kaplan, Martin F., and Steven Schwartz, eds. *Human Judgement and Decision Processes*. Academic Press, 1975.

Kleinmutz, B. *Problem Solving: Research, Method and Theory*. Wiley, 1966.

Kohlberg, Lawrence. *Stages in the Development of Moral Thought and Action*. Holt, Rinehart, and Winston, 1969.

Lau, Richard R., and David O. Sears, eds. *Political Cognition*. Lawrence Erlbaum, 1986.

Luria, A. R. *Cognitive Development*. Harvard University Press, 1976.

Margolis, Howard. *Patterns, Thinking, and Cognition: A Theory of Judgment*. University of Chicago Press, 1987.

Martin, Jane R. *Explaining, Understanding, and Teaching.* McGraw-Hill, 1970.

Mayer, R. E. *Thinking and Problem Solving: An Introduction to Human Cognition and Learning.* Scott, Foresman, 1977.

McClellan, James E. *Philosophy of Education.* Prentice-Hall, 1976.

McCulloch, Warren S. *Embodiments of Mind.* MIT Press, 1970.

Michalos, Alex C. *Improving Your Reasoning,* 2d. ed. Prentice-Hall, 1986.

Mischel, R., ed. *Cognitive Development and Epistemology.* Academic Press, 1971.

Neumann, John von. *The Computer and the Brain.* Yale University Press, 1958.

Nisbett, Richard, and Lee Ross. *Human Inference: Strategies and Shortcomings of Social Judgment.* Prentice-Hall, 1980.

Penfield, Wilder, and Lamar Roberts. *Speech and Brain Mechanisms.* Princeton University Press, 1959.

Piaget, J. *The Development of Thought: Equilibration of Cognitive Structures.* Viking Press, 1977.

———. *Judgment and Reasoning in the Child.* Littlefield, Adams, 1928.

Radford, John K., and Andrew Burton. *Thinking: Its Nature and Development.* Wiley, 1974.

Raskin, Marcus G. *The Common Good: Its Politics, Policies, and Philosophy.* Routledge and Kegan Paul, 1986.

Rescher, Nicholas, ed. *The Logic of Decision and Action.* University of Pittsburgh Press, 1967.

Richardson, John T., and Michael W. Eysenck. *Student Learning: Research on Education and Cognitive Psychology.* Taylor and Francis, 1987.

Rieke, D., and Malcom O. Sillars. *Argumentation and the Decision-Making Process.* Wiley, 1975.

Roth, Paul A. *Meaning and Method in the Social Sciences: A Case for Methodological Pluralism.* Cornell University Press, 1987.

Savage, C. Wade, ed. *Perception and Cognition Issues in the Foundations of Psychology.* Minnesota Studies in the Philosophy of Science, Vol. IX. University of Minnesota Press, 1978.

Scheffler, Israel. *Conditions of Knowledge: An Introduction to Epistemology and Education.* Scott, Foresman, 1965.

———, ed. *Philosophy and Education: Modern Readings.* Allyn and Bacon, 1966.

———. *Reason and Teaching.* Bobbs, Merrill, 1973.

Suzumara, Korato. *Rational Choice, Collective Decisions, and Social Welfare.* Cambridge University Press, 1983.

Swartz, Robert J., ed. *Perceiving, Sensing, and Knowing.* University of California Press, 1965.

Thompson, Robert. *The Psychology of Thinking.* Penguin, 1959.

von Wright, Georg H. *The Logic of Preference.* Edinburgh University Press, 1963.

———. *Norm and Action: A Logical Inquiry.* Routledge and Kegan Paul, 1963.

Voss, James, F., ed. *Approaches to Thought.* Charles E. Merrill, 1969.

Wallsten, Thomas S., ed. *Cognitive Processes in Choice and Decision Behavior.* Lawrence Erlbaum, 1980.

Wason, P. C. and P. N. Johnson-Laird, eds. *Thinking and Reasoning.* Penguin, 1968.

Weddle, Perry. *Argument: A Guide to Critical Thinking.* McGraw-Hill, 1977.

Werner, Heinz. *Comparative Psychology of Mental Development.* Science Editions, 1961.
Woolridge, Dean E. *The Machinery of the Brain.* McGraw-Hill, 1963.
Young, J. Z. *A Model of the Brain.* Oxford University Press, 1964.

Index

Achievement, high-level, and cognitive performance, 94–95
Action: and choice, 24; meaning, 5–6
Action focus, justification for, 25–27, 58
Actions: empirical, 38–58; intellectual capacity available for directing, 29–38; intellectual requirements for directing, 25–29, 38–70; minimum conditions for justifying, 26–27, 59–60; normative, 58–78; summary of requirements, 27–28
Argument, and justification, 69–71
Assumptions, unacceptable, 12–14
Athletic coaching, as model for inquiry, 4, 18

Benchmarks: development and use, 28, 73–74, 75; meaning, 72
Buffer variables, 65–66

Calculation: meaning, 35; role in knowledge creation and use, 35–36
Capacity and limitations, intellectual, 25–38

Causal assumption, meaning, 34–35, 53–55
ceteris paribus, role in theorizing, 55
Choice: as action, 24; influence of social context, 77–78
Circularity, avoiding in justification, 72–74
Classification: meaning, 34, 47; use for predicting, 47–50
Cognitive skill: improvement, 121–67; indicators for, 88–89; meaning, 1, 3–5; measurement problems associated with, 121–24; need for, 17–18; role in normative justification and argument, 14
Cognitive skill testing: evolution of test, 82–88, 96–104; preliminary findings, 92–96; questionnaire, 91–92; summary of results, 99–104
Cognitive skill training: based on theory transfer, 124–48; preliterate, 148–67
Cognitive training, results: large classes, 144–48; preliterate, 164–67
Collective terms, use of, 45

Concepts: problems with, 42–43; standardization of, 43
Concepts, normative, 60–67; defined, 60–61; measurements of, 66–67; and quality of life, 61–64; structure of, 64–66
Conceptual frameworks, 45–46
Conditionality, of knowledge, 55–56
Conflation, of effects of action on people, 75
Consensus of informed opinion, meaning and role, 70, 72–74
Consequences, as focus for justification, 59–60
Controlling events, meaning, 24, 51–52
Counterfactuals, importance of, 88, 95, 163–64
Criticism, competent, 49; knowledge claims, 37–38
Critiques, as a training focus, 133–38

Deductive system, meaning, 30
Definitions, types of, 42–43
Descriptions, common sources of error in, 41–46
Development orientation, content of, 87
"Discipline," meaning, 69–71; role in justification, 72–74

Empirical knowledge required for directing actions, 38–40
Equality, meaning, 21–22
Ethics, traditional: inadequacy for directing actions, 13–14
Evading the induction problem, 31–38
Experiments, natural state and laboratory, 57

Forecasting, with classifications; 47–50; with theories, 50–51
Forecasts, and classifications, 50–51; meaning, 34–35
Fundamentals, importance of agreement upon, 10–12

Generalizations, types required, 33–35
Goodman, Nelson, 88

"Harvard syndrome," 7
homo mensura, 21–22

Induction, meaning, 30, 68–69
Induction problem, as focus for inquiry, 29; organizing an evasion, 31–38
Informed opinion, meaning and role, 70–74
Input variables, meaning and use, 64–65
Irreducibility, of individual life, 76

Judgment, meaning and implications, 9–10, 36–37
Justification: empirical knowledge claims, 55–58; normative knowledge claims, 67–78; useful simplifications, 74–77

Knowledge: conditionality of, 55; meaning and relation to cognitive skill, 7–8; requirements for directing actions summarized, 38–40

Large classes, cognitive training in, 144–48
Lexical definitions, 42
Life, nonnegotiable character of, 76
Limiting conditions, function of, 37–38
Logic, limitations, 13
Long, Norton E., 70

Measurement problems: general, 44–45; with normative variables, 61–62; with respect to the quality of life, 66–67
Mill, John Stuart, 53
Model of the human situation, 20–21
Monitoring policy effects, need for, 28–29

Natural science as an inadequate model, 13

Nominal definitions, 42–43

Normative assumptions, primary, 20–22

Normative concepts: meaning, 66; structure, 54–67

Normative requirements for directing action: fulfilling, 58–78; summarized, 58–60

Piaget, Jean, 159

Policy, meaning, 28

Pragmatic criteria, need for, 31, 52

Precising definitions, 42

Prediction: with classifications, 47–50; with forecasts or theories, 50–51; meaning, 46

Preferences: justification, 68–69, 70–73; meaning, 67; and priorities, 67

Priorities: meaning, 35, 67; prerequisites for, 67–69

Purpose(s): fundamental, 3, 19–24; intellectual prerequisites, summary, 27–29; overriding, need for, 3–4, 20–22; second-order, 4–5, 22–24

Quality of life concept: meaning, 61–64; measurement of, 66–67

Real definitions, 42–43

Saint-Exupery, Antoine de, 14

Scaling, 44

Science, as model for inquiry, 13, 67–68

Social context, importance of, 77–78

Subjectivity, effects of, 44–45

Testability, conditions of, 28

Testing, cognitive skills, 81–104

Theory: as analogue to map, 56–57; development of, 53–55; function of, 51–58; justification and testing, 55–58; meaning, 34–35; and policy-making, 54; uses and limitations, 56

Theory of knowledge: analogy to coaching athletics, 18–19; proposed, 17–78; role in development of priorities, 2–3

Training, cognitive, preliterate, 148–67; attitudes and orientations, 161–64; experimental program, description, 153–67; experimental results, 164–67; foci for, 157–64; program design considerations, 150–53

Training, cognitive, theory-based: assumptions required, 126–30; for literate adults, 132–33; pedagogical considerations, 138–42; types of training, 125; very large classes, 142–48

Transitivity, need for in priority system, 26

Vagueness, conceptual, 42

About the Author

EUGENE J. MEEHAN is Curators' Professor, Political Science and Public Policy Administration, in the Department of Political Science at the University of Missouri–St. Louis. He is author of *Reasoned Argument in Social Science, Economics and Policymaking: The Tragic Illusion* and *Ethics for Policymaking* (Greenwood Press, 1981, 1982, and 1990, respectively).